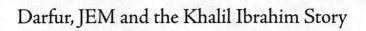
Darfur, JEM and the Khalil Ibrahim Story

Darfur,

JEM

and the

KHALIL IBRAHIM STORY

Abdullahi Osman El-Tom

THE RED SEA PRESS

TRENTON | LONDON | CAPE TOWN | NAIROBI | ADDIS ABABA | ASMARA | IBADAN

THE RED SEA PRESS
541 West Ingham Avenue | Suite B
Trenton, New Jersey 08638

Book and cover design: Saverance Publishing Services
Photos courtesy of the author and JEM

Library of Congress Cataloging-in-Publication Data

Tom, Abdullahi Osman El-
Darfur, JEM and the Khalil Ibrahim story / Abdullahi Osman El-Tom.
    p. cm.
Includes bibliographical references and index.
ISBN 1-56902-345-X (hardcover)
1. Ibrahim, Khalil, Dr. 2. Harakat al-'Adl wa-al-Musawah al-Sudaniyah. 3. Sudan--History--Darfur Conflict, 2003- I. Title. II. Title: Darfur, J.E.M. and the Khalil Ibrahim story.
DT159.6.D27T86 2011
962.7'043092--dc22
                           2010054144

To Nadia El-Tom Power

Contents

Preface

The purpose of this project is to expose the reader to the cultural background of Dr Khalil Ibrahim, his early dreams and aspirations and the reasons that led him to rebel and take up arms against the very system he once supported, the Government of Sudan, whose President, Omar al-Bashir, has been indicted for war crimes by the International Criminal Court (ICC). Most of the information in the book was gathered on my last visit to Justice and Equality Movement (JEM) rebels in Darfur in August, 2009. Additional data used are based on interviews in Libya, August, 2009 and Qatar in February and April, 2010. Numerous phone interviews were also used to clarify certain issues in the text.

The narrative in this work follows a particular style. The author ushers in the reader in a gradual way, laying out the scene and providing context to the story before handing over the entire voice to the main character of the book. Transliteration of the Darfurian names is always problematic. Official systems that are based on classical Arabic names do not serve our purpose. Darfur is marginal to the Arabic world and most names are pronounced in a way that compromises classical Arabic. Moreover, as with all Muslim parts of Sudan, Darfuris do not use surnames. Each person is known by his/her first name, followed by father's and then grandfather's first names. Titles, if any, precede first names, thus you have Dr Khalil or Dr Abdullahi and so forth. However, if the second or third name is unusual, then it is used in replacement of the first name and hence Izzaldin Bajji is referred to as Bajji and Ahmed Togot Lisan is called Togot. Bajji and Togot are rare names and serve as a better identifier for the bearer.

The preparation of this book has been a source of immense pleasure that far outweighed the solitary nature of writing. Its long journey, both in time and space, has taught me a lot—about my own people in Darfur and the Sudan at large: their culture, history, and struggle for sheer survival. Like any work of this nature, the book could not have become a reality without the help of so many people along the way. Dr Khalil Ibrahim, President of the Justice and Equality Movement (JEM) has been most generous with me. Despite his busy schedule of meetings, phone calls and media interruptions, he managed to make himself available to me with patience and self-denial. On numerous occasions, and to thwart continuous distractions, we started our interviews at 6am. While I did my best to be true to his narrative, I hasten to add that this book reflects my own version of his story and he is therefore free to disown any passage or word in the text if he so chooses.

So many comrades in JEM have also been instrumental in making this work possible. Commanders Cholloy, Sandal, Bajji, Abu Bakar Hamid, Togot, Adam Bakheit, Bishara Suleiman, Mansour Arbab, Jamous and many others provided protection and guidance throughout my trip into Chad and the war zone.

Back at home, Ruth McLoughlin provided editorial backup and undertook the tedious work of going through the manuscript, section by section and word for word. I am utterly grateful to her for excellent editing with a sharp eye for lack of consistency; for taming my wild syntax and curtailing some awkward expressions that cropped up in earlier versions of the manuscript.

Of course this work would have never been completed without the generous structural support and intellectual environment provided by the National University of Ireland, Maynooth (NUIM). The author is grateful to NUIM for this and would like his gratitude to be registered at the outset of this humble work.

While I fully acknowledge the contribution of all those who have assisted me in bringing this work to the reader, I humbly remain solely responsible for its limitations.

Who is Hinain?

"Who are you?" I say to Khalil Ibrahim, President of JEM. Khalil replies, "I am Hinain Ibrahim Mohamed Hinain Jurey Salim Taha Kuria Abdalla Baru Isi Omer Mohamed Daj. Hinain is a name that translates into Hilal in Arabic. In our language, 'L' is pronounced 'N'. We are known over here as 'off springs of Hinain or of Hilal'. It is common among our people, as indeed across the Sudan to commemorate an ancestor by naming an offspring after him or her. So I was named Hinain after my great grandfather."

"Wow, a dozen generations in one go!" I say, as I sit in the night desert, bewildered by the man's memory of his ancestors. Few of us Darfurians manage, or indeed care to string our names past a great grandfather. Our Arab neighbours in Darfur accuse us of not knowing our ancestors. In their obsession with their pedigrees and their derogatory mocking of other Darfuri whom they call Africans, a Darfur Arab nomad once said, "The Darfuri African is like a young camel. He does not know who is his father. Every Arab in Darfur can easily count his ancestors up to ten generations and some can connect you direct with Prophet Mohamed."

As I reflect on this statement, Khalil seems to falsify the assumption of our fellow Arab Darfurians. But in as much as I am impressed by Khalil's knowledge of his ancestors, I am also left terribly confused, so I intervene, "But why Hinain and where is Khalil in this pedigree?"

1

I straighten my squat on the soft carpet spread on the sand of a water valley in North Darfur. This is July and the valley is still dry and the locals are worried about yet another bad harvest this year. The two edges of the valley are dotted with Acacia trees. Four guards stand a few meters away at the four cardinal directions, carrying their machine guns. These are the presidential guards of the president of JEM and you see them hanging around wherever he goes.

The stars shine over our heads despite the strong moonlight. Every now and then, some soldiers resting nearby break the silence of the place. Occasionally, a fox, a wild cat or a hedgehog arrives and reminds us that we do not have a monopoly over the vicinity. The ban on lighting fires or using torches at night for security purposes adds to the tranquillity of the place. This is JEM HQ, a transient camp that can relocate at very short notice. There are around one thousand of us in this location, divided into small units. The units are scattered around in the valley, forming a circle around the HQ.

Khalil's silence seems to last forever. I cannot wait to crack the riddle of the name Hinain. I have known Khalil for over six years, and yet, this is the first time I hear the name Hinain. Over the years, we gave Khalil numerous aliases to disguise his identity and location during our long distance phone calls. Hinain would have been a perfect one, but to my surprise it has never been used.

I pretend to adjust the position of my digital voice recorder in front of Khalil but only as a subtle reminder that it is time to proceed with the interview. He tries to resume talking but holds back, waiting for me to wag away a mosquito that is buzzing near my right ear. The mosquito reminds me of my childhood tales, that mosquitoes do not like the blood of dead people. In order to ensure that its victim is alive, the mosquito buzzes him in the ear so that he moves and proves good for feeding.

Mansour, Secretary for JEM Presidential Affairs, appears from nowhere and interrupts our interview. He is speaking on his satellite phone and worse than that, is carrying a folder in his hand. It is never easy to get Khalil away for a private chat. Khalil recognises this and so he decides that we sit here, away from everybody.

Mansour hands over the phone to Khalil for while. A commander of a JEM mobile force 500 kilometres away proceeds to brief Khalil about his progress and possible engagement prospects. Khalil instructs him gently to be on the alert, choose his battlefield and avoid populated areas. He then turns to someone else at the other end of the line and I get lost, for he is now speaking in the Zaghawa language. I delight myself in picking up on one of a few sentences I have learnt in that language so far. It is the common Zaghawa greeting formula at the start of Khalil's conversation, 'Awaja tino da', meaning 'we are alright' or 'there is no problem'.

Failing to follow Khalil's conversation, I now focus some resentment against the satellite phone commonly known by its trade name, Thuraya. This has turned into a real pest ruining almost every single attempt that I make at an interview. But then, where would JEM or all the Darfur Movements be without the Thuraya. Of course JEM uses the old fashioned radios for communication but these are bulky, inefficient and immobile. But the Thuraya too is far from perfect. It is bulky compared to normal mobile phones and only works well when you are in the open, away from building structures and trees. Aesthetically speaking, Thuraya designers have a lot to answer for. Their artistic talent ranges between paucity and complete nonexistence. At a US$ per minute transmission charge, the Thuraya is one of the most expensive phones in the world.

The reader is justified in wondering how on earth JEM commanders manage to keep their Thurayas in credit, given that they operate in a terrain with no banks, no modern shops and certainly no credit cards. Well, it is easy. As I sit in my office in Ireland, the phone rings and I lift the receiver to hear, "Hello Brother, this is commander Ali. I am sorry I cannot be on the phone for long. I am low on credit and will be on the move soon. Please top up my phone if you can. You've got my number that ends with 09."

As soon as I finish the call, I make a few brisk moves. JEM commanders rarely ask me for money or cards because among all of us in the Diaspora, I am one of those who make a regular contribution to the organisation. That makes the phone call even more pressing. When they ask me for help, I know they are in a desperate situation.

I hurriedly make phone calls, texts, emails to JEM members across the western world and particularly those who are not short of disposable income. Regretfully, most of the Darfurians in the Diaspora are refugees or asylum seekers and are unemployed. In responding to Commander Ali's plea, this sad fact has to be factored in. The exigency of the situation means that I have to act—and quickly—so I text a JEM friend in the Middle East, "Please send me 15 Thuraya cards. Your money will be in the Western Union within half an hour."

I dash to the Western Union office and dispatch money to Bahrain. I text a money transfer number to my Bahrain friend and I get a positive response promising to deliver the cards' numbers to my email account. This is the beauty of the Western Union. Although it is notoriously expensive, charging around 5% depending on the destination, the Western Union is most efficient and is suited to developing countries. Its transfer is instant and can be cashed either in local or hard currency. This feature of the Western Union is not to be underestimated, particularly in countries with restricted access to hard currency. But the real drive behind popularity of the Western Union in poor countries lies somewhere else. Clients with neither a bank account nor an identity card can also avail of its services. The identity of the recipient can simply be verified via an agreed password.

Back in the office, I switch to my computer email section waiting for the phone cards and there they are, within less than an hour of Ali's phone call. I text Ali the pin numbers divided into three separate groups. Remaining faithful to his habit, Ali confirms reception of the phone cards. Sometimes we get fake cards but not today. There is no complaint from Ali following the dispatch.

I get a bit impatient when Khalil ends his phone calls only to start discussing a draft speech prepared by Mansour. Khalil will be addressing the meeting of JEM Executive Board tomorrow and had asked Mansour earlier to compile some points. Thinking there must be some confidential points to be raised, I suggest that I leave them alone for while. Both Mansour and Khalil say it is not necessary but I still think I should give them some space so I pretend to go for a pee anyway. A water vessel is always kept at hand in the camp for the ablution necessary after toileting and most particularly for Muslim prayers. The dusty environment of the area makes the water vessel indispensable for other needs as well. You have to wash your face every now and then with water and clear dust from your eyes. Across the Sudan, the Chinese have now replaced the traditional clay and tin water vessel with a cheap plastic design but have kept its most important feature. In a terrain where water is as expensive as petrol, the vessel has a very small valve that ingeniously conserves water by releasing it in tiny trickles.

A few metres away, I pass by one of the guards sitting on the sand, holding onto his gun. He stands up, gives a salute and then asks for a cigarette. Smokers, including myself, are issued with packets of cigarettes every now and then. But with little to occupy them, soldiers go through their rations very quickly. I keep my rationed cigarettes, but for smokers who do not appreciate my own brand. Theirs, sold by the brand name 'Fine', are much stronger and they seem to prefer them over my Silk Cut brand. I reach into my pocket and hand him a couple of cigarettes, trying to light one of them for him but he declines saying, "Not in front of the boss. I will smoke it later."

I move along contemplating this archaic Sudanese interpersonal habit. This guard is in his mid twenties and still does not smoke in front of Khalil. It is not polite for young men to smoke near their elders who can be any acquaintance of their parents' generation. Even though Khalil and the guard do not belong to the same ethnic group, they seem to act as relatives. I too picked up this habit from Khalil and am now in the habit of addressing anyone below the age of 30 as son, meaning my son. The manner in which the guard hides his smoking habit from Khalil but at the same time borrows cigarettes from me is certainly not flattering. After all, I am older than Khalil, reasonably senior in JEM and have a head of hair that is whiter than that of anyone else in the entire camp? Am I insulted? Of course not! "Thank you my son, you will come again to borrow another cigarette tomorrow!", I say to myself and walk away from the guard.

Going for a pee at night is not an easy venture in the camp. You need courage and a strong pigeon-like sense of navigation. The place is infested with snakes, scorpions, lizards, super-size cockroaches, fat rats and God knows what other creatures, all ready to jump at you as you walk at night. Scorpions are a picnic, relative to the others, and nobody bothers about them. With our army boots, we just crush them as we walk. But the problem is the snakes. Depending on which part of them you tread, a nearly two foot snake can strike high above the boot or simply through the trousers. If it is any consolation, snakes here are not terribly lethal, particularly when they hit you in the leg, the furthest point away from your brain. And snakes are not innately malicious; we must give them credit where it is due. Snakes do not run after people and do not creep about looking for a human being to bite. Far from it, they do their best to avoid contact with human beings, sparing their bites for defensive or pre-emptive purposes. It is easy to avoid snakes at night. The motto is simple—make a little noise with your boots as you walk along and slow down to give them time to move out of your way. Other than that, there is little to do except muster your courage and pray for Allah to save your feet.

As I walk away from the guard, I become very conscious about landmarks around me. It is easy to get lost over here and stories abound about seasoned soldiers who lost their way back to their camps following similar short walks. Yesterday I lost my way in broad daylight. Luckily, after twenty minutes of utter disorientation, I spotted one of our cars at a distance and one of the soldiers had to bring me back to my camp. If that can happen in the middle of the day, my concern at night cannot be reduced to mere paranoia. But my prospects of identifying landmarks are limited to trees and stars. Almost all trees over here are Acacia and it is hard to distinguish among them. As for the stars, they are good for establishing cardinal directions but notoriously unreliable for short walks. And so I study my surroundings. To my right now is a dead tree falling eastwards. To the left of it is the tallest tree within sight, with a little shrub next to it but in the direction of a guard with whom I had just spoken. With delight, I spot a medium size 'toothbrush' tree ahead of me. It is greener and thicker but above all, it is not Acacia as are the rest of the other trees. It is now to my right, therefore it should be on my left when I come back.

I now turn to stars for further clues. I wonder whether our rich folk-knowledge of stars can help me get back safely. Otherwise, I will spend the night in the open and the mosquitoes will get a delightful feast. Unfortunately, the northern star is not visible tonight. It has been a dusty day and the horizon is covered in haze. The 'milky way' is now right over my left eye and I am not sure how useful it is. That cluster of stars, we call 'the chicken and its chicks', is right over my head and so is 'the scorpion'. I forget about them because any star that sits over your head makes a poor navigation lead. But my best clue comes from those stars we call 'the funeral bed'. One of the four stars, forming the left hind leg of the bed, points eastwards with a slight tilt to the north. Exact east can be worked out by forming a line between that bed leg and another star down below, spoken of as the third mourner following the funeral bed. From where I stand, that line is right on Khalil's head. I fail to locate the bouquet of stars we call 'the leather water bucket'. My failure gives me a feeling of discomfort. My prolonged absence from Africa is robbing me of wonderful knowledge that I mastered during my childhood. Embarrassing as it may be, I now share the same impoverished navigation skills of any European citizen who requires a GPS to find his/her way in his/her birthplace.

Believe it or not, I manage to find my way back to the carpet. Delightfully, I find the pair of them talking about Khalil's child-hood, which interests me, so I go along with it and forget about Hinain for a while. Mansour leaves, claiming to be tired but I know he is playing the same game that I did half an hour earlier. He simply does not want to listen or eavesdrop on what we are saying. Strange to say, I knew Mansour over the phone like many other senior members of JEM but I cannot recall meeting him in the flesh before my arrival to the Military Base. In the Executive Council of JEM, Mansour is replacing Jammali Jallal Eldin who was killed in the invasion of Omdurman (May 2008).

As Mansour leaves, I urge Khalil to take me back to what he has been telling Mansour. They were talking about Khalil's early childhood but a tree was intriguingly inserted into the family history. Without waiting for me to stop adjusting my voice recorder, Khalil clears his throat and says, "Believe it or not, I was not born in a village or a town. I was born under a Sidr tree at a nomadic camp, or in the wilderness if you would like to say so. The tree is still there bearing my name, Hinain. We were people of animals and my family was always roaming around in search of pasture and water as the seasons dictated. But we have a village too, called Kayra, about twelve kilometres south of Tine town. My documents say I was born in 1958 but I don't think that is right. I was probably born a year or so before that. As you know, we, and yourself too, belong to that generation whose birth dates were not documented. There were no maternity hospitals, no trained midwives and no birth forms to fill. Our birth dates were later based on estimates negotiated between health personnel and our relative a decade or more after our actual birth dates. Of course this is still the case in most rural parts of Darfur.

I was the sixth of eight children. They were Nadeefa, Abu Bakar, Hawa, the twins Husna and Husain, Gibriel, myself and Mohamed. I also have another brother from a different father. You know him well of course. That is Abdel Aziz Ushar who is now serving a death sentence following the JEM invasion of Omdurman."

Khalil senses my confusion over something and he is absolutely right. The Sudanese are notoriously forgetful of the age of people but it is rare for anyone to miss where he belongs among his or her siblings. Khalil should be the seventh child and not the sixth as he says. Khalil realises my predicament, quickly spotting the cause of my confusion. So he clarifies, "Two of my older siblings were twins and I was the result of my mother's sixth pregnancy. I did not have a chance to know my father. He died when I was a baby and it was my good mother who brought me up. My mother married again so I had a stepfather. He was also a relative, a first cousin of my late father and hence he was never a stranger to the family. In our culture as you well know,

9

if I were to be orphaned, as it happened, he would have been obligated to come to my help anyway. But a lot had happened before the second marriage. Following the passage of my father, the family moved back to my mother's village so that she could avail of her brothers' help."

Khalil pauses longer than usual for he is a man never short of words. I get worried that the interview has inadvertently revived a difficult memory of growing up without a father. Apparently, I am wrong. Khalil is thinking about his mother, a woman he reveres and holds in respectful love and admiration. So he continues in an impassioned voice, "My mother is called A'iba which means in our language 'have you seen her?'. This is a beautiful name that eulogises a woman and extols her virtues. She is A'iba Idris—Sultan—Abderrahman Firti. Sultan Abderrahman Firti was also a paternal uncle of my late father and was a Sultan with a royal copper drum. Like many other ethnic groups around, copper drums are symbols of royalty and only kings or sultans are allowed to keep them. The current Sudan border splits the Zaghawa into two countries, Chad and Sudan and the dividing line now runs on the grave of Sultan Firti. His line of pedigree goes back in a succession of 25 Sultans to Sultan Kuria, the ancestor of the Kobi branch of the Zaghawa people. To be exact, Sultan Bakheit Abderrahman of Umjaras Palace on the Chadian side of the divide is number 24 in that line of Sultans. His relative Mansour Dosa Abderrahman Firti, on Sudan's side of the divide, is number 25, and we meet at Sultan Abderrahman.

My mother is a formidable woman and I cannot express how much I am indebted to her. She did everything to take care of us following the untimely death of our father. But for want of a male guardian, it was my maternal uncle Salih who acted as our father figure. My mother was not short of brothers and I can say I was fortunate to have had numerous uncles to take care of me. In addition to uncle Salih, my mother had two other full brothers—Basher and Nur Eldin. But she had many other brothers too, or half brothers to be precise. Altogether, there were 22 brothers and sisters in her family so we were comfortably protected. That was in addition to ten more younger uncles who were born later."

At this moment, I stop writing. Khalil notices this so he pauses for a while. Khalil is intrigued by my ability to write in darkness, a skill that many anthropologists have. It is unwise to put full trust in a digital recorder and I use notes as back up. Writing in darkness comes with its problems particularly when it is in the Arabic language, which is notorious for dots. Almost every second letter in the Arabic language has one to three dots, either below or over it and this is my headache when I write in darkness. Dots always fall in the wrong place and in order to avoid the consequences of memory lapses, they have to be revised and adjusted at the earliest opportunity. Having overcome his amazement about my writing, Khalil proceeds to clarify himself, "Yes, my mother had many siblings out of her grandfather's forty nine marriages. Her father was a sultan and sultans had many wives in the past. Of course Islam restricts the number of wives to four at a time but there were always ways around that. Sultans wanted more and more children and they would keep getting married, abandoning older wives as time passed. I am glad to say that this archaic Zaghawa tradition is now waning and women are now treated much better than before."

My mind sails back to my own family and in particular to that of my maternal grandfather. Well, I must confess my mother's father was dwarfed by Khalil's grandfather's nuptial enterprise but not the number of descendants left behind. Altogether, there were twenty children of six or possibly seven wives of my own mother's father. Add two or three generations down the line and you have a whole lineage in both families of Khalil and myself. I get a strong urge to get Khalil talking about his uncles and their family but then I pull back. In as much as I want to guide and manage the direction of the interview, I equally wish to leave Khalil free to talk about what is important for him. After all, this work is meant to be an exposition of his life and nobody is more adept in determining what matters in that biography than the man himself. We adjust our squats and I let Khalil indulge in his royal connections, "Through my mother and father's families, we are connected to many Sultans, both here and in Chad. Sultan Mansour who escaped the current war and is now living in Khartoum is the 25th in our Sultanate line. He is Mansour Dosa … Abderrahman and that is where he connects with my mother. My mother's full name is: A'iba Idris Abderrahman. On your way towards us, you were hosted by the family of Sultan Bakheit of Iriba in Chad. Those people are also our cousins and are descendants of Haggar, who was another brother of our ancestor Sultan Abderrahman. At a different level, we are also related to a King of Umbaru of North Darfur as well as relations of Brigadier Tigani Adam Tahir through a grandmother.

Similarly, we also share ancestors with Sultan Hasan Bargo of Kabka and of Chad. Among the groups that stretch across Chad-Sudan Borders, we are linked to no less than ten branches of Bedeyat of the Zaghawa. That is where my family relates to Idris Deby, the current President of Chad. But our pedigree also connects us with non-Zaghawa people. Prince Tigani Ali Dinar of the Fur ethnic group is also related to us. His mother Mastoora was the daughter of Sultan Abderrahman. We are also distantly connected with Sultan Terab of the Fur. His mother, Fatima Guria, known in Arabic as Zareeba, was a sister of Sultan Haroot and Sultan Taha of the Kobi branch of the Zaghawa people and were children of Hinain (Hilal). In my genealogy, Taha appears seven generations above me, on my father's side. Guria, Taha and Haroot were children of king Kuria Abdalla Baru. In Zaghawa language, Kuria is nicknamed 'ina kuria' which

12

translates in Arabic as 'the mounting king'. According to local
exegesis, he appeared in a large convoy of horses and camels.
Thus, he distinguished himself from other strangers who came
on foot".

Khalil takes a sip of his soft drink can and offers one for me
but I decline. He is at full tilt, humbling me with knowledge of
his ethnic connections. To say I am impressed is an understatement. I am indeed mesmerised by the whole experience and do
not wish to disturb the flow of the narrative. He continues with
the same confidence and passion, flattering me with the title
'Professor', "You know Professor, we Darfur people are ethni-
cally more mixed than people dare to admit. This aspect of our
population fascinates me and I always go out of my way to learn
about it. Mohamed Yousif, the current Federal Minister of Youth
and Sport comes from a royal Fur Family. Nonetheless, we are
relatives sharing one ancestor. The Rezeigat Arabs are connected
to us through our common ancestor Ahmed Alkarobi. As for
the Tunjur ethnic group, we meet somewhere high up at our
common ancestor Ahmed Almagoor. Through the Tunjur, we
also have multiple connections with Bedeyat and in particular
the Briera lineage. We link with them at Ahmed Almagoor and
Abu Zaid Alhilali. Darfur is a spectacular locus of ethnic mix.
We have a very rich tradition of local history but many people
are not aware of it. In one of these stories, three bothers and a
sister appeared in what is now known as Umkardoos area near
Nyala. They were the earliest Muslims in the land. One of them
settled in Dar Sila in Chad and formed what has come to be
known as the Dajo Sultanate.

The second brother settled in Tama Land forming Tama
Sultanate. His descendant, Sultan Baroud of Gereida, is now
ruling his people in Chad. The third one established the Kobi
branch of the Zaghawa ethnic group that was subsequently
divided into Chad and Sudan. As for their sister, she was wedded

to the Sultan of Gimir and her offspring became Gimir to this day. Thus we have the Tama, the Gimir, the Dajo and the Kubi, all descended from the same family. Local traditions refer the link back twelve to thirteen generations ago.

Like all Darfur people, my people explain their Arabisation in genealogical terms. We mentioned earlier a man called Ahmed Alkarobi, say more than a dozen generations ago. Alkarobi is the ancestor of what are called Karobat Arabs in Darfur and Chad. As an Arab, Alkarobi was known in Zaghawa as 'Sunutair', meaning 'white or light coloured man'. Sunutair produced a child called 'Sunu Beri' meaning the 'white/ light coloured Zaghawa'. Your friend Izzadin Bajji belongs to this Zaghwa group. They are much more Arabized and some say are slightly lighter in colour. My family connects with them on both sides of my mother.

As you can see, I am a product of many ethnic groups including some Arab ones. In my calculation, I am connected to no less than 52 ethnic groups. So far I have focussed on men but I have hundreds of female ancestors we have not yet covered. Despite all this ethnic mix, I can say I am a Zaghawa, that is, in terms of my culture, language, origin and sentiments. Of course there is nothing called a pure ethnic group and hence there are contradictions here. All Darfur people are equally mixed, much more than they realise. Darfur is rich in local history and if Darfur people are taught their history and where they come from, lots of the problems we currently have will simply dissipate".

On this note, I feel the session has come to its natural end. As we exchange good night wishes, Khalil instructs one of the guards to show me the way to my camp. He knows the area very well and with my poor sense of navigation—take one wrong turn around a tree, and you will spend the rest of the night looking for your way.

Back in my camp, Abdel Karim Cholloy, Commander General of the JEM Forces is waiting. He is half lying on a carpet next to his pitched mosquito net. Next to him is Ahmed Togot Lisan, the Chief Negotiator. He is inside his tent, faintly visible in the dark but struggling to overcome sleep and take part in the chat. A few meters away is my mosquito net waiting for me to erect it. Soldiers are scattered, forming a circle around us, some asleep and some chatting in a low voice intermittent with laughter. It is generally peaceful at night so the guns have already gone under pillows and I am glad to see no barrel is pointing in my direction—just in case—as nobody knows what dreams they may have in their sleep.

The Commander offers me a cup of sweet tea from a flask. The tea is barely hot as it has been there for a long time and no fresh fire is allowed at night. We talked for a while about the battle for El Fashir, led by him in 2003. It was a historic moment that catapulted the Darfur uprising into a credible armed struggle. The then Governor of Darfur who is an accomplished army general described the execution of the invasion as the envy of every army general, combining surprise, swiftness and withdrawal with minimum casualties. The assault supplied the fighters with weapons much needed for establishing themselves as an armed Movement. Prior to that, Khartoum propaganda dismissed the Movements as no more than amateur bandits. Commander Cholloy was badly injured during the assault. He fainted in the middle of directing his forces.

I fiddle with my recorder to capture this glorious moment of the El Fashir invasion. Sadly, the Commander falls asleep on me. I turn to Togot but he is already snoring. I know there is no history of tsetse fly in the area so I cannot say he is a victim of one. To my knowledge, Darfur languages lack terms for the fly in their vocabularies. Those of us who were fortunate to have visited schools have learnt about the fly in biology or public health classes. I feel envious of Togot and Cholloy. Despite their formidable responsibilities, they are able to sleep so easily. But I also understand. We spent the whole day in meetings. From half past eight in the morning until sunset, we were squatting under the same tree, discussing endless JEM problems. The shade of the tree kept moving and so it was our carpet throughout the day. Of course we had short breaks for food and prayers but that was all.

I wish the Commander good night and he responds with apologies for not being able to stay awake. Unlike me, he will get up very early and phone his instructions to different battalions across Darfur and beyond. But believe me, when I say early, it is early; somewhere around five o'clock in the morning. As for the likes of me who gets tempted to stay a little longer in 'bed', we have our own alarm clocks. These are the machos and there are many of them in any army. They cannot be bothered about mosquito nets and prefer to sleep in the open. And if you sleep without a mosquito net, you have to get up early as flies will awaken you at the crack of dawn. Early risers make sure we are up as well. They hang around chatting, praying, making tea or being a nuisance to late sleepers.

I crawl under the mosquito net and try to catch some sleep. I think about safety for a while. Night guards are nowhere in sight. They are perhaps far away, positioning themselves at an outer circle around the base. Government planes do not bomb before late morning. They require daylight to fly and the nearest military airport is a few hours flight from here. We do not expect them at night and if they ever show up, it will be well after sunrise. My mind goes a bit hazy with sleep. Suddenly, I wake up, disturbed by the chase of two puppy-like animals passing swiftly between Cholloy's mosquito net and mine. Of course they are not puppies for there are no dogs in the camp. These are either foxes or a fox chasing a rabbit or some other poor animal. A few seconds later, I hear the howling of a fox in the distance. This is surely one of the guilty culprits. Foxes are abundant in the area, and like other scavengers, they sneak into the base at night looking for food. And there is no better place for food remains than this military base. Three camels were killed early today to feed us and there are no bins for hiding the waste. Food remains are simply thrown a few meters away from the camp, to the delight of foxes, hedgehogs, squirrels, rats and God knows what other creatures. The chase leaves me wide awake and with my mind wandering all over the place. My trip to the base seems to prevail over other thoughts and that is what I fall asleep thinking about.

N'Djamena City

It is a mid July day and Paris is sunny with a temperature well over 20° Celsius. I am wondering how it is in Sub Saharan Africa. I struggle to identify my seat in an Air France plane bound for N'Djamena, the capital of Chad. Luckily, the plane seems to be ready to leave at 3pm as scheduled. I try to read for a while but my mind is too scattered for anything of substance so I turn to something lighter, or so I think. I take out two manuals: one for a digital camera, the other for a digital voice recorder and wonder where to begin. As I fiddle with my camera, the air hostess comes towards me looking somewhat agitated. It does not take her long to discover what I am up to, so she turns away with a big smile. It didn't occur to me that taking photographs of fellow passengers has also joined the list of forbidden acts during air flights. On reflection now, I must agree that banning the use of cameras in airplanes does make sense, for who wants to be photographed by a stranger in mid-air? A glance around me makes things clearer. There are about a dozen EU soldiers in full uniform among the passengers. Many other passengers in civilian clothes must be UN and NGO employees heading for the same destination. Chad is host to well over 400,000 Darfuri refugees and some of my fellow passengers are on their way to take care of them. But they too have their own safety concerns, and hence, taking their photos without permission is a matter of concern to the airhostess.

It is around 10pm and our plane has just landed at N'Djamena International Airport. Well, 'United Nations International Airport' would have been a better name for the place. Our aircraft is the only commercial passenger carrier at the entire airport. There are perhaps a dozen other planes, all of which are either UN, military or cargo planes, presumably flying in personnel and supplies for refugees and their EU peacekeepers (EUFOR).

The humid air of the rainy season gives me a spectacular African welcome and makes me feel at home. The smell of fuel pouring out of the engines of the plane fails to confound the wonderful aroma of the air. As the passengers descend the stairs of the airplane, they go into an orgy of stripping off their clothes. One by one they remove their jackets and hang them over their shoulders. If you think Paris was warm earlier on in the day, it is a relative term when applied at this moment to Africa. Yet, speaking for myself, I cannot say it is hot either. The rain that has fallen prior to our arrival has created a pleasant temperature, but not cool enough for European jackets.

I walk towards the main entrance of the airport and struggle to suppress my pitiful reflection about the country. Chad is 128,4000 square kilometres, bringing it to more than twice the size of its former colonizer France, 2.34 to be exact. And yet, the country has neither national nor private airline and this is its International Airport. To make matters worse, Chad has no highway network to speak of either. The thought gives me concern about the trip that lies ahead of me. I quickly cast that aside for it is a problem for another day and for a different place.

The passport control zone is relatively small but still gives the impression of having more airport staff than passengers. This ratio reminds me of my home, Sudan, a poor country where the State is the biggest employer as well. There are far too many employees for the work to be done. To call it 'disguised unemployment' is to miss the logic behind it altogether. Government employment provides the only barrier against destitution for employees and their extended families and hence in a poor nation, the bigger the public sector, the better. But this phenomenon is also driven by its own logic. African governments rely on inflated public employment to stay in power. Providing a dubious road to power, public employment becomes the only viable device for the generation of legitimacy, safeguarding the loyalty of the masses.

I am just about finding my way in the queue when a young Sudanese man approaches me and introduces himself. Welcome to the informal world of Africa. This young man is now mingling with the passengers right behind the passport control cubicles. As I come to learn, he is a representative of the JEM office in N'Djamena and a son of a high-ranking JEM officer who was a classmate of mine during my school days. I never met the lad by the name of Isam before, but he claims to have recognised me from my photographs on the internet. Well, I must say I am flattered and resolve to boast to my friends back in Ireland that someone, somewhere in the world, recognizes my face in the same way as he recognises celebrities he has never met in the flesh. He may be the only one who recognizes me in this way but that is good enough for me to boast about.

Isam and his companion, a Chadian airport employee in what looks like a military uniform, take my passport and lead me to a small office by the passport control cubicles. There are only two desks in the small office shared by three employees, a woman and two men. They are also in military uniform. It is very clear that the woman is the senior of the three. She has an air of authority, wears a more decorated outfit and has the whole desk to herself. Her uniform is of better fabric than the others and looks like it has come straight off an ironing board. The senior official welcomes us with a smile and directs us to start with the men sharing the second desk. The two men go into what looks like an unnecessarily complex operation of scrutinising my three documents: a passport, a copy of a faxed entry visa and a set of airline tickets. The men look friendly and relaxed and reassure me that they are not on the look out for a fault. It takes them a few minutes to do their scribbles, signing and stamping the documents before passing them to their boss for extra signatures. The encounter is, to say the least, a spectacular fusion of French bureaucracy and Chadian informality. We are treated like acquaintances but with full commitment to official processes. The operation is soon accomplished but has produced more work for me and other Chadian employees in the city; I am to reproduce my documents and get my passport re-stamped at the Immigration Office within three days. Some fellow passengers whom I left at the queue are still there when I pass on my way out of the airport.

Two senior personnel of JEM are waiting in their car for me outside the airport. These are Bishara Suleiman, Secretary for International Affairs and Commander Izzadin Bajji, Secretary for Financial Affairs, and the person who organised my visa. Bishara is a short stocky man who is often quiet, carefully weighing his words when he speaks. He is a shrewd businessman and can spot a crooked person a mile away. Bishara was running a successful business in the Sudan until the problem of Darfur started. Like many Darfurians, he had to leave Sudan and his unfortunate choice was the Gulf countries. There too, his business flourished, but not for long. Following a petition from the government of Sudan, Bishara was ejected together with other successful businessmen and is now living in Chad. But Bishara is smart. He has adapted himself to this nomadic existence and has spread his business over numerous African countries, a strategy that protects his business against the turbulence of African politics. No wonder Bishara handles the international aspects of JEM.

I never met Izzadin Bajji before in the flesh but have known his voice over the phone very well. Bajji is in N'Djamena for a short break and has taken the duty of ferrying me across the border into Darfur. Bajji is renowned for being an excellent army commander. But the man also has other qualities that are no less important for JEM. He is a wheeler and dealer, a practical man who knows how to navigate around difficulties and get a job done. Send Bajji into a shop to buy an item and he will come out with it as a gift, free of charge. That is Commander Bajji.

Both Bishara and Bajji are familiar with the city and have established an impressive web of connections across the nation and beyond. Their position is helped by having numerous relatives living in the city, some of whom work for the Chadian government.

The 20 minutes journey to the hotel is short but equally informative. N'Djamena has been known for being one of the poorest capitals in Africa but that image is gradually being challenged by the new flow of oil. The city looks like a forest of cranes and JCBs; roadwork signs and new buildings abound everywhere. This is my second trip to the city; the first was five years ago but it was of too short duration, lasting only about six hours. At the time, the Chadian government was at loggerheads with JEM and our trip was confined to meeting Mr Deby, the President of Chad and mending the relationship between the two sides. The mission was a spectacular success leading to an enduring and healthy relationship between Chad and JEM. But the trip taught me nothing about the city. My companions and I were taken to a hotel where we waited for the President to have time for us. Following a short meeting with the President, we drafted an agreement and then headed straight to the airport and out of the country. The few spare minutes I had in the city was consumed by eating and greeting, a prime feature of Chadian hospitality that I will come to later.

N'Djamena now looks much more militarised than a few years ago. Military check points and armed guards are a common sight at every turn. But there is something reassuring nonetheless: the soldiers appear very relaxed and unconcerned about the traffic and the passers-by. The blasé posture of the soldiers is understandable for they are not deployed to keep the city dwellers in check. Rather, their duty is to defend the city against rebel invaders from Sudan. Luckily, over 1,000 kilometres distance from the borders to the Sudan gives these soldiers ample cause to be relaxed in discharging their duties.

We reach Hotel Sahel just before midnight. Our car has to manoeuvre its way over water drainage cover to enter the hotel. According to a previous visitor, I was to stay in a JEM guesthouse in N'Djamena. Well, apparently not. The guesthouse is full and Hotel Sahel is now used for the overflow. There are two rooms booked for JEM in Hotel Sahel, one of them is to become my home for a while. The room can be shared by a couple of people if necessary. This brings back a wonderful memory of my childhood in Darfur. My father was a merchant and our house always received many guests, many of whom were retail traders who would regularly visit my dad to restock their shops in neighbouring villages. They used to come with a camel or two and buy one sack of sugar, a chest of tea, a box of soap and so forth. Their business might entail lodging with us for a night or two. We had a large guest room where I had my bed, together with four other beds. Between the beds was a large mat that was also used for sleeping. Whenever we had an extra important guest, I had to crash on the mat and leave my bed for him. As the weather was always hot, the courtyard in front of the guest room made a better space for sleeping at night. Our house was large enough to sleep over a dozen male guests. Female guests stayed inside the house and had no shortage of space either. Thus, in Sudanese style, the two rooms reserved by JEM in Hotel Sahel could go a long way.

My room in Hotel Sahel is by all means ok, though it is pretty basic with running hot water, mosquito net, a fan that works only at full speed and an efficient air conditioner, if you can bear its noise for an extended period. Overlooking the electric sockets that protruded out of their positions, the room is adequate but does display a remarkable comical feature. The bathroom door is made of clear glass leaving the toilet seat constantly in full view from anywhere else in the room. What the designer thought about possible occupants of that room was indeed a curiosity. He must surely have imagined that the occupants and their guests would be so resolutely intimate as to answer the call of nature in full view of each other. Well, my entire period of stay in that room failed to produce even a single person with whom I could share such a cosy affinity; that is, if such a bond ever exists among adults. On a number of occasions, either my guest or I had to leave the room to allow use of that wonderful bathroom. Mind you, as I now realise, I do share the room with others who do not mind me, or who may even delight in me using the bathroom in their presence. These are a couple of mosquitoes, one or two cockroaches and a beautiful small gecko, barely an inch long which takes the liberty of leisurely sneaking in and out through an opening under the door. I must say, I sort of like the small gecko and accept that it has the same right, if not more, to share my space in Hotel Sahel.

I get up fresh in the following morning, ready to explore my surroundings. I take a short walk around the block but find nothing to attract my attention. I might as well be walking around in any big city in Darfur. So much for the capital city of N'Djamena! Back at the Hotel, Bishara and Bajji are sitting at a table in the open, in front of their room. They are ready to have tea and coffee when I arrive. The weather is just perfect and there is no need yet to look for shade provided by the trees a few meters away from us. It is a good time to catch up with news but equally to learn more about the place which is now buzzing with residents waking up for their work.

Hotel Sahel is a single storey building with rooms on the sides facing an inner open courtyard. The design makes it look more like a horse stable than any other structure. Several trees scattered around the courtyard provide pleasant shades for chatting, doing business and sheltering cars from the heat of the sun. In some way, the Hotel evokes a memory of the detested apartheid system, for European residents occupy one side of the hotel with better rooms, leaving the rest of the hotel for African residents, including the likes of us, Sudanese and Chadians. Peace-keeping and relief operations bring in a large number of western personnel to Chad but only the most junior among them end up at Hotel Sahel. We refer to them as the Mitsubishi tribe for they often opt for expensive air-conditioned and chauffeur-driven 4W drive Japanese cars. The laptops and brief cases they carry do not match their tourist posture of shorts, t-shirts and sandals. In sharp contrast to the row of lavish cars of the Mitsubishi tribe are the other vehicles on the African side of the divide—dirty, dilapidated and always left unlocked.

Communication between European and African residents in the courtyard is perplexing to me as I sit among them. The Africans cast their sharp gaze at any moving object in the vicinity. Once they share space with others, the Africans stop seeing them as strangers and look for an opportunity to engage. But the Europeans react differently. As they move around, they make minimum eye contact, preferring to withdraw into a mode of polite non-interference, walking around with minimal eye contact. There is no air of unease or feeling of enmity between the two sides. It is simply a cultural clash where friendliness and concern about welfare of the other are discharged in different ways. The end result is an awkward lack of communication that combines proximity with distance at the same time.

It is now well after 8.30am and the shade provided by Bishara's room wall is failing us. Two young men join us and are waiting to do some business with Bishara. They are also JEM members looking for help to find work in the city. The sun is already getting hot and will soon force us to take refuge under a Neem tree a few meters away. We are sipping sweet tea and eating bread with jam and processed cheese. It is a pitiful breakfast indeed but will keep us alive until we organise lunch, a short drive from the hotel. As we sit there, we entertain ourselves by watching a bunch of white storks constantly rebuilding their nests in the tree. These are familiar migratory birds in Sub-Saharan Africa, appearing regularly during the rainy season. They are almost domestic, preferring to nest in trees in populated areas and never in the wild. But they are noisy and irritating at the same time. Their nests are so badly constructed that the twigs keep falling at every move. To keep their nests in shape, the poor birds spend the whole day flying up and down the tree to retrieve fallen twigs. But some of them are more honest than others. Every now and again, one of them steals a twig from the adjacent nest and a mighty fight between the two neighbours ensues. No wonder Darfur people see these birds as epitomising anti-sociality and lack of neighbourly spirit. We give Bishara a hard time, for the bird proliferated in his native Zaghawa land and hence is called 'Zaghawa bird'. We recall how industrious the Zaghawa are and admire their capability of turning even the most piteous opportunity into wealth. Rather than giving them credit for their creativity, other groups in Darfur stereotype the Zaghawa as deceitful, anti-social and intent on enriching themselves at the expense of others. We catch one bird stealing a twig and make a comment confusing Bishara as to whether we are referring to dishonest Zaghawa birds or Zaghawa people. Bishara concedes that he is outnumbered by us and takes our mockery of his people in good spirits, proceeding to shower our own respective ethnic groups with no less demeaning stereotypes, ranging from cowardice to treachery and destitution.

Isam drops in with a friend and finds us sitting under the same tree. He introduces me to a friend by the name Ateem (not his real name) who works in the 'intelligence' end of the airport. We seem to hit it off and he promises to fix me a flight to Sudan's border and thus save me the hassle of going by road, a trip that takes at least 'two nights' in the way he expresses it. I delight in finding a new friend who looks genuine and is well connected in the city. Ateem is a Sudanese from Darfur, turned Chadian. Within minutes of exploring his biography with him, I discover that I know many of his cousins and relatives who attended secondary school and university with me. These connections dispel my apprehension about befriending someone with a connection to the Chadian National Intelligence. Ateem and Isam take my passport and promise to take care of registration as ordered at the airport.

Isam and Ateem are replaced by two other visitors to Bishara. They are busy talking in Zaghawa language. I do not speak Zaghawa so I get lost and turn to my notebook to jot down a few observations. Both of the new guys are called Mohamed and I am not able to remember their father's names. What is striking about both Mohameds is that they have two mobile phones each. To my surprise, I discover that Bishara also has two mobile phones. But there is somebody else in the company I forgot to mention. His name is Ibrahim and he has a business in the city. Ibrahim is certainly much smarter than the Mohameds. He shows me something called a dual simcard mobile phone, something I never knew somebody had taken the bother to invent at all. But here it is in front of my eyes. I carefully examine the new device and get really impressed. I too use a separate mobile phone when travelling abroad and in fact I have no less than ten simcards for different countries, but they are useless because I cannot find them when I need them and that means five minutes before my drive to the airport. What I was looking for before at Heathrow Airport sometime ago was not a dual simcard phone but a multiple simcard holder, something like a business card holder where you can store your spare simcards. But Ibrahim's phone looks cool and I feel this strong desire to procure one as soon as I find my way to the market. God bless China for they make things cheap in this country. I don't care how clumsy my dual simcard phone would look or how many years it would last. Mind you, back in Ireland, we change our mobile phones once every 18 months. And so what if my Chinese phone wouldn't last long. It is not the end of life.

As we sit there chatting, I get intrigued by the Chadian, or shall I be honest and say, Chadian-Sudanese use of mobile phones? A different etiquette for handling mobile phones seems to be in play over here. The phones are constantly ringing and one needs no apology for answering the phone even in the middle of a conversation with companions. Occasionally you are drawn into the phone call and asked to say hello to the person at the other end whom you do not know and have never met. In Chad, in the same way that you get introduced to someone you meet, you can also be introduced to someone through the phone and with minimum background information. Imagine being asked to talk to someone in that manner. What are you going to say? I suppose you can say, how are you? How is your family—in a broader sense—because you do not know whether the person is married or not, say a few things about the weather, which Africans rarely talk about and that is it. You cannot ask such a person about work just in case you end up hitting a communication block; the other person might not be working at all or the business might be going through difficult times. Either way, the communication is bound to be limited and meaningless, but here you go.

Chad has two rival phone networks, none of which seems to be reliable. At any given time and zone in the city, one of them or both could be off air for a while. Moreover, they are unpredictable in the promotion offer they launch every second day: 'top up now and get free texts for the next three days, top up now and get free minutes within the Server.' And so forth. The Chadians delight in this and play the two servers against each other. They do their best to use the cheapest at any given time and that is why they subscribe to both simultaneously. If you cannot afford to have two phones, let alone a dual simcard phone, you carry an extra simcard in your pocket, just in case.

Chadians also use the so-called 'flash system' in common with other African countries. To flash someone is to phone and disconnect the moment the destination phone starts ringing, what we call 'sending a missed call'. The other person knows that you want to talk to him/her but you are short of credit. More often than not, it is not a matter of being short of credit. Rather, it is a smart recognition that the person you flash is a higher achiever than you and hence has no problem in obtaining credit. Flattery it may be, but it seems to work well in Chad.

Well, you might say, who am I to judge whether the mobile phone is a curse or a blessing in Chad, but I am going to stick my neck out and say something. The idea of two or three people sitting at a table, each speaking on his phone is certainly bizarre but why should I care about that. They are free to say the phones connect six people, a better connectivity than that which can be generated by a company of three people at a table. Let the Chadians go on disrupting their conversation with their mobile phones. In the meantime, I can't wait to get my dual simcards mobile phone.

The Best Food on Earth

A beautiful girl (lead singer)
Bring her to me (all together)
Her lips are dark (lead singer)
Bring her to me (all together)
Her chest is high
Bring her to me
Her hair is long
Bring her to me
I want her now
Bring her to me
Her bum is …..

I rush towards the singers to catch their words. To my surprise, they run away giggling, feeling embarrassed about their words. Having lived abroad for a while, it seems to have escaped me that young boys in their twenties do not sing such songs in front of their elders. This is not flattering but I have to accept that I am old and have long parted company with young men. My white hair obliges these young men not to flaunt their sexuality in my presence. Performed in perfect Darfur Arabic, the song flaunts every rule in the Arabic language but also breaches religious sensibilities and political correctness of at least an older cohort of Darfur people. I gracefully accept that I am in that cohort and I am not a bit offended. Far from it, I find the song very amusing and that is why I want to record it. Bajji, whom I have accompanied to this location finds the episode very amusing and can't stop laughing. I feel a bit embarrassed. What an idiot I am making out of myself!

These young men are JEM soldiers packing their pickup truck in front of a JEM guesthouse where they are staying. They are preparing for their return to Darfur, a journey of over 1,000k. The pickup truck, a sort of SUV, is being loaded with belongings, on which more than a dozen soldiers are to sit for the journey. A few more trucks are on the way but they have not arrived yet. The young men line up at both sides of the pickup holding a rope. The song helps them to pull the rope and tighten it in unison. The lead singer says a verse and those on the right side of the truck pull the rope towards them as they chant, "bring her to me". These kinds of work songs are still common in Darfur in communal work requiring movement coordination. You hear them at water centres, in threshing grain at harvest time and in loading or unloading lorries in the market.

The truck is parked in front of a guesthouse rented by JEM for the purpose. The house is large and facilitates more than two dozen JEM soldiers. Some are there for treatment following injuries in war but many are there for private matters. A few of them are there trying to locate relatives displaced by the Darfur war. Having lost their villages in the war, Darfur survivors scattered around, are trying to eke out a living in Chad. And there is no better place for that than N'Djamena, a city booming with its newly discovered oil. The whole place looks like a jungle of cranes and roadwork signs dotting every road. The city is bustling with pedlars, hard currency dealers and international aid workers. There is indeed a bit of work to do for industrious workers.

Like myself, these young men are going to Darfur or rather returning to Darfur, 'the field' in our parlance. For over five years, I had been acting as Head of Bureau for Training and Strategic Planning of JEM but have never been able to visit the field before. My portfolio designates me as a member of the Executive Council of JEM and in particular for dealing with non-military medium to long term plans of the Movement. Mind you, that does not absolve me of accountability for military ventures of JEM. Following JEM's invasion of Omdurman (Khartoum, May 2008), the government of Khartoum declared me a criminal, and a wanted enemy of the nation. My photograph, together with many others, was splashed all over national newspapers and Sudanese citizens were ordered to cooperate and facilitate my speedy capture. I do not know whether that is frightening or flattering but the fact remains that to this day, I do not know the difference between a Kalashnikov and an AK-47 assault rifle. Maybe there isn't one anyway.

The Executive Council of JEM meets at least twice a year. But there is a formidable challenge in gathering the members of the council in one place. Members are scattered across the globe in three continents, Africa, the Middle East and Europe. Many Members of the Executive Council carry limited travel documents that only allow restricted border crossing. Other members like myself have difficulty attending meetings due to work commitments. To that, one may add military commanders who have to travel through one or more countries and sometimes to attend meetings without recognised official identity documents. Leaving travel and accommodation costs aside, organising a meeting of JEM Executive Council is a daunting business to muster. For this reason, no meeting can be fully attended and many members have to relay their inputs by phone.

I struggle hard to find someone willing to give me the words of the song but the boys collude to tell me nothing. The exposure of my recorder seems to have complicated the encounter. Who on earth wants to go down in history, caught with coming up with such lyrics? As I struggle to overcome my predicament, Bajji comes to me and says we have to be somewhere else and very quickly. We are invited for dinner somewhere and there is no way out of it. The idea of attending such a social occasion appeals to me very much for I want to meet some local people and learn more about the city. Never mind the other side of the rendezvous, the handshaking and the over eating that goes with it.

By the way, if you think I am exaggerating the length of time we spend on greeting each other and eating, you are wrong. In the week that I spent in N'Djamena, I must have added weight that would take me a whole month to gain in Ireland. And I must have clocked a total of 24 to 30 hours of shaking hands. In Chad, it is an experience to meet an acquaintance after some years of separation. You start by hugging and shaking hands uttering the usual phrases: How are you, brother? How is your family? Hope your people are alright; May God keep you in comfort and sound health; Delighted that Allah brought us together again ..... endlessly. Don't worry if you get stuck for new phrases. This is a ritual that needs no imagination and any inventiveness is foolish and counterproductive. Just go back and repeat the exact formula from the start. Then you sit down for a while and try to catch up with news. But just as you are about to leave the greeting business behind, your friend stretches his hand towards you and you start all over again. Then you move towards enquiring about relatives and, of course, somebody like a parent, a sibling or even a close friend must have died since you were last together. Oh God, this requires another round of hand shaking by way of condolences, occasionally coupled with reciting the opening chapter of the Koran that every Muslim knows all too well.

Condolences have their own strict formats, so off you go: May Allah bless his soul; May He take him into the heavens; May Allah receive him with mercy; May He forgive his sins; May Allah bless his offspring; May He admit him into the league of the righteous believers......

As for food, Chad is a land of feasting. Forget the poverty that hits you in the face when you land in the country and never listen to that stuff about food shortage. Those people take their revenge on poverty and lack of food by feasting big. During the time I spent in Chad, I never needed to eat a single dinner, the main meal of the day, in a hotel, and here is how it works, but only if you belong to well-connected people like my hosts. The Chadians save for a while and spare no money for marking their social occasions with a big feast and there is always a gathering for something and an event to celebrate. In a circle of relatives and friends, say around 200 or so, something is bound to happen every three or four days that requires proper commemoration by a banquette: marriage with its several stages, naming a newborn, circumcision, arrival of a brother or friend from the Diaspora, launching a business, new house and so forth. To that, you may also add funerals or remembrance of a deceased relative a year or so later. Thus every second or third day, you are invited for a feast somewhere in the city of N'Djamena. And if you are not invited, not to worry! You don't need to crash the party, for a friend can take you with him. Of course you do not need to be off work to attend these feasts. Your lunch break is there to give you a chance for partaking in the feast and tough luck for top government officials who are concerned about lost working hours. However, if it comes to the worst and you get worried about being late getting back to work, bring your boss with you to the feast and you will be sorted out.

My heart goes out to those Chadians who have to organise these lavish banquettes. Of course for such a feast, one has to map out a substantial budget, labour and time. But it is their use of space that I find most intriguing. To have around 200 men around, not to mention women who slave inside the house cooking, you do need plenty of space. Luckily, a whole industry seems to have flourished to facilitate this obsession with extravagant feasting. A huge rented canvas is used to create a shade complete with plastic mats to squat on. The shelter is pitched in front of the house and takes over the whole street extending nearly up to the door of the opposite house. The traffic is diverted to another street, for no car can pass through. As for neighbours, the host need not worry about them. They are part of the party, but be warned, for this is a man's world; their women are cooking inside the house while the men help in entertaining their neighbour's guests.

Never miss the opportunity if you are invited to one of these gatherings. The food is unbeatable but some of the rules involved may seem somewhat bizarre. When you arrive to the house, you just slam the doors of your car and abandon it anywhere nearby. Most cars in Chad don't lock anyway so you needn't worry about that. Your first problem is how to identity your host, possibly squatting among 100 or so men. That is, of course, if you are a legitimate guest and actually know the host. The Chadians wear this elaborate outfit, a garment that is far too big and wasteful and a Tuareg turban; and it is this turban, locally called Kadmoul, that causes agony for outsiders like myself. The Kadmoul looks much more like a balaclava than anything else. It covers the whole head, ears and all. It is an equalizer where all men look exactly the same but somewhat in disguise. The face is exposed but only just. You can see from half an inch above the eyebrows, down to the eyes, the nose and mouth, and that is all the clues you have to recognize a friend. The chin and the cheeks are hidden and so is the neck. Needless to say, the age of the person is also disguised by the attire.

By the time you reach your host in the mist of the crowd, you would have shaken hands with about 20 men. If you know them, you have to shake hands with them even if you have met them earlier in the day. If you don't know them, remain unconcerned; you will get introduced to them and you have to shake hands with them as well. The only people you are spared shaking hands with are those who are busy eating at the time of your arrival. But don't hold your breath. As soon as they finish eating, they get their share of greetings as well.

Having finished with the business of greeting, now it is time to choose a spot to squat on and that is not an easy matter. The men are divided into smaller groups of five to seven each. Each group makes a space for you and invites you politely to join them and you wouldn't know where to go. You don't want to let any group feel you are rejecting their invitation or that you prefer another group. This is indeed a very delicate matter and you have to weigh things carefully. If you are lucky, someone might just grab you down and bring an end to your diabolical diplomatic agony.

In attending one of those feasts, you need no appetizer. The wonderful aroma of spicy food devoured by groups near you will do the job. After waiting for a while getting distracted by newcomers, our food finally arrives on huge silver trays each carried by two young men. One of these trays lands in front of us. The tray is about 70 centimetres in diameter and comes with a colourful cover made of palm leaves. The cover is a work of art displaying skilful handcraft common in the area. We get asked to sit in groups of ten, so we do, and pretend to be able to wait until everybody is properly seated. God help those women inside the house. They must have been cooking the whole day and a greater part of last night. I count 14 different dishes arranged in a well-defined order of size. It is a real spectacle. No matter how fastidious your taste, you will surely find a dish or two that suits you on our tray: roast meat, meat in sauce, vegetable and meat cooked together and vegetarian dishes. In between the dishes sit piles of a local version of pitta bread.

We besiege the tray and gaze at the wonderful food, waiting for a signal to start. It is not polite to attack food so we hold back and pretend to be in full control of our craving. Only wretched and destitute people attack food and who wants to be confused with one of those miserable creatures. After what seems to be a century of waiting, a wonderful man says, "In the Name of Allah, Most Merciful, Most Compassionate, let us start guys". And we descend on the food like hungry vultures. Unashamedly, our hands are already in the dishes long before we finish uttering the prayer's word "Amen".

I sample different dishes but remain undetermined where to settle. Suddenly, I shift my mind away to the French who colonized this country and ponder about their audacious claim to having the best cuisine in the world. Let the French forget their chateaubriand, chicken chasseur and ratatouille and come and join me right here at Amadu Street in N'Djamena. This is where the best food par excellence is and don't give me that stuff about French food, for I have seen it, tasted it and cooked it as well. Poor French people! It is bad enough that they have been expeditiously defeated by Indian, Italian and Chinese cuisines at the international level. Now I am calling them to bow in front of their former colony as well. How more painful could it be?

But there is something agonising about these feasts, and their occurrence in an open street makes the experience even more troubling. As I struggle to eat more, I cannot overcome an immense feeling of guilt. We are, in fact, surrounded by an army of hungry children staring at us. The children are between the ages of six and thirteen. Some of them are clearly attending a Koranic school nearby for they are carrying wooden slates inscribed with some Koranic verses, or their homework, so to speak. Every child carries a receptacle of some sort or another: a tin, a plastic container, a plastic bag and so forth. Every time a tray is sent back after eating, the children rush forward and are given a chance to strip the tray bare of its leftovers. Given the amount of food served in each tray, there is bound to be plenty left on it but the number of children is not small either. Moreover, the children also want to save some food for later, or for their siblings at home. I have been told that at the end of the feast, there will be special food for these children but there are simply too many to satisfy.

Well, the ugly sight of these children reminds me of what I have read about the history of Europe and its culinary habits. In the 18th century, the French and the British Empire enacted laws regulating banquettes and specifying in great detail how food should be served per a banquette guest. The empires were clearly worried about wasted food that could be spared for feeding the hungry among their populations. As late as the 1990s, India too followed suit and introduced laws regulating marriage banquettes and the maximum amount of rice and meat to be served at wedding feasts. Perhaps the Chadians should take a leaf out of that book but what is the guarantee that saved food will reach these children?

To the Field

It is 10 o'clock in the morning and we are sitting at the court-yard of Hotel Sahel sipping tea and coffee and eating bread with jam. The day is unusually busy for we will soon be on our way to Darfur, inshaalla (by Allah's will) as we say. Actually we should have left half an hour ago but time is taken with incredible ease in this country. One wonders why bother wearing a watch in this part of the world.

We take shelter under our favourite Neem tree and ponder about our surroundings. The problem is that the storks that share the hotel with us also favour this tree and will certainly mark you if you sit directly under their nests. It is getting drier now and the smell of the rain of the past few days is replaced by hot, dusty air. While the heat seems to have slowed down our life a bit, it does not seem to have affected our fellow creatures around us. The birds are busy renovating their nests as usual, the Hotel cat is chasing the geckos around but catching none, and the flies and ants are determined to share our breakfast.

Two top officials of JEM fly in from Egypt and join us at the Hotel. They are Ahmed Togot Lisan and Sulaiman Sandal Haggar, simply known as Togot and Sandal. As I say Togot and Sandal, I reflect on how different is our system of naming compared to its European counterparts. To call the first Togot and the second Sandal gives the impression that we use the middle name in formal contexts. That is not true and we have neither middle names nor family names as such. At least for us in Darfur and other parts of Muslim Sudan, the full name consists of the name of the person, followed by the name of the father and then grandfather, all on the male side of course and irrespective of gender of ego. Thus, we have the siblings Mohamed Adam Ali and Fatima Adam Ali. Should you not like to use the tripartite full name, then stick to the first name only, irrespective of the context or the social distance between the addressed and the addressee. However, if the full name includes a name that is rarely used, then you use that irrespective of the context. Togot and Sandal are rare names and have better distinguishing power and hence they are chosen over other possibilities. Let us now get back to our newcomers.

Togot is the Chief Negotiator of JEM. He is a lawyer by profession but has long drifted into the politics of Darfur. Like many Darfuris, Togot is rendered homeless by the Darfur crisis. He is based in the UK but is rarely there. His family lives in Egypt but he is rarely there either. Most of his time is spent travelling to different countries for talks and consultations on Darfur. Togot is fluent in English, Arabic and Zaghawa and has an encyclopaedic memory of all major events that JEM have experienced since the onset of the Darfur crisis. Togot is perhaps the only person who can name, at any time, the well over 30 resolutions and agreements that have been issued on Darfur/ Sudan and can back that up with dates, contents and lists of signatories.

Sandal is in charge of the Intelligence Division of JEM. He is an accomplished lawyer but had to close down his Khartoum office and flee the country at the start of the crisis. Sandal is an avid reader and is often seen with thick Arabic and English books. He is always a great talker who can captivate his audience with his hilarious sense of humour. In addition to that, Sandal is an excellent commander with a leaning towards the minutiae of battles fought by JEM. He is a wealth of knowledge regarding the military history of JEM, a chapter that is yet to be written.

Togot answers his constantly ringing phone but this time his conversation catches our interest. He is now talking to Bajji who left yesterday with the soldiers to the field. Bajji tells Togot that they are already a third of the way on their journey but Togot remains unimpressed. He tells him that the first 300 kilometres are paved and it is easy to travel. The soldiers have a long way to go but at least they are moving and not sitting on their bums, like ourselves, under a tree getting worried about bird droppings. Ateem will be here anytime and take us to the airport. The man and his plane crew have no concept of time so there is nothing we can do except to sit and wait. Togot laughs at me when I remark that our luggage is way too much for flying. He reminds me that we will be in a transport plane that has no limit for personal luggage. I look at our luggage and remain unconvinced. In addition to our bags, there is a military kit for each of us. These are the same as the military kits displayed on Sudan TV following the invasion of Omdurman in May 2008. In its propaganda, the Government wanted to show its supporters that JEM was financed and fully backed by rich foreign powers and was awash with money. The kit was displayed, valued and compared to kits of the Sudanese army. I must agree that JEM military kit is excessively luxurious and far too heavy for combat movement. It has a huge waterproof canvas mat about the size of a double bed sheet. This is used as a mat but you can also fold it around you when it rains. The kit also has a mattress that looks like a small duvet, a pillow, a mosquito net and a luxurious blanket that you can find only in decent hotels in Africa. Moreover, the kit comes with a military uniform complete with a pair of fine leather boots that I find utterly heavy and impractical. Of course there is no military kit without a gun but that cannot be issued to us in N'Djamena. I needn't worry about that since JEM is unlikely to waste a gun on me anyway. Guns are reserved for trained personnel and not for 'politicians' as they like to call us.

Togot and Sandal joke about my experience with the military kit and can't wait to see me in military uniform. When I received the kit yesterday, I told Bajji that I did not need any for I had my sleeping bag and prefer to wear my civilian clothes.

But Bajji was in no mood for compromise. He told me that all JEM visitors to the field must be in camouflaged military outfit at all times. As for my sleeping bag, he thought it was only fit for western tourists and should remain behind in Hotel Sahel. I don't need to worry about the military uniform now for Ateem says we must board the plane in civilian clothes.

Ateem rings and tells us that he is on the way and we have to be quick. Otherwise, we miss the plane, which is now being loaded at this very moment. At 12pm, we leave the Hotel in a rush. Ateem appears in civilian clothes today and I enquire about his military uniform. He tells me he has to switch between civilian clothes and military uniform depending on the task at hand. He does not elaborate and leaves me wondering whether we will feature in his investigative report later on in the day. Our position in Chad is always precarious and the Chadians must work out what we are up to when we are passing through their country. The Chadians are not to blame, for Sudan always looks at Chad as its backyard and has always meddled in its affairs.

The traffic is smooth and we reach the airport within 15 minutes. We park the car under a tree near the gate of the airport and stay in it while Ateem goes to investigate the plane. We are at the airport but have no tickets and no guaranteed seats in the plane. The three of us are foreigners and in the name of security, the State can easily restrict our movement to the capital if they so wish. The trip looks like clandestine work or a work of espionage that can go wrong at any time. But 'JEM' is a password in Chad that can get you a long way. In Chad, JEM ID is more important than any European passport. When the Khartoum-backed Chadian rebels invaded Chad the previous year, JEM intervened and brought its troops to N'Djamena and successfully defended the government. It is true that JEM was defending its interest and not the government of Chad as such. Having a pro-Khartoum government in N'Djamena would have been catastrophic for JEM. The intervention raised the profile of JEM in Chadian government circles and reduced previous apprehension about the organisation.

We sit in the car and pretend not to be worried. If we fail to board this plane, public transport will remain the only option. That means a trip of 900 kilometres to Abeche and that is only half of the agony. From Abeche, we have to hire a private car to the Chadian border where we can be collected by our troops. We have to map at least three to four days for that, not to mention the cost. I keep thinking about the French idiot who picked N'Djamena to be the capital of Chad. The city sits at the very edge of the country and only a river separates it from Cameroon. From most parts of the city, you can gaze at people roaming around across the river in Cameroon. Small fishing boats sail up and down the river and I wonder whether they know which country they are in as they chase their fortune in the water. Happily, we see Ateem rushing towards us with a huge grin. Never mind that he interrupts my contemplation about the fishermen. We say 'Alhamdulilla', meaning thank God, and rush out of the car, flinging its boot open and nearly breaking it. It is not easy to carry a military kit and a luggage bag each, but somehow we manage.

As we approach the main checkpoint hall, I realise that we are the only passengers in the airport. As usual in all Chadian offices, there seems to be more staff than clients. The staff appears to be relaxed and somewhat disinterested. We are asked to put our bags on the security belt so we do, but our military kits fail to fit. They are far too big for the security chamber so we just pass them around without having to unwrap them. As we pass through gates and come around to collect our bags, one of the staff gets somewhat agitated. Apparently, the security screen has just shown a little toy in Togot's bag. Well, Togot never fails to amaze me. He has a gun in his suitcase that security and Ateem are examining and talking about in a language that I cannot understand. I needn't worry for none of them looks bothered. Togot goes on to show them a piece of paper that I later learn to be a gun license. The gun is to go in the cockpit with the pilot, to be retrieved at the other end of the journey. The crisis is over and off we dash, out into the vast empty space of the deserted airport. Ateem leads us to our plane, which is easy to identify, as it is the only plane in the whole airport.

I must say the plane looks somewhat strange to me. Given its load, the plane is huge and far too big and I wonder why they cannot get something smaller. The rear door of the plane is open for loading with a flap coming straight down touching the tarmac. The flap has an electric conveyor belt that moves things up and that is where we put our luggage. To our surprise, we discover that there are no stairs for us to climb up the plane so we bid Ateem farewell and follow our luggage on the belt and up into the miserable monster. The inside of the plane is something else. It looks much more of a cave than anything else. I get somewhat confused about where we are going to sit but I soon discover benches that you pull down on the inner sides of the plane. They look like low shelves but you can sit on them. Two African men in civilian clothes join us inside the plane. The noise of the engines is deafening and adds to the heat inside the plane. The air-cooling system is at full blast but it is making no impact as the plane is sucking in heat and dust coming out of its powerful engines. The crew have now appeared and are arguing with two Chadian airport staff at the back of the open plane. Ateem looks at them with some amazement, gazing at one of the crew who is holding Togot's pistol, looking as though he is ready to use it if needs be. We cannot hear them because of the noise of the engines and I cannot establish what language they are speaking. After some heckling, the crew moves towards the plane and the rear door moves up slowly, locking us inside. We sit sweating but relieved that the crew is now moving towards the cockpit. There is nothing reassuring about the plane at all. The crew who are clearly Eastern European hardly resemble pilots. They are wearing dirty jeans and clumsy t-shirts with their big bellies sticking out. I look around and examine the no-less comforting surroundings. The plane has certainly not been swept for a few weeks. Empty soft drink cans and soda water bottles are littered everywhere. A few objects that look like aircraft spare parts are piled near us. The only object among them that looks useable is an old spare tyre. This is the first time for me to see an airplane tyre in such close proximity. It is bald and covered in dust looking as big as a tractor tyre. I cannot see any air valve on it so I assume that it is tubeless and has no air like car tyres.

We sit for a while, struggling to manage the heat. It soon becomes apparent that the two Africans we saw earlier are not passengers. They are stewards or whatever you might call them. Each one of them pulls down a bench and lies on it. One of them is reading a book while the other covers his face and gets ready for a sleep, never mind the time of the day. I cannot say I am worried about my safety but I cannot hide my feeling of apprehension and nervousness. I have never before been in a plane that has no seat belts, no exit doors and certainly no safety jackets. What would you do with safety jackets in the middle of the desert anyway? Never in my life, have I experienced fear of flying but this plane is different. Nothing in it says it will not crash. I struggle to drive this thought out of my mind but it keeps lingering in the back of my head. In a self-delusional way, I conclude that if the man opposite to us can go to sleep in front of us, this plane must be safe enough.

Sandal tries to involve me in a discussion he is having with Togot, but without success. My mind is firmly set on the safety prospects of the plane. I try to distract myself with my notebook and pretend to jot down some description of my surroundings.

In the middle of the plane sit two piles of boxes held together with tapes. They are about 1.5 square metres each. I read the contents of the boxes: soup, biscuits, chocolates and something called Nestle puree that I have never heard of before. These are destined for EUFOR in Iriba, the city to which we are flying. I stop writing and contemplate the ludicrous nature of this charter plane and how wasteful the EU can be: the entire load of the plane, including three crew and two attendants, amounts to no more than 500 kilograms of goods. I must be looking at the most expensive soup in the world. It just simply does not make sense to me.

The plane gradually moves along and we get airborne. The noise subsides a bit now and it is possible to talk without shouting. N'Djamena looks deceptively beautiful from the air. Its graceful winding river with little fishing boats adds a charm to the city that I failed to experience while on the ground. You can see Cameroon on the other side of the river and wonder about the interplay between nature and politics in Africa. Here is more or less one place divided by a river into two cities and two nations. The N'Djamena side is poor, turbulent and unstable. The other side is, by African standards, prosperous, peaceful and stable. Even the phones work better over there while they remain rebellious and unreliable on the N'Djamena side of the divide. I wonder whether N'Djamena politicians take time to think about that.

N'Djamena gets smaller and smaller and we shoot up towards the sky. Whether it is by design or otherwise, the pilots take a very steep climb up before they decide to straighten up the plane. For a while, the near vertical ascendancy of the plane threatens to send the boxes rolling down towards its tail. It is getting quieter and I can even hear the man lying on the bench snoring. His snoring gives me comfort for he must feel safe enough to fall asleep so easily. I ask Togot about the make of the plane and he says Antonov in a tone that sounds callously casual to me. My heart jumps with the mention of the name Antonov. I am on my way to the field and will almost certainly be bombed by one of those planes. How stupid am I to be worried about flying in this plane; I shouldn't worry when I am inside it, I should worry when it hovers over my head in the field.

Togot's mention of the Antonov throws me into a state of utter unease and anger. This is the plane that is causing horrendous death and destruction in Darfur. Well, it is not this one but some of the same make. Up to now, over 4,000 villages have been destroyed, with hundreds of thousands of lives lost in the process. I have lost many friends, acquaintances and relatives to Antonov bombing. God forgive the Russians. The history book of Darfur shall remain tainted by the dual Russian contribution to human suffering—of the Antonov and the Kalashnikov.

This is a transport plane flight and the cockpit crew seem to confuse us for the load they are carrying. Throughout the flight, they say nothing and I can't work out if they have any public address system in the plane. An hour or so ago, one of them came out of the cockpit and made a few cups of tea or something and went back through the door that is kept open throughout the flight. He said nothing to us and did not offer us tea or coffee or anything. Those guys are not unfriendly but they simply do not want to have anything to do with us. Maybe they don't think we share a language in common and prefer to save us any embarrassment. It doesn't matter whether they talk to us or not but we are glad they are giving us a lift free of charge.

The plane is now descending and the topography under us is gradually taking shape. We are supposed to land at Iriba, a town close to the borders of Darfur and one of the major posts for fleeing refugees. That is why the town is also a military base for EUFOR. The refugees are picked up by EUFOR and driven to safety in the nearest camp further inside Chad. Iriba is in the heartland of the

Zaghawa and maintains a strong affinity with Darfur Zaghawa across the borders, 60 kilometres away. The town takes its name from its water availability as indicated by the suffix 'ba', which means 'well' or 'water source' in Zaghawa language. In a desert area like this, water becomes an important defining feature of a place, with the amount of it being crucial for the size of habitation it can sustain and the general prosperity of the entire area.

The plane circles for a while and gives a panoramic view of the town. The town seems to be reasonably planned with mostly straight streets of different width and a few zigzag lanes. The houses are mostly single story rooms of brown mud with inter-mittent grass huts. All buildings seem to have flat roofs, a style of architecture common in deserts where it doesn't rain much. Two structures stand out from the air. These are the palace of the Sultan and the EUFOR base. The Zaghawa have a hierarchical system with a Sultan at its apex in every area. Over the years, Zaghawa Sultans have lost most of their official authority to government but have retained strong traditional influence among their own people.

The EUFOR base is located near the airport. It is a huge fenced place with high walls made of sand and barbed wire. From the air, the walls are dam-like raised sand with high observation posts. But there is something odd about the base that makes it an alien imposition in the town. Straight lines and right angles dominate its architecture. It is as though the architects want to teach the Africans about western geometrical order. The base is cramped with tents, vehicles, military tanks, containers as big as rooms, helicopters, etc, all arranged in straight lines. From my window in the plane, I get a spectacular view of EUFOR base whose western wall is no more than 150 meters away from the runway of Iriba Airport.

The landing is reasonably smooth with the plane gradually coming to a halt in the middle of a dust ball. The dust gradually settles away before the back door of the plane is opened for us and our luggage. Before I work my way out of the plane, I notice one of the pilots getting out and running away from the plane. I feel a sense of panic coming on for a moment and look at Togot for an answer but he is equally bewildered. I soon realise there is no cause for panic at all and that I must stop being paranoid. The poor pilot must have been bursting in the cockpit for he is now standing with his back towards us and peeing at the barbed wire-fence barely 50 meters away from the plane. His legs are spread apart and he is peeing like a camel. It must be that tea that he didn't want to share with us earlier in the flight. I am delighted to see him paying for his meanness.

We get out of the plane only to discover that we are safe and well guarded. The plane is now surrounded by 15 EUFOR soldiers positioned in a circle of 50 metres diameter around us. They carry their machine guns but seem to handle their job with little concern. I am pleased to spot a fellow countryman among them, an Irish soldier with freckles on his face. I wonder whether he realised that we happen to belong to the same nation: Long Live the Republic of Ireland! I must say the whole exercise looks like a silly joke. I do not know what these soldiers are guarding: the Antonov plane, the eight passengers or the soup. But I understand. Doing a worthless job is better than doing nothing at all. Well, they have earned their soup and I hope they enjoy it.

As we descend from the plane, we notice a civilian car approaching the airport. The open airport has no check-in building and a car comes right within a few meters of our plane, ignoring the EUFOR soldiers. The driver waves at a soldier near him and moves towards us, starting the usual lengthy Chadian-Sudanese greetings. Apparently, the car belongs to JEM and is there to take us to our residence in the town. We thank the aircrew and drive off into town.

Iriba is a small town of about 8,000 inhabitants. By local standards, the town looks relatively prosperous despite its desert surroundings. EUFOR military base has been a blessing to the town bringing in both cash and employment. Refugee camps scattered around the area have also transformed the once sleepy town into a giant flourishing market for food and other necessities.

We drive carefully through houses scattered around at the edge of the town. Some of these houses are inhabited but many are half finished and are there for the purpose of staking a claim on space rather than to provide homes for their owners. Scores of sheep, goats and camels are being driven in and out of town, apparently to chance their luck in the animal market of the town. Gradually, we get into the main street of the town with shops attached to houses at both sides. Women traders sit in small shelters selling sundried food items. Water sellers are busy taking advantage of the lack of water pipes.

We stop at a huge stone house in the centre of the city. Our host by the name of Mohamed Haggar is out of town but will soon come back. Opposite the house is the palace of the Zaghawa Sultan of the area who happens to be the eldest brother of our host. We seem to be under royal guardianship, untouchable, and can never be more protected. We sit for while under shade provided by a roof attached to one corner of the high walls of the house. To one side of us is a room that looks like a store used for guests of lower status. In front of us is the 'saloon', a sort of VIP guest room for important male visitors. We seem to be some of those VIPs so the saloon is unlocked for us. The saloon is huge, almost like a classroom or around 4.5 X 8 metres in size. An expensive carpet covers the floor, almost wall to wall, with cushions thrown around everywhere. Comfortable armchairs are scattered around but most people prefer to sit cross-legged on the carpet in this part of the world. One can squat on the cushions or simply use them for support against the armchairs. A huge TV set is pitched at the corner operated by a satellite dish fixed to the roof of the house. Four vertical side fans stand at each corner of the room. A small generator supplies power in the house for there is no electricity in the town. We sit on the carpet and Togot finds his way to the TV set. It doesn't take him long to find a live British soccer match that he prefers over the repetitive Al Jazeera News. Well, no place on earth is safe from the omnipresent British soccer and Iriba is no exception!

I am tempted to sit on a chair but have to give in and join the rest on the carpet. Sitting on the chair will look odd for I will be at a level that is higher than everybody on the carpet. Only an arrogant person would entertain such a high seat among a company of equals. Togot, Sandal and a young son of our host seem to favour the carpet so I join them. It is uncomfortable for me to sit cross-legged so I lean against one of the chairs, spreading my legs in front of me. I am embarrassed about how much space I am taking but nobody seems to be bothered. We have already been fed and we are now waiting for our host who is on his way back to the house. As we watch the TV, our young host and a friend of his compete to display their hospitality. We are entertained to tea, coffee, soft drinks and even sweets that seem to attract no one in the company except the boys.

News of our arrival has already spread to the troops in Darfur. Fortunately, there is good mobile network coverage in the area and there is no need to use our expensive satellite phones. We exchange news with JEM field commanders in Darfur and the President of JEM too catches up with us over the phone. Most importantly, we learn that the Chief Commander of JEM is on his way to take us across the border into Darfur. The three of us are now busy talking on our phones in the proper Chadian style. Togot and Sandal outdo me in phoning for they have now taken out their satellite phones as well but are only using them for receiving incoming calls. We will soon move out of normal network coverage and become dependent on satellite phones.

Suddenly, our host, by the name Mohamed Haggar enters the room and we all arise for the usual greetings. Haggar seems to know Togot and Sandal well so he turns his attention to me and gives me a very warm welcome in Iriba. As an influential person, not to mention his royal connection, I am not surprised that he addresses me as a guest of the whole town and not only his house. Haggar is a small and unassuming man with a goatee beard but it doesn't take you long to discover the power and charm behind the little man. He is a merchant whose business trades on almost everything that one needs in the area. In Iriba, he is the man to turn to for grain, animals, transport, fuel, shop supplies, not to mention an audience with dignitaries like the Sultan. Then our host switches to politics and I realise that we are listening to a different man altogether. His deep knowledge about border politics and squabbles between Khartoum and N'Djamena gives me the impression that Haggar cares about his politics just as much as he does about trade. Like most people in border areas, Haggar talks about Sudan and Chad without a hint of which side of the divide he belongs to but the mixed, if not conflicting allegiance is evident in his analysis. He is a man of two nations and handles both nations with the same intensity of emotional engagement.

Then Haggar turns to talk of JEM. After sympathetic and flattering remarks about the organisation, he dips his hand in his briefcase and takes out his laptop. To see a laptop in Iriba is mesmerising, but to find one in use is something different altogether. For a long time now, laptops count among gadgets that one finds inside international NGO offices but never in the houses of ordinary Africans living in towns with no electricity supply. I get confused about what document Haggar wants to show us on his laptop and wait impatiently for the screen to light up. Well, it is not a document that our host is about to display. Rather, it is a collection of photographs that Haggar wants us to view of the visit of Dr Khalil Ibrahim, the president of JEM, to the house. As he goes through the photographs, Haggar talks about Khalil with tremendous admiration. Astonishingly, his knowledge of Khalil dates back a long time. Furthermore, Haggar knows Darfur and its politicians very well, for he has gone to Sudanese schools with many of them. This is an aspect of the area that many visitors do not know or comprehend. Despite its failings, Sudan commanded better schools than Chad and many border ethnic groups took the liberty to make use of Sudan's education system. The Zaghawa in this area are semi nomadic and have traditionally treated political borders with utter disdain. Sadly, Darfur war has brought cross-border relations to a halt and most schools in Sudan's side of the divide have been destroyed.

Commander Cholloy: The Hero Of El Fashir City

We are just about to finish with laptop photograph viewing when a score of visitors arrive and everyone jumps up for greetings. It is the convoy of the Chief Commander of JEM, a healthy looking man of close to 6 foot tall. His name is Abdel Karim Cholloy, most famous for the daring occupation of El Fashir in 2003. Cholloy was badly injured in the operation but continued to direct his troops until he lost consciousness due to excessive bleeding. The occupation of El Fashir was a turning point for the Movements, supplying them with arms, vehicles and most importantly confidence in the ability to defeat the professional government army. Commander Cholloy's appearance brings back a memory of comments made by Lieutenant General Ibrahim Suleiman, the Governor of El Fashir at the time of the occupation. He said, "The operation combined elements of military surprise, accurate timing, clear targeting and swift entry and exit with minimal casualties, a dream of every military commander."

Commander Cholloy is a man of few words who makes little attempt to mark his presence in a group. But Cholloy has many understated impressive qualities. He is sharp, with a highly developed sense of observation. Cholloy is famous for his extraordinary sense of orientation. He has a GPS kind of brain that guides him in a desert terrain that has little to show by way of landmarks. Above all, Cholloy speaks his native language of the Guraan ethnic group, as well as Zaghawa, Fur, Arabic and some English. With all of these languages under his belt, Cholloy speaks as little as possible and instead prefers to listen to his companions; a model I should endeavour to emulate if I can.

Meeting Cholloy in the flesh is more than sensational for both of us. Over the past few years, I have spoken to Cholloy fairly regularly and sometimes twice a week. We have grown accustomed to each other's voices but we have never met before. The phone bonding between us seems to have worked for we are now talking like old friends, with him constantly relaying to me greetings of many JEM commanders that I know fairly well but have not yet met.

After being entertained to a good supper, we arrange ourselves on a huge mat spread in front of the Saloon. We are to sleep in the open, a delightful experience that I have not had since my last visit to Sudan six years ago. From now on, this is how I sleep, in the open air looking at the beautiful stars the whole night. The generator is now switched off and we are engulfed in complete tranquil darkness. I must be the only bad sleeper for within five minutes, I find myself surrounded by a

53

bunch of men, all fast asleep and snoring. The view of the stars is a bit hazy as the clouds are building up. We do not have to worry if it rains, for we can simply pull in under the sheltering veranda near us.

I get woken up at around 5.45 am in the morning. Someone near me launches into prayers at that time of the morning. I know this cannot be Togot for he is not known for being diligent about his prayers. I look around and find it to be Sandal. Togot and Cholloy are awake but are still motionless. The air is cool and pleasantly humid, a rarity in a dry desert climate. The flies are busy and determined to get us up so we do so rather hesitantly. The town has already come back to life and I can hear some people exchanging greetings in the street. Desert people get up early to take advantage of the cool morning and we too have to organise ourselves for our long journey into Sudan.

Haggar, our host, suddenly appears, followed by his son, a young teenager carrying a tray with a teapot and half a dozen tea glasses. In this part of the world, you start your day with sweet tea and if you are fortunate, you get a cup of coffee immediately afterwards. But coffee is more expensive and is often taken by better off people like our host. Breakfast comes an hour later, around 8 to 8.30am.

A few minutes later and we squat around for breakfast. A huge tray is positioned in the middle of us. A round heap of millet porridge about the size of a soccer ball sits on a dish surrounded by spiced yoghurt and tomato sauce, a perfect rival of the Indian korma relish. The smell is so delicious that I cannot wait to taste it. Next to the porridge is another huge dish of roasted meat. It looks good but I have no interest in it at this hour of the morning. I know that it is the meat that interests everybody in the company but that is alright with me. Haggar is taking his time washing his hands and we cannot start eating until he joins us. He tells us to start eating but we resist his call.

54

It is not polite to start eating until everybody joins. As our host, the rule becomes even more pressing and there is no way out of waiting for him. Just as he is about to join us, his phone rings and you can sense the disappointment on the face of everybody. Haggar signals to us to start but nobody is willing to go first, so we sit waiting, struggling to contain our impatience. No wonder a Darfurian proverb says, 'waiting over porridge while hungry is as difficult as guarding a lion.'

Luckily, Haggar's phone call does not last long and we make space for him to join us. We follow his prayers saying, "in the name of Allah, Most Compassionate" and start eating. We go slowly on the food, for that too is a cherished cuisine rule in this land. "Never attack food like a vulture", was what my late father repeatedly taught me in my childhood. 'Devouring' the breakfast goes at an incredibly slow pace, interrupted by polite conversation and laughter. But my mind is somewhere else, far away from the food we are eating. I am in a magical flight back into my childhood. We, the Darfurians and the Chadians, have much more in common than we care to acknowledge. What I am eating now is exactly what I had, countless times throughout my childhood. Even the dishes and tray seem to be exactly the same make and must have been manufactured by the same company and designed by the same designer. I get a strong urge to close my eyes, the better to see members of my family back home in Broosh, nearly 800 kilometres away, sharing this food with me. I pull back and simply look down at the goat meat, the chillies and lemon squeeze in a separate saucer and the porridge relished by this wonderful yogurt sauce—all of which bring back a long gone family, right in front of me. I can even imagine the chickens, the domestic pigeons and our cat that were never far away from our eating spots. As I drift away in my wonderful daydream, Haggar pushes a bony piece of meat towards me, urging me to try it. I oblige and grab it, amid his complaints that I never touched the meat at all. Perhaps Haggar's people too share with us the saying, 'the best meat is what is adjacent to the bones.' We are in a land where hospitality is never complete without food containing meat. As a host, he takes pride in making sure that his guests are well fed. He is indeed a perfect host and will send us away with a good memory of our brief encounter in Iriba.

We finish breakfast and another round of sweet tea is waiting for us. I call it sweet because there is more sugar than tea in it. The invisible women inside the house who laboured over the lovely breakfast we just had, have decided on how much sugar goes into the tea; a small power that women still retain in a male chauvinist land and I am not complaining. So sweet is the tea that the possibility of the rim of the tea glass getting glued to your lips should not be discounted. Well, I must confess that in my childhood, I appreciated sweet things and the more sugar in it, the better. Living in Europe for a couple of decades corrupts that taste and develops an aversion to sugar that does not go down well in Sub-Saharan Africa. In this part of the world, sugar is a valuable product and tea and coffee are coveted precisely because of their sugar contents. Putting on weight is not a problem here. Far from it, and with everybody as thin as a desert snake, the more weight you can muster the better. After all, thinness is a mark of poverty and a bit of flesh indicates success, wealth and high class. Slimness, or more aptly to look like a hypochondriac person, is an attribute of misery, destitution and peasantry background. Western doctors can go to hell—welcome sugary tea, for who wants to count among those miserable creatures.

Our breakfast and tea are followed by frantic activities to get ready for departure. Now I come to the most interesting part of my journey. From now on, we all have to be in camouflaged military uniforms. Togot and Sandal are already in their military outfit and so is Commander Cholloy of course. There is no way out of it for JEM has a strict rule that all the senior members visiting the field must be camouflaged in military uniform and if necessary engage in combat. As I later came to know, the rule is flouted by only one person and that is Sulaiman Jamous, a member of the Executive Board of JEM and Head of Humanitarian Affairs. A veteran of the Darfur uprising, Jamous joined JEM later, following his defection from the Sudan Liberation Movement (SLM) of Abdel Wahid and had negotiated this deal prior to joining JEM. Lucky man, he neither wears military uniform, nor carries a gun, a fine principle that suits his age as well as his solid connections with international NGOs. Well, he is only few years older than me but he is able to get away with it.

I sneak into the bathroom and after a quick wash, I slip into my military trousers and shirt. My worry here is not about how to put on military trousers and a shirt. Apart from the colour, there is little difference between the military uniform and my usual civilian attire. Surprisingly, my worry now shifts to the wash I just had. This is perhaps the last decent wash I have for the next two weeks or so. Water is scarce in the field and reserved for other pressing needs. Well, as long as I do not develop lice, simple sweat and foul body odour can be managed.

I come out of the bath looking like a perfect army general, shame about the missing Kalashnikov. Cholloy admires my uniform and remarks about my bare head. Like all Darfur Movements, soldiers wear a Tuareg's kind of turban instead of an army cap. The Turban which is part of my army kit is called Kadmoul or also Kadmoun as many Kobe Zaghawa do not recognize the difference between 'L' and 'N' and switch freely between the two sounds. In the area of my upbringing in North Darfur, Kadmoul refers to a fabric belt used by women to keep the waist sari in place. Over there, men use a different type of turban, much shorter and less elaborate compared to the Kadmoul.

I hold the Kadmoul in my hands and look confused as to where to start. Togot can't stop laughing at me and I get rather embarrassed. Here I am with all my experience, failing to tie the Kadmoul around my head, a job that every young teenager in the area can handle. As I examine my brand new Kadmoul, I judge it big enough for ten heads and yet I am expected to wrap it around an average size head like mine. With a width of 2.5 feet, the Kadmoul may look smaller than a bed sheet. However, a bed sheet is no match for a Kadmoul when it comes to its length, a whopping 12 feet long. Yes, that is right. A Kadmoul is 2.5 X 12 feet large!

Cholloy tells Togot off and comes to my help. Gently, he tells me where to start and off we go. I am delighted to be in the company of a sympathetic teacher. Without him, it will take me several hours to wrap that thing around my head and make it stay. Here are Cholloy's instructions, for you too may need it one day, "Take one end of the Kadmoul and let it down to a few inches below the heart on the left side of your chest. Move with the rest of it upwards, covering your left ear and proceed to spread it over your head covering the scalp and forehead about a centimetre over your eyebrows. Move along downwards covering your right ear and straight below the chin and round again until you get over your left ear again. Hold the Kadmoul with your left hand just over your left ear. With your right hand, fold the Kadmoul and go on wrapping it around your head clockwise. Go around as many times as it takes until you get to the other end of the kadmoul. Insert the end of the kadmoul firmly to the side of your scalp. And here you are—a perfect Tuareg man and a JEM fighter".

Now let me invite you to put away the illusion that the Kadmoul is an unnecessary invention. That is precisely what I thought before my journey into the field. But far from it, the Kadmoul is the most useful and versatile attire ever invented. It is a head cover, a pillow, a handkerchief, a towel, a bed sheet, a coverlet, a balaclava, a bandage and if you are killed in action, a probable incident in combat, the Kadmoul serves as your shroud. The Kadmoul has a layer just below the chin. For disguise, you simply move it to cover both the mouth and nostrils. The forehead part of it can be lowered to rest on the eyebrows and you end up with a perfect balaclava showing only the eyes. The dangling part of it on the left side of the chest is used as a handkerchief proper. It is good for drying your hands, cleaning your face from dust and wiping your sunglasses or spectacles if you wear any. You just cannot beat a good Kadmoul.

The Kadmoul comes in different colours depending on your taste, purpose, age and eccentricities. Any colour other than white can be used. Of course Kadmouls used in the field have to be non-reflective. Thus, for camouflage, brown, black and khaki colours are preferred while yellow and white are avoided.

In my peculiar academic naivety, I thought we would be immediately on the road following breakfast. Oh no, I now realise it is not that easy. For better or for worse, I am travelling in the company of two of the most important officials of JEM. These are Cholloy, Chief Military Commander of JEM and Commander Sandal, Chief of Security of JEM. Sandal is in charge of both internal and external security of JEM; in US parlance, FBI and CIA combined in one office. I wonder how large is my own dossier in his collection. Pretty hefty, I suppose.

Cholloy, Sandal and Togot move aside to be briefed on what is happening at the other side of the border. Three men connected with JEM have just arrived to see them in Haggar's house. I sit aside jotting down a few notes but try to follow them at the same time. Their talk is a mixture of Arabic, Zaghawa, possibly Bedayat, relished by a few English and French words. This is a land of free tongues and people are not shy of stringing together words belonging to different languages in the same sentence. To make matters worse, their talk is riddled with military jargon, names of villages, hills, Janjaweed leaders, Chadian rebel leaders and chieftains that I cannot recognise. My clumsy Google maps prove no help to me in making sense of the discussion. They too must have realised that I am beyond help so they decide to march off without my participation.

The briefing is over and we sit debating our exit from Iriba. It is now 12 at noon and the journey ahead of us is at least five hours. If we get stuck in the sand, it will surely be longer and we do want to get to our destination before darkness. But there is a problem. The palace of Haggar's brother, the Sultan, is opposite our house. If we visit the Sultan, he will probably kill a sheep and have us waiting for a long time. Fortunately, Haggar says it is not important to visit the Sultan this time as he is busy with some visitors. He will make him understand that we are in a hurry. This is a delicate issue and has to be managed carefully. Haggar does not want us to travel in the dark and certainly not to spend the night in the middle of the desert. That is a risk that far outweighs offending the Sultan. He tells us to make it up to the Sultan in our coming visit to the town, and we agree with a great sense of relief.

We are now packed and ready to leave but one of our cars is not there. It has gone for water and fuel. In a desert terrain, water is a most important travel companion. So scarce is water that its source gives names for towns, people and animals alike. As for fuel, you have to budget for two to three times your distance. It is easy to get stuck in the sand, sometimes more than once in a journey. Hitting a single bad stretch of 100 metres could easily double your fuel consumption.

I stretch out my map for Commander Cholloy to show me our way. Well, I can euphemistically call it a map for it looks more like a black sheet of papers with zigzagging lines showing the borders between Chad and Sudan. The place is almost uninhabited with exceptionally few villages dotted around. The absence of villages does not mean the absence of people here and there. Cartographers have a reckless disregard for nomadic camps and have yet to devise a culture of offering them a space on their maps. The deceptively empty terrain in our map is also home to numerous nomadic groups roaming the area around the year. Some of those now count among the dreaded Janjaweed with their characteristic disregard for political borders. This is why we have to travel in daylight, giving our fully armed guards a panoramic view of the landscape.

We finally manage to say goodbye to Haggar and embark on our journey. We are in a convoy of three cars, relatively small but well armed. Cholloy's car is a seven-seater Mitsubishi SUV. Cholloy decides to drive so I sit next to him with the back seat occupied by Togot and Sandal. The driver and Cholloy's two bodyguards squeeze in at the back of the car.

Two Toyota pickups with their tops completely cut off, form the rest of our convoy. Just over a dozen soldiers ride on them. We ease our way towards the edge of the town, manoeuvring to avoid an odd chicken, a goat, a dog or a child. As we approach the edge of the town, the Kalashnikovs come out with their barrels glittering under the sunshine. We are now on our own, with nothing between us and our enemies except bullets. But there is little sign of life as we leave Iriba. The landscape resembles a sheet of yellow paper, a complete desert with little evidence of life; legendary evidence of how resilient human beings can be. Trees around the town have long been wiped out for fuel or for house construction, and the hungry animals have long devoured the remaining grass and shrubs that have no use for the town. The air is still humid from the drizzles of last night but the soil is too dry to sustain any new grass. The deadness of the environment is stunning; there are no grasshoppers, beetles, butterflies, or birds. No foxes, squirrels or mice either. This is a dead land, a desert, full stop.

It is not quite clear who is guiding whom on our journey, Commander Cholloy or his guards. Sometimes we lead the convoy, sometimes we are in-between the two trucks and at another time, one of them moves ahead and waits for us on top of a sand dune. Cholloy and his soldiers have not yet discovered the joy of GPS. Maybe the GPS is of no use in the desert. There are at least three satellite phones, or Thuraya, in the car, but nobody seems to consult them. Instead, Commander Cholloy seems to rely on his old natural pigeon-style orientation gift. Mind you, there are some guidelines here as well. The sand is riddled with tracks of tyres of every conceivable size of vehicle and drivers of our convoy cars are spoilt for choice. Sometimes, they leave the beaten tracks and make their own. No roads means free roads and one can move in any direction.

I get somewhat worried that we might get lost. It is true we have plenty of water. Food is not seen as that important for one can survive for several days without it. It is the absence of water that kills people in a desert. But there is some exotic food in the car if you can stomach it. Yes, if you can. Cholloy brought with him a bag of roasted locusts. The wings are gone but the rest of the little things are complete with eyes and thighs. These are desert locust one can buy in the local markets of Darfur and Chad. When you eat locusts, resist the temptation to throw away the green stuffing of the insect. That is pure grass and tree leaves and high in medicinal value—or so they say.

As we move further away from Iriba, trees start to emerge and signs of natural life gradually replace desert death that we are leaving behind. Nomads too start appearing with their scraggy camels, sheep and goats. Still the terrain is too dry for cows, so we see none. I am now less worried about getting lost and gather my own old way of identifying the cardinal directions as we travel. I can work it out at least from some of the natural signs. As you get past noon, the sun moves towards the west, providing a good clue about the four cardinal directions. Tree shade also falls to the east, thus giving you another clue to direction. No wonder nomads prefer not to move at noon where the sun is in the middle of the sky and tree shade falls directly underneath them. As for the travelling by night, stars provide clear guides that even a child of ten can easily read.

It is now two hours since we left Iriba. Fortunately, we had only a small problem where our car got stuck in the sand for a while. The soldiers rushed to our rescue and their shovels did the miracle in no time. Then we stop for a while for a drink of water and the usual Muslim prayers. We are now travelling north parallel to the Sudan Border on the Chadian side of the divide. Sudan, or rather Darfur, is no more than 20 kilometres to our right. Our car stops at the ruin of a deserted village in the middle of nowhere. Togot thinks this miserable spot has played an important role in the current Darfur crisis. We are still in the Zaghawa area and Togot's birthplace is not far from here, but technically in a different country. Back in the colonial era, the British and French empires had separated Togot's village and this deserted one into Chad and Sudan. Togot is familiar with this area very much, having visited it during his childhood with his people and with total contempt of modern political borders.

Sometime in the last century, a man packed his family and belongings and abandoned this deserted village. At the edge of the village, he marked his departure with a song that is commemorated in Zaghawa legends to this day. These are the words of the song extolling the futility of the village he was leaving behind:

> 'You barren granite land
> I dig a well and find no water
> I cultivate a farm but gather no harvest
> I marry but my wives bear no children

I set a trap but catch no game
I am leaving you, you fruitless land, for good'

With these words, the man left and settled among the Berti in Tawaisha township, deep in the eastern part of Northern Darfur. The man in question was Tibir, the grandfather of the current Governor of North Darfur, notorious for the facilitation of atrocities against Darfur people, and in particular, his own people, the Zaghawa. In Zaghawa tradition, only the lower caste of Hadaheed set traps. The Hadaheed, literally 'tinkers', dealt in iron works where men smelted iron for agricultural tools and fixed metal pots and trays. Their women worked in pottery. The Hadaheed were stigmatised and socially dispossessed. Other Zaghawa kept their distance from them in marriage, companionship and even in the sharing of food. Needless to say, this unjust situation is now slowly but steadily wearing out.

Like all Zaghawa names, Tibir was Arabized to be Kibir, as in the Governor's name Osman Mohamed Kibir. Kibir senior did not only change his village and his name. He also changed his ethnic group. His grandson, the Governor, now counts as Berti and not Zaghawa as his ancestors were.

A Taste Of Darfur

At just before sunset, our convoy arrives at the border town of Umjaras. It is not size that qualifies this place to be called a town. Rather, it is its conspicuously modern façade in the middle of nowhere that gives it the title. Umjaras is the hometown of President Deby of Chad and his oasis of retreat during the fasting holy month of Ramadan. As in most African countries, the birthplace of the president attracts public investment even when people refuse to move into it. Umjaras is no exception. It has a small modern airport, solar powered lit roads, offices and houses for government officials and an army complex. The palace of the local Sultan is modernised to serve as a guesthouse for the President and his VIP visitors. Other than that, Umjaras has little to show for itself, nor to vouch for a place on any respectable map. If you look hard, you can see little cottages scattered around in the horizon. They cluster in two to three houses here and there, a pattern that is characteristic of nomadic sparse settlement. The souk has a few shops that seem to have more staff than customers. As a market juncture, Umjaras thrives on its position on the way to Libya with trucks stopping for a little rest, for food, tea but most importantly water. But the market is also dependent on JEM. The proximity of Umjaras to the border and particularly the Darfur area under control of JEM, makes it an important centre for non-military supplies. No wonder rival movements refer to Umjaras, sarcastically, as the capital of JEM.

In the JEM base of Umjaras, we are entertained to tea, soft drink and a meal of goat meat. I spend the evening delighting myself in catching up with old friends including voice friends whom I now meet for the first time. Meeting people whom you have only known through the phone is a fascinating experience. From the voice, conversations and jokes, you work out how the person actually looks. You occasionally get it just about right but most times you are way off target. The person turns out to be of different age, height, physique and temperament.

Our cars are also attended to, for Umjaras base also houses one of JEM's main garages for maintaining their vehicles. We are now ready to venture into Darfur. However, a vast and elusive terrain stands between us and our destination. A chain of mountains, streambeds and soft sand dunes do not allow a direct crossing of the border. We have to move further north along the same truck dirt tracks from Libya and later branch off eastwards into Sudan. Our convoy has grown larger for other vehicles have also joined from Umjaras base. The area seems to be livelier with nomadic camps, small villages and flocks of camels in the way. The air is still humid from some showers that have fallen in the past few days. A miracle has already taken place, for the once dead and dusty sand is now covered with a carpet of thin green grass. Much more, the rains have rejuvenated the whole landscape and repopulated it with birds, squirrels, rabbits, foxes and autumn insects like butterflies, grasshoppers and fireflies. It is amazing how a few showers can bring back life into a completely barren terrain and in a matter of days.

As we move along, our convoy continues growing bigger and bigger, with more vehicles joining us by the hour. Welcome into the Republic of JEM for we are now in Sudan proper without me noticing it. The trucks that are joining our convoy are also on the way to the same meeting that I am pursuing. Every now and then, we stop for a short greeting of new recruits into our caravan, sometimes without disembarking. I try to count the number of cars in the convoy but stop at 35 for they are moving too fast in all directions for me to follow. All of the cars are camouflaged in brown colour spray that matches the terrain very well. The only one that is not dark in colour is ours but its white paint is fully disguised with brown mud.

Just an hour or so before sunset, Cholloy stops his car telling us our travel for the day is over. We are to camp here and resume the journey early in the morning. We have one hour of sunlight and that is just enough to enable us to light a fire and cook dinner. After darkness, no fire is allowed and cars remain stationary. We are now in the middle of nowhere. The trees around us are too sparse to make a forest as such. We quickly pitch our beddings on the sand. There is no need for mosquito nets as there is not enough humidity for the mosquitoes to breed and there is a good breeze to drive the odd ones away. The clouds are gathering and there is a slim chance of rain. I say slim chance because the lightening we see in the horizon is too far to the east and that means the rains will fall too far to the south of where we are. In local wisdom, the lighting has to be in the northeast horizon to produce rain. This is not the case this evening. We needn't worry if we get a drizzle tonight for we are all supplied with rain proof sheets. This is an old nomadic trick well incorporated into the JEM military kit.

We busy ourselves exchanging visits and getting introduced to each other. My discovery that I am not the only stranger in the place gives me some comfort. Many new recruits are meeting other JEM soldiers for the first time. Operation Long Arm that took place a short while before has raised the profile of JEM and as a result volunteers flocked to join the Movement. Indiscriminate government bombing and the racist response of Sudan's security agents that followed the JEM invasion of the capital and bigoted revenge against Darfur people also led many to desert the government army and register with JEM. Many of these new soldiers are now looking for their relatives who happen to be in the convoy. A few of them are from my own area and have heard my name and are now coming to meet me in the flesh. I find the experience exciting but also embarrassing. They all know my name but I do not know theirs. They are much younger than myself and some of them have gone to schools with my younger brothers. I however know their families and perhaps some of their older folks. Either way, we are pleased to meet each other and recognise that we share a few things in common: a homeland, an ethnic group and a cause that we are fighting for.

While some of us are busy getting acquainted with each other, the kitchen squad is working frantically to prepare the food and extinguish all fires before darkness. Their diligence pays off, for just before dusk the food appears and we divide ourselves into small groups for eating. To my discovery, each cluster of soldiers is referred to as 'dhara', a Sudanese word for the 'communal eating place' that you find in most villages. A huge tray is placed in front of us with sufficient food for 8 to 10 men. The dinner, a typical desert meal, consists of millet porridge relished with a fine sauce of sundried ingredients: meat, onion, okra, pepper, tomatoes and chillies. With mostly two meals a day, the kitchen squad is always assured of a healthy appetite and little leftovers on the trays to discard. Nobody over here talks about cholesterol level, caloric intake, dieting or any other strange terms I often hear in Europe. Over here, food is an equalizer where everybody shares exactly the same diet. As we devour the food, I glance at the open spot that comprises the kitchen a few metres away from us. The meal is carefully designed to save on washing up afterwards; and mind you, it is water and not labour and time that are to be conserved. I contemplate how many utensils I need in my house back in Ireland to feed a dozen people. It is by far too many compared to the work of our kitchen squad. Over here, the kitchen squad requires a mere one pot for cooking porridge, one for making sauce and one tray for serving the food; altogether, three receptacles to use for cooking as well as for eating. And delightfully, ladies and gentlemen, you end up with only three kitchen wares to clean afterwards; a dream of every chef, every wife and every husband on earth. How foolish can we be in our so-called civilised part of the world?

It is now 8 o'clock and we have spread our sleeping packs that the soldiers have unloaded from the truck on the sand. Commander Cholloy, General Sandal, Togot and myself are in one cluster separated by a few metres each. Soldiers have scattered themselves around, maintaining a distance of 10 to 15 metres away from us in every direction. Some of them are still chatting but their voices are too low for me to follow their conversation. They chat at whispering level for fear of disturbing us. It looks rather strange that they want to chat and yet they stay far apart from each other. I quickly work out there is a security logic behind the arrangement. The soldiers are forming a circle around us for we are in the company of the Commander in Chief of JEM. As I soon discover, this is only the inner circle around the Commander. Our group is a division of the Fifth Brigade. The rest of the Brigade is in Jabal Moon, more than a hundred miles away. Like the rest of us, Commander Cholloy is on his way to the Executive Meeting scheduled to start tomorrow. Our larger convoy has divisions of other Brigades as well, each accompanying an Executive Member or two to the meeting. As far as I can remember, I noticed earlier in the day some cars bearing signs of the 1st, 2nd, 4th 7th and the 11th Brigades. These other Brigades have pitched their camps away forming the outer security circles around us and in such a way that any unfortunate intruder into the circle will be a target of fire from multiple directions.

I feel tempted to study my map and find exactly where I am but I am not allowed to light my torch. Cholloy tells me we are deep in North Darfur following Wadi Hawar, or—Hawar Valley—the longest streambed in Sudan. Tributaries of Wadi Hawar come from Chad as well as Sudan and consolidate in one giant valley in North Darfur. In the rainy season, the valley zigzags its way northeast and feeds into the River Nile, close to the Egyptian border. Throughout the dry season, and in sparse spots, the valley retains shallow underground water that forms little oases in the desert.

Gradually the soldiers go quiet and their laughter gets less and less intermittent. The air is exceptionally fresh with a gentle breeze coming from the north. The clouds are forming but there is nothing to worry about. My mattress is positioned on one half of my canvas leaving the other half ready to turn over me if it rains. As we go quiet, other life starts around us, disrupting the serenity of the night. Foxes, wild cats, hedgehogs, rats and rabbits take over the camp but with little peace among them. Occasional fireflies display their beautiful light and assert their entitlement to join in the feast of the tranquil night. I am sure that is not all; the crawlies too must be in full force but they are too humble to profess their presence among us. With the exception of the evil mosquitoes, none of these creatures have any interest in us. It is strange that in Europe we never sleep until these creatures are either dead or completely out of bounds. Over here, they are a good omen. They assure us of life and if we do not welcome them, we do not worry about them either. I tuck myself under my blanket and fall asleep.

It is 5.30 in the morning and I am disturbed by a burst of life around me. Commander Cholloy has just finished his morning prayers but is still sitting on his knees facing east. I have to stand in the queue for water to brush my teeth. There are limited water vessels circulating around and I have to wait for my turn. Some keep them far too long for they have to do their ablution of prayers.

The kitchen squad are busy with their glowing fire. It is time for tea and the tea glasses are being cleaned. No breakfast will be served yet. It is now time for sweet tea but food has to wait until our next stop. Fortunately, we do not have long to go and will surely be fed before noon. In accordance with the Commander's order, we quickly gulp our tea and start moving. Some cars have already gone ahead of us and the whole desert is now roaring with the noise of vehicles moving in an eastwards direction. The track we follow is not straight, for we have to manoeuvre our way around sand dunes and cheat a few wet spots as well. Every now and then, we come across camel nomads who look unconcerned about our appearance. Some wave at us by way of greeting. Others focus their attention on their disturbed camels galloping in all directions in utter fear of our vehicles. In the midst of all that, a column of 30 to 40 vehicles appears from nowhere and joins our convoy. As it turns out, this is the 12th Brigade of the President of JEM. We stop for normal salutes and greetings. I have not seen Hinain, or rather Dr Khalil, as he is better known for some time. The last time we met was two years ago when we visited Cairo for a meeting with the Egyptian government. Since then, Khalil decided to abandon France, his former place of residence and remain in the field, venturing out only for important meetings in neighbouring countries.

Khalil seems to have put on weight and looks as though he has also grown taller. He towers over me for a hug and expresses his admiration for my military outfit. He stretches his hand to loosen my Kadmoul just below my chin. He thinks I am wearing the headgear too tight, failing to allow air to circulate freely around the neck. I feel somewhat embarrassed but concede my poor knowledge of how to handle the turban. My experience with the Kadmoul evokes a similar problem I had when I first started wearing a necktie. It took me a while to get that superfluous attire right. The Kadmoul is just the same and I shouldn't be bothered if I am not perfecting it now.

Luckily, our travel lasts only a short time. Just after half an hour of our stop, we come to the end of the journey. We end up in a thin forest at Wadi Hawar. A mixture of numerous trees dot a depression in the valley and that is going to be our camp as well as our Executive Board meeting place. With a bit of luck, the destiny of future Sudan will be determined under one of those trees.

Our car comes to a halt under a thick Acacia tree. The mud smeared over the car is now fading and hence the vehicle has to be hidden, literally inside a tree. The forest in which we are situated, is the thickest I have seen so far. Trees of every height, colour, thickness and leaves are there. I struggle to recall local names of some of the species around me, for we have almost all of them in the area where I grew up. Thus I can see around me four or five species of Acacia trees in addition to Arrad (Albizia), Heglig (Balanites), Mokheit (Boscia), Gaddeim (Grewa), Nabak (Ziziphus) and toothbrush trees (Slavadora). There are many small shrubs that I had not seen in my early childhood. The air is fresh with the beautiful scent of roses that attract hundreds of colourful butterflies, yellow wasps and bees. I hate to think about mosquitoes at night but there is no point in agonising about that right at this moment.

It is now just around eleven and we sit under the biggest tree in the compound. It is a huge Acacia tree selected for its size, its shade and its location right in the centre of the base. The shade of the tree is carpeted for us to squat on, moving every now and then to adjust the carpet, or rather carpets that are joined together, with the moving shade. This is now the office where the Executive Board of JEM will convene for three days. There are 18 of us sitting in a circle waiting for the Chairperson to appear. The best seat in the shade is at the stem of the tree and that is reserved for the boss. It is the stem of the tree that marks this seat 'presidential' for the stem can be used as a back support. We are yet to introduce ourselves formally. In the meantime, we are entertained to tea, soft drinks, soda water, sweets and dates. Commander Cholloy signals to one of the guards to bring in my coffee jar. Apparently, the Commander noticed my undiminished addiction to coffee and my bizarre habit of adding a spoonful of coffee into my tea. Nobody drinks coffee here and I find it embarrassing and unpractical to request a separate glass of boiled water for my Nescafe. Instead, I sneak in a jar of coffee and invent my own concoction. I simply sprinkle some coffee into the teacup and maintain the supply of caffeine in my blood. Wonderful! This strange practice flouts every rule and ritual evolved for the consumption of tea and coffee in the land. My comrades must pity me and wonder whether I need urgent professional help for no sane person will come up with such an invention. But as long as my caffeine level is right, why care about what others think about the habit?

As I sit listening to reports of various offices of JEM, a strange buzzing sound attracts my attention. The sound propels me back to my childhood in Broosh, my hometown in Darfur. This is almost the same sound made by a domestic wasp when it hovers inside a water pot. The wasp goes into a water pot to gather moisture for building its clay nest. The pot amplifies the sound made by the flying wasp and that is exactly what I am hearing now. As I contemplate about my childhood wasp, Togot looks at me with a huge grin and says, "That is Hajji Waham, the friend you have been wanting to see."

A burst of laughter comes from everyone and I grab my camera and dash away from the tree shade. Togot is absolutely right. It is indeed my friend, Hajji Waham, far away in the sky about a size of a sparrow but far too small for my cheap camera to photograph.

Hajji Waham, which translates as 'the deluded hajji', is the term coined by JEM soldiers for the enemy Antonov bomber. Antonov planes make daily flights over JEM camps and that is why the term 'hajji' is given to them. To avoid surface to air missiles, the bombers fly at high altitudes of well over 30,000 feet, leaving little chance for detecting what is underneath them and pinpointing targets. Designed as a transport plane, the Antonov is loaded with barrels of explosives that are pushed down through its rear door. When one of those barrels lands, it bounces and explodes, sending hot shrapnel around a meter or so above the ground. Shrapnel can cause injury above the waist. The soldiers know this and stay flat when they see the barrel falling from the sky. In the words of one solider, you need a stunning bout of bad luck to end up a victim of Antonov bombing. The barrel literally has to fall directly on your back to kill you. Worse than that, the Antonov is off target by two to four miles. Of course the Antanov can be lethal when attacking unarmed civilians from a low altitude. All this seems very reassuring but I would rather not see the wasp over my head.

Our meeting is now adjourned for half an hour to allow Hajji Waham to go away. We are ordered to scatter around and avoid the possibility of wiping out the entire Executive Board of JEM in one go. We walk, as commanded, in different directions and I approach a group of soldiers playing cards under a tree. Unlike me, they prefer to remain focussed on their game, completely unconcerned about the Antonov circling over them. All of a sudden, I hear a thunderous sound in the distance, a barrel or two must have hit the sand. A soldier tells me that is not all—"This white Antonov carries 12 barrels. The darker one carries either 18 or 21 barrels", he says.

I stand there and watch as the Antonov plane comes and goes in a rather haphazard way. Every now and then, I hear an explosion somewhere in the distance. As I learn, the bombs fall about 3 to 4 miles away from us. The wasp sound subsides and we go back to our tree and resume our meeting.

Hinain, The Camel Boy

I sit with Hinain just a few meters away from the tree that has turned into JEM's main office for two days. It is just after 7pm and the night is fresh and full of the laughter of soldiers in the dark surrounding us. The stars are glittering above, accentuating the eternity of nature and the power of the vast surroundings that enfold us. In as much as the emptiness of the space about us is appealing, it is also troubling, for it is a powerful reminder of our relative insignificance, if not total nothingness, in this universe.

Despite our long meeting earlier, that continued throughout the whole day, Hinain appears fresh and ready to chat the whole nightlong. Through his cunning and skilful manoeuvring around difficult issues, Hinain was able to contain numerous rivalries and the interests of diverse offices that arose during the day. Throughout that time, Hinain focused on his notebook and remained silent yet attentive, intervening only when it was essential. But it was his sparse interventions that guided the meetings away from explosive issues and conflicts that arose from them. His apt silence and sympathetic hearing paid off, but now it is time for him to talk.

To accompany Hinain on a journey in Darfur is to know the man as a nomad at heart. He is passionate about animals and knows how to care for them. Hinain's mood easily turns into anger at the sight of a weak and unhealthy herd. Every time he passes a flock of camels, goats or sheep, he scrutinizes the beasts like an animal trader. He is ready to interrupt any important discussion and take time to comment about the animals; their breed, their health and the care they are receiving from their minders. He just knows a thirsty, hungry or sick animal when he lays eyes on one. The scraggy camels he encounters are in that state, not because of inhospitable terrain that offers almost no pasture—rather, it is because the lousy herder is too lazy to take better care of his flock. Hinain loses no opportunity to volunteer his praise or convey displeasure about herders and their animals alike—these camels should be resting and regurgitating now, not feeding; these animals should start trekking towards the nearest water centre; these animals have not been given slat for far too long; these shrubs are of no benefit for these camels to feed. These animals are under the care of an excellent herder—and so on.

I notice Hinain's face under the moonlight. It reflects a pilgrimage—the experience of his childhood journeying with animals. It is clear that this is where Hinain's heart lies. He is at peace with animal herding much more than with politics. This is understandable given the turbulent experience Hinain has had in his political career. Hinain hesitates as though he does not know where to start. He removes the Kadmoul from his head, straightens his squat on the carpet and begins.

"I must have been five or six years old when I first started minding goats. At age eight, I was herding cattle and by 10 or 11, I was already a camel herder. At the time, I was living in my grandfather's village. Like everybody else, we combined farming with animal husbandry. We had goats, cows, camels, horses and a few donkeys. In the rainy season we stayed put in the village where the farms were. It was easy to feed animals in the rainy season, for grass and water were plentiful there. In the dry season we turned nomadic and the availability of pasture determined where we would be. Different families kept their animals together so we minded our animals and those of our mother's brother together in one herd.

The Humble Goats

Minding goats was an easy job. We had to be careful in the rainy season for we had to keep the goats away from farms near the village. In the dry season, goats required little attention. You had to keep an eye on them and hang around to keep away wild animals and occasionally eagles that preyed on them. I must have been around 6 when I came across a young goat, newly born and abandoned by its mother. I took the goat home and minded it for a while. My family was not able to find its owner, for some people were constantly on the move in search of pasture. Some weeks later when the goat was big and healthy, an uncle of mine who worked as a medical assistant in a neighbouring village came and insisted the goat was his and wanted to take it with him. I told him how I found the goat and that he could get it back if he could produce a reliable witness to support his claim. Given my age at the time, the man was amused by my challenge. He laughed and laughed and kept telling the story to everybody who came to the house, for he was lodging with us. When he left, he didn't take the goat. He let me keep it. The man was a cousin of my mother and must have found it mean to take a goat from a nephew, especially that had I not rescued the goat, it would have perished anyway. The goat grew up very well with me until disaster hit. Once, while I was walking the goat, an eagle hit it and burst its belly open in front of me. It was a horrific sight for me. I cried so much on that day for that was the first goat I owned in my life. Other goats that I took care of belonged to the family and were not particularly mine as such. I had hopes to produce a whole herd out of that goat but that evil eagle came and ruined my dream. Even though we were only young boys, our presence would protect goats against attacks by foxes and hyenas. These animals were scared of people so they would never come near goats even if they were guarded by a young boy. The eagles were different. They could snatch a young goat within a few meters of the herder.

I have wonderful memories of my animal herding time. There were so many enjoyable things to recall from those good old days of my early childhood. I remember I had a dog, which I called Barous, sort of white with fluffy fur. I found him in the bush while I was herding. He was a small male puppy and his eyes had just opened when I found him but he was weak and hungry. He was just born and was too frail and slow to catch up with his nomadic owners. I took the puppy with me and milked a goat for him. I gave him the name Barous because of his white colour. He accompanied me all through my goat herding. Barous grew stronger and much bigger than other dogs and was always following me like a dear friend. At age 8 I used to ride it. It was able to carry me on its back and gallop with me behind the goats. My friends thought the whole thing was so hilarious and my relatives did their best to stop me riding the dog but with little success. They saw the funny side of it but they were concerned about my safety. Time sorted the issue out as I grew up and put an end to the bizarre habit. At the time, it was good fun and I enjoyed it very much.

People now think it must have been hard for such a young child of 6 or 7 to be herding goats away from home but that is not true. Quite the contrary, it was easy and enjoyable. With goats, you never strayed far and you were always within running distance of a village. In the morning, I used to get fed and then would take some water in a gourd and would stay out until just before sunset. Sometimes I took some dried pancake with me but most days there was no need for that. We are talking about a time that was long before recent drought and desertification. There were plenty of nuts and fruits that we would collect. We had gum from Acacia trees and nuts and berries from other trees like Nabak (Ziziphus), Homeid (Sclerocaraya), Mokheit

(Boscia), Giddeim (Grewia), and Ardeib (Tamrindus Indica). When we were confused, we simply followed older boys and girls to show us which was edible and which was not. It did not take us long to implement their advice.

Milk came fresh and straight from the goats we minded but often we visited nomadic camps where we also got free yoghurt and fresh milk. Frequent contacts with various nomadic camps formed an important aspect of the social life of herders. They furnished us with knowledge of pasture, lost animals, outbreaks of animal diseases, and any sighting of strangers in the area. Information gathered in these camps enabled us to revise our strategies and devise a better way for handling our animals. Food was central to the hospitality of nomads and guests were never allowed to pass by without partaking of some sort or another of food and drinks.

Hunting was also an important pastime activity while we were herding. Older boys were more successful than us and were constantly setting traps for birds, digging out and chasing little animals so we were never short of roasted rabbits, squirrels and birds. While in the open with the flock, hunger was never part of our vocabulary but we were scared of jackals which went after goats, or at least that was the worry of the younger herders like myself. As for the rainy season, it was a picnic. We never even needed to carry water with us. There were plenty of open pools for us as well as for our goats. For extra moisture, we knew all the plants that had juicy roots you could suck to quench your thirst. We were allowed to raid farms and obtain melons, cucumbers, beans, nuts, sesame and sorghum stalks that we chewed like sugar canes. The farmers themselves shared food with us when we visited them. Mind you, they all knew our families and wanted our cooperation to keep our goats off their farms. They had to be nice to us to protect their farms against our animals as well as from stray animals. I can tell you we never felt hungry while in the bush with our goats. Furthermore, goats were easy to mind. You would just park under a tree and keep them within sight. Other than that, there was nothing you needed to do. Instead, spend the whole day chatting and playing games with other children and away from the interference of adults. We would dig out mice and geckos out of their holes for fun and we trapped squirrels and rabbits, caught locusts and raided every bird's nest we could find for food. Most days, our bellies were full and we needed little extra food when we made it home.

The Feeble Cows

By age 8, I had graduated to minding calves that were left behind by the main herd. Calves were separated from their mothers and kept in the vicinity of villages. People who had cows kept kraals for them way outside the village. Our kraal was about one mile away from the edge of the village. Just before sunset and before the big cows arrived, it was my job to get all the calves inside. My older sisters would milk the cows one by one and it was my job to release the calves one after another. Only women were allowed to milk cows so my job was to control the calves. Every time my sisters went to milk a particular cow, they would shout to me and tell me which calf to release. They all had names and there was no confusion regarding which one to release.

Milking took a long time and we liked it because we also got fresh milk on the spot. The milk was warm and beautiful and we didn't mind that it was raw. Milking took a long time because our cows were combined with my uncles' cows in our kraal. Occasionally I fell asleep at the gate of the kraal and my sisters had to carry me all the way home.

I must say my experience with herding cows was bitter. That was not because there was anything wrong with cows. Far from it, I loved my cows, had wonderful moments with them and still relive great memories of that part of my life. But to be honest, the whole episode was a disaster. By the time I moved into herding cows, nature changed course and turned against us. The pasture deteriorated rapidly, water wells dried up and the cows simply failed to cope with the climatic change of the day.

Cows have to be kept within no more than 20 miles of a water source. We watered them every third day but there was a problem. Water sources attracted many animals and the pasture around them was always exhausted. That meant there was little grass for cows to eat in their slow journey for water. Sometimes we would spend a whole day trekking the cows to a water centre, only to discover that the well was drying up. Often we got only a little bit of water and had to wait a few hours for more water to collect at the bottom of the well. By the time we finished watering, we would be utterly exhausted and the cows too were equally exhausted and hungry. I remember one day when we were coming back from a difficult watering session. It was late at night and we were walking back from the well towards our base. There were a number of us walking close by and somewhat scared of wild animals. All of a sudden, we discovered that one of us went missing. It was a young girl, a teenager of around 13. We went back looking for her and there she was, standing upright and fast asleep. She had a tray on her head and a leather water bucket in her hand. That was how exhausted we used to get trying to save our poor cows.

1973 was a difficult year for us and our cows. That was the year of famine referred to as Julu famine—the famine of going astray. It was such an expressive name for that famine because people abandoned their communities and escaped in all directions in search of food. We entered that year with a good wealth. We had 48 cows, plenty of goats and some camels. By local standards, we were doing very well, and if not the wealthiest in the area, we were pretty close to that. By the end of 1974, we were almost destitute, but every family had the same fate.

There was very little food in the area and people were hungry. I was in the camp at the time struggling to keep the cows alive. Young men left their nomadic camps and visited other camps pretending to be looking for lost animals. But there were no lost animals! In fact, they did that hoping to be invited for food in these camps. In our tradition, visitors would be offered food whenever they arrived. But there was no food to be shared in those years. Once I was roaming around with some cows when I stumbled across a cow struggling to stand up but it was too weak to do so. I tried to lift the cow up but it was too heavy for me. The owner of the cow was nearby but I did not see him. He joined me and we were able to lift the cow up and moved it slowly to a tree so that it could graze on its leaves. The wife of the man came to us with breakfast on a small dish. It was a miserable breakfast! It consisted of porridge with sauce made of leaves of Sareh tree (Maerua)—perfect famine food that no one would eat in normal years. I sat with the man and had one mouthful when he said to me, 'Please leave this food for me, for I have not eaten for a whole day.' His face was engulfed by shame and sadness, for no decent adult would refuse to share food with a guest. I understood the situation, left the food for him and followed my cows, without knowing what to say. It was such a bad time in which social life came to a total halt. For a whole year or so, there were no celebrations of weddings, circumcisions, childbirth or naming ceremonies.

We had to do something quick to save the cows. We split the herd into two and sent half of them to some uncles of ours who lived in South Darfur, near Nyala city, some 400 kilometres away. We knew that some of the cows would not make the journey but we had no choice. It was usual for the Zaghawa to share the care of animals they own with their relatives. Surplus animals would be given to a relative who took the milk and later shared the offspring of the herds. That was also a perfect way for helping relatives to establish their own herds.

We moved with the other half of the herd to West Darfur, close to Gineina city. That was the land of the Masaleit and the Iringa who were somewhat hostile to us and saw us as thieves, troublemakers and unwelcome strangers. The journey itself was arduous; the grass was depleted and water was scarce. As nomads we had to tread very carefully for our animals were too weak to walk and it was difficult to keep the cows fed and watered. There was a real dilemma, for where there was water, there was no grass and where there was pasture, there was no watering well within reach. Occasionally we had to employ some eugenic measures and save only the cows that shared history with the family. These were the cows that had been in the family for generations. We knew them and they knew us. Other breeds that came later into the herd had to be sacrificed, or to put it differently, left to starve. We would climb trees with a leather bag and raid bird nests to collect grass for favoured animals. A bird's nest would only give you a handful of hay and you could not feed every cow that. Difficult choices had to be made, otherwise, you would end up cow-less altogether.

Yes, we treated some cows almost as family members and did everything to save them during the journey. These cows also knew us much better than newer animals. Nomads knew this fact but ignorant city people found it bizarre and unbelievable. I remember once in that journey I lost a favoured cow by the name Mittey and went in search of her for days. Mittey, meaning 'orphan' in the Zaghawa language, was a third or fourth generation animal in our family and it was painful to lose her. I eventually found her and was walking her back to the herd when I passed a Masaleit village. There, I was suspected of being a thief and was brought to the house of the village chief. I was chained and Mittey was kept in a kraal usually reserved for stray animals. The Chief told me to wait, thinking that the owners would come looking for their cow. In the morning, they brought me in front of the kraal for further investigation. They were perhaps disappointed that no one had come in search of the cow. The Chief was debating my case with a half dozen men near the kraal. They were speaking Masaleit so I could not follow their conversation about me. I gathered that they could not believe that a Zaghawa boy of 13 or 14 could own a cow and so they assumed I must have stolen the cow from somewhere. I was a total stranger in the area and had no material evidence to prove ownership of the cow so I told the Chief that I could prove the cow was mine if he would just open the kraal. This he did and I started calling the cow by her name—'Mittey, Mittey, Mittey.' The cow came towards me, ignoring all those in the crowd. Then I continued calling her and moving around the group while Mittey followed. Then I started jogging around the kraal and Mittey sped up behind me. I passed in front of the Sheikh and his friends and ran out of the village with Mittey galloping behind me. The question of the ownership was settled and the crowd remained in their places shaking their heads with amazement. That was Mittey, the cherished member of our family.

Well, it breaks my heart to say Mittey did not make it that year. Neither did the other cows. Out of all the cows we had, we were left with only 18, part of the dispatch to the Nyala area. Camels were better. They survived the drought and became the mainstay of our nomadic life.

Some years later, my bother Gibriel came back from Japan where he did a Ph.D. in economics. He wanted to get married. In our system, we had to raise about 40 head of animals, usually a mixture of cows and camels by way of a dowry. On top of that, there was an extra dowry payment of a few more animals and money. The family of the would-be bride told us that we were poor and would not be able to raise the dowry. I was so insulted that I jumped on a horse and travelled towards Nyala to get the cows that we entrusted to our uncles over there. Surprisingly, news had reached them about Gibriel's intention to get married and they sent the cows towards us. I met them half way—altogether 16 cows. To that we added some camels and also collected more from relatives and were able to establish Gibriel's house. I must say it really helped that Gibriel himself came back with some money. At the end, we were able to go through with the wedding without any problem. We paid 40 head of animals, a mixture of cows and camels. We also paid one cow for the bride's mother and anther one for her uncle who presided over the ceremony, as was dictated by Zaghawa marriage rules.

The Zaghawa had a very diabolical system of marriage and I am delighted it has since changed, though not totally I may say. When a suitor, or more precisely, suitors, approached a family for marriage, the relatives of the girl would give very little away. They would simply say, 'We would need some time to consult her uncles and would be delighted to host you on such and such a date to give you an answer. If Allah allows, you will get the girl'.

On the assigned day, the family of the groom would arrive, only to discover that they were not the only suitors. More often than not, the suitors would have known the intention of their rivals and would have factored that into their strategy. The highest bidder would normally win. I remember a famous case of a girl in the village of your friend Bajji who took care of you in N'Djamena. In that case, groups representing 13 different suitors arrived in the village. They were all vying for the same girl. The host family accommodated the visitors in different shelters, treated them well and launched into the bargaining. A committee representing the girl shuttled among the visiting groups checking their dowry offers. After intense bargaining, one group won while the rest had to go back empty handed. Not surprisingly, each group would strive to excel in extolling the virtues of their suitor and scorning those of their rivals. They would say, 'We are a big clan, courageous and wealthy. The children of your daughter will grow up surrounded by numerous wealthy uncles. They will be well protected and cared for. We are rich and in a position to offer such and such as a dowry and shower the mother in-law and her brothers with good animals'.

Then they would turn against their rivals and deride them, 'Do not go for those other suitors. They are so few in their clans and cannot even protect themselves against invaders. If a bull of theirs falls in a well, they have to seek the help of others to lift it out, for they have not many men around. Those people are destitute and will surely kill the children of your daughter with hunger. They are mean and do not know how to honour a guest.' And so on and so on.

The bidding could go on for days without conclusion. Of course the girl in question was involved but the final say was skewed in favour of her male guardians. She too had to think about how much she could fetch out for that meant esteem and status in the community. Other constraints had to be taken on board as well. The bride had to think of the future wealth of her family and particularly her brothers, if she had any. Her brothers would need animals for they too had to pay a high dowry in marriage. The bride had to weigh all that carefully before responding to the final choice of her male guardians. In a Zaghawa family, brides brought wealth into the family. Of course they too would take some to establish their own families but in general, and unlike bridegrooms, they were a net gain to the family. The woman with the 13 suitors I told you about did very well. She secured 60 head of animals, more than any other dowry I can remember.

The contribution of Zaghawa women to the household was, to say the least, substantial. Schools have now changed things, but in the past, the burden of work carried by women was unbelievable. By the time the girl was eight or nine, she would have been well trained to help at home while herding goats like myself. By age 12, a Zaghawa girl was able to cook a meal for the entire family without any adult assistance. She would also do the normal household jobs like cleaning, childminding and nursing sick relatives. From age 13 or 14 onwards, a Zaghawa girl carried almost the same workload as an adult woman. She would take full care of the house, mind goats and cows, fetch water and firewood and trade on processed food if necessary. The only thing I did not see Zaghawa girls do was fighting a war, but I am glad I did not need to test them on that. God help the Zaghawa girls of those tough days.

In Love With Camels

Throughout my herding experience, it was the camels that I loved the most. Camels were wonderful animals—friendly, faithful and easy to manage. They were also resilient and were able to adapt to the changing landscape of the time. In my experience, the most useless animals were sheep and I am glad I did not have to do much with them. They were slow, picky in pasture and had no endurance for thirst.

Cows were nearly as bad. Though they were not as thirsty as sheep, they still had to be kept within 15 to 20 kilometres of a watering centre. Camels were far better and we were able to herd them within a radius of more than 30 kilometres of wells. As desert animals proper, camels could stay away from water for more than a week and still survive with no bother. Moreover, camels were able to beat the lack of pasture by their sheer height. In areas where grass was depleted, you could not keep cows or even goats. But in the case of camels, you could do so if you could find suitable trees, for they could subsist on grazing on high branches that other animals could not reach. But camels also had an additional advantage that made them superior to other beasts. You could carry everything on them—your belongings, water and other things. With camels, you would never run short of cash. You could carry lots of forest goods to the nearest markets; things like the sundried meat of wild animals, ostrich eggs, fodder, firewood and fruits and nuts that you would gather in the wilderness. That was why camels were deemed to equal wealth.

But camels had one danger. They attracted camel thieves and we had to be on guard for them at all times. Stolen camels could be taken several hundreds of miles away within a few days. A search party could follow the tracks of the stolen camel on the sand for a whole week without catching up with the thief. Fortunately, the Zaghawa were a close-knit society and had an impeccable communal system for retrieving stolen animals. Within minutes of a camel theft, a whole community could be mobilised and rigorous pursuit of the thief would ensue. We were also good in reading the tracks of animals on the sand. During my herding time, I could recognise the track of my camel on the sand out of those of ten other camels. That was a skill all nomads had and could not survive without. It was the ABC of nomadic life.

We too took our precautions against camel thieves. There were always good camels that thieves would be after. Their target had to be strong and fast for a quick get away. These were also our favourite camels and we kept them constantly within sight. I still remember, not without some nostalgia, one of those camels. It was my real companion and I never allowed him to move far away from my base. At night, we arranged the camels in our sleeping place. Camels parked at night and regurgitated their feed. Camels preferred to park against the wind, and that meant a north-south direction with their backs to the north. Like all other herders, I used to spread my sleeping canvas in front of my parked camel for the night. The camel would stay put, re-chewing its food. Every time the camel flushed a new bout of food from its stomach for regurgitating, I got this awful smell that came with it. It was bad at first but soon I got used to it and it never bothered me after that.

Sleeping within a yard or two in front of a camel was a deterrent against theft and there was a good logic behind the practice as well. From a parked position, camels moved forward and hence that sleeping arrangement. There would be no way for the camel to stand up and move forward without stumbling on the owner and causing injury to him. A good camel would never stampede and injure its owner on purpose. Instead and if necessary, the camel would have to crawl sideways before standing up, waking up everybody in the camp. That was why thieves avoided camels kept in that position at night. The best position I enjoyed with one of my favourite camels was to lie by the front side of the camel and use the left knee of the camel as a pillow. Most times, the camel stayed in the same position and did not disturb my sleep. At other times, the camel had to lie on one side and stretch its legs. Like all good camels, mine always lay on the right side and then stretched its legs for a while, repositioning itself so that I could resume my sleep. Camels always lay away from their owners and I have never heard any camel that crushed its owner in his sleep, a likely possibility given its weight compared to that of a human being. I must say, it was true that camels were domesticated animals and enjoyed being close to their owners.

We always approached a camel from the left side and that was where we slept at night at well. The halter of the camel stretched back at the left side of the camel's head. To immobilize the camel, we put the hobble on the left knee of the camel. We also rode the camel from the left side and there was logic behind that too. You stood on the left leg and lifted the right one over the saddle. That was why you had to be on the left side of the camel.

Among all the camels I had, there were five that I loved most. Every one of those camels was unique and had a different personality, temperament and quality. One of them was called Oriterr, a name that translated as the young (Ori) white (Terr) camel. Oriterr retained the same name even when he was no longer a young camel. In fact, Oriterr was not that young even when we got him, for his back teeth had already emerged. I think we got Oriterr as part of bride wealth we received for the wedding of my sister Nadeefa. Oriterr was the fastest camel we had in running, if not for walking as such. He was certain to be a winner in racing but we never tested him in that. He was also wise and courageous and was never disturbed by wild animals when travelling at night. That was a good quality for travelling at night and safer for the rider. Oriterr was also strong and tolerant and able to carry his load for a long distance without getting tired. I think Oriterr was bred by troublesome people, possibly bandits who got involved a lot in conflicts. In our view at the time, Oriterr was bred by the Kababish nomads of Kordofan. That it witnessed lots of fights was clear to us. His tail was severed and he had the scars of previous injuries on his skin. I loved Oriterr very much and he was very domesticated and faithful to me.

Then I had another camel called Hore, meaning 'blonde' in Zaghawa language. It took the colour of a white horse with a dash of black on it and that was why we called him Hore. Among all the camels we had, Hore had the softest back that would send you to sleep within minutes of starting your journey. That was a good quality for he never tired his rider. We got Hore from West Darfur, in particular the Sirba area. In those parts, men travelled between nearby towns trading in local markets, each of which was held on one day of the week. Their camels were trained to walk gently because some of the wares they transported were fragile. Hence, Hore was drilled to walk gently without rattling his load. Because of his soft and gentle walking, Hore retained his toenails intact throughout his life. That was an aspect of soft walking, for rough walking eroded the toenails. Hore was indeed an animal of burden. It could carry a substantial load without getting tired.

Hasanain was another fine camel we owned. Strangely, his name was a human name common in some parts of the Sudan. The name was derived from the root 'hasan', meaning goodness, and 'hasanain' was the plural of it. It was a new name in the area and I did not know how our camel ended up with such a strange name. Hasanain was fast but was equally a rough walker. He was certainly not a camel for a lousy rider. Bad camel riders never stayed on Hasanain's saddle. Hasanain's galloping made your stomach churn and you had to fasten your Kadmoul (cloth belt) around the stomach to keep your intestines in place. His pace was so fast that you felt the horizon rushing towards you. As it galloped along, Hasanain threw the sand sideways and broke the grass, making a rhythmic sound that frightened snakes and other little creatures out of his way. As if he knew his quality, Hasainain sped away with confidence mixed with an air of enjoyment. In a playful way, Hasanain fanned his tail left and right, tapping the cheeks of his buttocks as he sped away. In Zaghawa language, we referred to Hasanain's brisk walking as 'Kuru'. It was the fastest travel you could ever dream of in those days. I remember I did around 100 miles in one overnight with Hasanain when I had to travel south tracing some lost cows. Hasanain was the Mercedes Benz of our nomadic time.

Of course we also had she-camels (niag) that were not kept for travelling as such. She-camels were the anchors of the herd. In addition to breeding, the she-camels kept us alive for they supplied us with milk around the year. We used to compose songs extolling the virtues of their milk. Camel milk changed with the age of the camel and the length of its lactation period. Younger she-camels gave sweeter milk but the amount of sugar content in the milk deteriorated with the age of the camel as well as that of her lactating calf. For that reason, we drank the milk of younger camels and left the milk of older ones for making yoghurt and butter. When we were near local markets, we sold yogurt and butter for extra cash.

There were a few occasions when more than a single hobble was needed for a camel. For maximum immobilisation, we hobbled all the four knees of the camel. That was important when we branded our camels or performed surgical operations. Each camel bore a brand of the lineage of its owner. Branding was important for identification but equally for pride in the lineage itself and its wealth and achievement. A hot metal was used to inscribe the lineage brand on the backside of the camel. The operation was painful and hence the camel needed full immobilisation. When the owner's parents came from two different lineages, their respective brands were put on the camel. If the camel passed from parents to children, the latter too might include their brands if they were different from their parents. The Zaghawa inherit the lineage of their fathers but their mothers might come from a different lineage. In this way, camels became an extension of the family, bearing the lineage origins of more than one generation. Had it not been for camels, our experience of the drought would have been an utter disaster for the family. Our cows were decimated but the few camels that survived kept us going. I wouldn't be exaggerating if I said our very survival was due to those camels.

I must have been about nine or ten when I spent my first night in a camel camp. I still remember how I took to fresh uncooked camel milk. Yes it was salty, but sweet at the same time. It was so heavy that a gulp of it would drive away hunger for hours and hours. But I was also thrilled with my first night in the camp for another reason. It gave me the feeling that I was not a child any more and had already moved into the adult world. By the time I was 13, I was well versed in the intricacies of camel herding. A year or two later, I earned fame for being an excellent camel herder. Whenever I lost a camel, I followed its track the whole day. At night when I was not able to see the track on the sand, I slept on it and resumed my pursuit in the first daylight. I was famous for being able to fetch back stray camels, no matter how many days that took. People would say that entrusting a camel to Hinain was like leaving a garment in a bushy kitr tree (Acacia mellifera). Nobody would dare to go near that garment at all. That was because Kitr thorns were sharp and poisonous and their injuries were difficult to heal.

The drought of 1972/1973 forced us, along with many others, to shift towards camels. The drought time and the years that followed coincided with some developments in our family. My sisters started getting married one by one and their marriages brought many camels to the family. Although the girls brought cows too, it was not possible to herd both at the same time. Terrain change made it impossible to keep camels and cows in one herd for both required a different pattern of grazing.

Gradually, we got rid of cows and stopped investing in cattle. We became camel nomads proper.

My commitment to camel herding continued for a long time. It did not cease even when I went to schools. Throughout my school years, I spent almost every school holiday in camel camps. There was only one vacation when I did not go to the camel camp. That was the vacation when I had to focus on my study for the Sudanese Certificate or Leaving Cert as some would call it.

Herding camels did me good and I got more out of it compared to what I got out of education. Even at schools I could say that I was much more mature than my classmates. Herding camels toughened me and made me independent and able to take difficult decisions from early childhood. The camps also taught me how to withstand loneliness for very often herding required isolation from others for an extended period. That proved a useful disposition in my school days. Studying sometimes required a solitary existence away from friends and I learnt that well.

Of course herding also taught me practical survival skills, like axing, milking camels, riding, drawing water out of deep wells, building and rope making. Like all nomads, I also learnt to navigate by reading stars at night and that is knowledge I find very practical to this day. To survive in the open, one had to command knowledge of the fauna and flora of the region. Halfway into my teenage years, I knew every plant, every animal and every insect that existed in Zaghawa land."

The Koranic School

We have so far clocked several hours of recording and I still do not know the mystery of the name 'Hinain'. It is a twist in the story that Hinain wants to retain for a little while. What I find bewildering is that I have known Khalil for nearly seven years now but have never heard of the name Hinain before. I adjust my digital recorder and let Hinain resume his narrative of his school time, "It is strange that minding animals had kept me away from schools. And yet, it was the animals that drove me into the classroom. While I was herding animals, I also attended a Koranic school, at least when I was not away from our village. As all over Darfur, we referred to the Koranic school by the name Maseed, a rich word that conjoins several meanings. The Maseed is a Koranic school, a village mosque, a social club for men, an informal court and a reception space for strangers and dignitary's visitors.

In my younger years, goat herding was a day business. I took the goats out of the village just after breakfast and stayed with them in the bush until late afternoon. Then I moved back towards the village and was there before sunset. Like most children in the village, I went to the Maseed for an hour or two every night around 7pm, with the exception of Thursday night which was our night off. The Maseed was only a few houses away from our house and there were around 15 children; mostly boys attending but a few girls dropped in every now and then too. Some of the children attended primary school as well but there were many like me who didn't.

The Maseed was right in the centre of the village. It had a grass room enclosed by a bush fence. There were four large Ziziphus and Balanite trees inside the compound. These trees provided shade for men to congregate and convene their mediation council meetings for resolving public disputes. The Maseed dealt with conflicts that involved strangers who came to the village to discuss matters like camel theft, damage to farms and fights over water.

The Maseed was also used for eating the evening meal, just at the end of the Koranic study session. In our village, Kayra, no man ate dinner at home. Food was brought from various houses, and all men ate together near our learning spot. Older boys could partake of this meal but younger ones went back and ate at home. Older boys were also needed to serve the food, help pour water for washing hands and fetch extra sauce if necessary.

Our Koranic teacher was Nur Aldin who was also my maternal uncle. Unlike other Zaghawa villages, Kayra people took great pride in having four men who had learnt the Koran well. Nur Aldin spent more than a decade in west Darfur where he learnt the Koran in the famous Koranic schools of the Fur ethnic group. In the Fur schools, Nur Aldin committed the entire Koran to memory and earned the title of a Fekki (Plural: fugara) and came back to establish his religious career among his own people in Kayra.

Fekki Nur Aldin became a well-respected man in the village and presided over all ceremonies that required reciting the Koran, such as at weddings, funerals and the naming of newborns. Nur Aldin was also our only Imam who took care of prayers in the one mosque we had in the village. In his free time, the Fekki used his knowledge of the Koran to make some money. He used the Koran for almost everything, such as preparing Koranic drinks for sickness, success in business and protection of property. He also made amulets that people wore to ward off attacks, including firearms, devils and other malicious forces. Traders commissioned his work for attracting customers, and herders took his medicine to increase the size of their herds. We never made use of these services but other people did.

Fekki Nur Aldin also hosted other fekkis who visited the village for the purpose of preaching and delivering services for money. These were the wandering fekkis who spent most of their time roaming different villages across Darfur. They made their living on offering Koranic medicinal drinks and amulets. In return, they were paid in cash or in kind. Clients who did not have cash, paid in animals, grain or any other valuable object.

My first visit to the Maseed was memorable. At first, I was quite scared of the teacher because he kept his cane near him and was always threatening to beat us with it. I hid myself between my two older brothers and stayed quiet for a while. We sat on the sand forming a crescent shape, facing the Koranic teacher. In front of us was an open fire lit by older boys before our arrival. That was the only light we had, for no kerosene lamps were used. Each of us brought a piece of firewood to keep the fire going. That was the only thing I took to the Maseed for I had no wooden slate to write on. In fact, I never needed to learn how to write like older boys. Senior students took great pride in decorating their wooden slates. After the session, most of them left their slates in the Maseed and only a few took them home with them.

Like most of the children in the Koranic school, I spoke no Arabic at all and communicated with the Fekki in Zaghawa. As far as learning the Koran was concerned, I didn't miss not speaking Arabic. Mind you, primary school boys who spoke Arabic did not understand the Koran better than us who didn't. The language of the Koran was far too sophisticated for a young Zaghawa to comprehend. Instead, we just memorised whatever chapter the teacher gave us. We were like parrots, repeating things we didn't know, nor did we care what they meant. We knew that the Koran was the words of Allah and it was good to memorise as much of it as possible. We made no effort to understand what we learnt, for that was of no importance for us.

I still remember vividly my first evening at the Maseed. I sat with my brothers and every student loudly recited his or her chapter of the Koran. Some read from wooden slates, but most from memory. Suddenly, the teacher noticed me sitting, not knowing what to do. I was the only one who was not shouting Koranic verses. He smiled and told me to repeat loudly after him, a sentence that I later learnt to be the first verse of the opening chapter of the Koran. He kept asking me to raise my voice higher and higher until he was happy. He wasn't hard of hearing but he insisted on us shouting as loud as we could. Following that, he just left me repeating the same verse over and over and turned to other kids in the company. I kept repeating that verse without a hint of what it meant. I just knew that it was what Allah said and it was good to learn. After about ten minutes, the teacher came back to me and was happy about my progress. He then shouted over the next verse and ordered me to run it together with the first one loud and clear. Every now and then, he corrected my pronunciation and moved on to someone else. Every time our voices flagged down, he touched his cane pretending to be ready to use it against us. We immediately responded by raising our voices and he smiled and dropped the cane. I did well in my first night at the Maseed. I was able to learn a whole chapter. It was short, consisting of only six or seven verses but that was a lot for my first session. As I was going home, the teacher praised me saying it was unusual for a child to learn the whole chapter in one night. He then ordered me to spend the next night reciting the same chapter so it would get fixed in my head.

The following days were much easier as I knew how to learn. I was going so fast that sometimes I learnt two chapters in the same night. I also stopped worrying about the cane for I knew that if I kept my voice loud and clear, I would not be punished. I also learnt not to giggle when someone cracked a joke near us.

The Koranic school was also open for adults to visit. Occasionally, some men dropped in and sat with us reciting their chapters. At the time, I thought it was strange that some were memorising longer chapters while others were just starting like myself. The adults were not reliable and they never came regularly. Some days, the adult students were away from town or perhaps in the camps with their animals. The beauty of the Maseed was in its ability to allow each learner to follow his or her own pace. Some pupils spent a longer time on the same verse and the teacher didn't mind at all. One boy, by the name Mohamed, kept switching to Zaghawa in his recitation and it sounded quite funny. We couldn't laugh at him for we would be caned if we did that. The teacher didn't mind. He just kept correcting him and ordered him to start all over, again and again. When I started staying away with the animals in the camps, I missed a few days here and there. Whenever I was back, I just resumed from where I was before and there was no problem. That was the aspect of the Maseed I admired most. It was not like primary schools, where your absence left you behind your friends in the class.

I still think it was hilarious how we were yelling at the top of our voices, each with a different speed and pitch. We often competed for loudness and clarity, to show off and to impress the neighbours of Maseed with how good we were. Our voices reading different verses at the same time was comical. Whenever the teacher touched his cane, we went wild and sounded like a bunch of chickens being attacked by a fox with each squawking in utter disarray. Despite this, the teacher was able to spot the pupil who had forgotten his line. Actually, when we got stuck and forgot the next word, we just repeated the last word like a broken record. The teacher immediately came to our help and told us what was next and off we went.

It is true that in the Maseed, each pupil recited a different Koranic verse. There were, however, a few occasions when we recited things in unison. That was when we learnt the Five Pillars of Islam, the Names of 25 Apostles and the Ninety-nine Most Beautiful Names of Allah. With little Arabic at the time, I thought I was learning the Koran when I recited those in Maseed. Later, I realised that those items had nothing to do with the Koran. Rather, they were some of those theological texts that we had to learn and be able to recite.

From Hinain To Khalil

My Maseed time was cut short by my herding responsibilities and later by joining the primary school. By the time I left the Maseed, I was able to command all the knowledge required for performing prayers. I learnt how to do the ablution, call for prayers and say my prayers complete with all the relevant Koranic passages. That was not bad for an irregular Maseed attendant. The Koranic Chapters I learnt in the Maseed were of great help for me in the primary school. For the first year at least, I did not have to learn a single new Koranic verse. I had them all in my little head and from Fekki Nur Aldin. The accent of the primary school teacher sounded different but the verses remained the same. It did not bother me that some children frowned at my Maseed accent. Unlike them, I at least knew the verses before the teacher uttered them and I was not shy to demonstrate that in class when the opportunity arose. That was enough to win me the praise of the teacher and fend off those jealous classmates.

Was I the child who decided to go to school without the consent of his guardians, as you suggested the other day? The answer is yes and no at the same time. The most important lesson I learnt in herding was to take action without seeking approval of my guardians, but within reason I must say. The Zaghawa were in the habit of pooling their resources and keeping their animals in one flock, minded by one or two relatives. As my fortune dictated, I lost my father early and my mother had to move back to her parents' village. My mother's brother took care of me and I grew up under his guardianship. I had two brothers, Gibriel and Abu Bakar. My uncle had only one son at the time and we grew up together, almost in one home split into two. Eventually a decision had to be made about school while taking account of our camels. Unfortunately, the decision was not in my favour. Namely, I was to take care of camels belonging to my mother and her brother. Abdullahi, my uncle's only son and my two brothers were to be sent to school leaving me uneducated. The decision seemed fair at the time but as the years passed by, other things happened and I changed my mind.

One day while I was doing my usual herding duties, a disaster hit out of the blue and I was engulfed in crisis. A few weeks old calf belonging to my uncle had a nasty accident. Like all young camels, the calf was very inquisitive and took great risks to satisfy its curiosity. The calf was walking in front of me when we came across an anteater's hole. In its characteristic nosiness, the calf stuck its head in the hole. I noticed that but simply thought it was an amusing sight and didn't bother about it. All of a sudden something happened and the calf panicked and twisted its neck and broke it. The calf was dead within minutes and all hell broke loose. I was so traumatised, for it was such a beautiful calf and I adored it ever since it was born. I rushed to the village and was crying when I got there. My uncle understood but his wife was furious. She wondered, why should I cry over a calf that I had 'just killed'. I was very upset with her unfair and callous words. A neighbour overheard the dispute and came to my help. She criticised my uncle's wife's comments telling her I was not to blame. She told her to be grateful for me who minded the camels and allowed her son to go to school. My uncle's wife was livid and uncompromising. In her anger, she responded saying, 'those who have surplus milk make yoghurt.' Her choice of that particular proverb was simply hard to take. In plain words, it meant my mother had several sons and hence could spare a son as herder. She herself could not, because she had only one son. I was therefore that disposable surplus. To be honest, the incongruous use of that Zaghawa proverb became a turning point in my life. It made me think about the value of herding compared to education. The very idea that I was a mere surplus boy, destined to remain an uneducated herder was hard to forget. For days and nights following that incident, my mind was tormented by one thing and that was how to abandon herding and go to school like my older brothers. I still loved herding, for it was the only thing I knew at the time, but the idea of going to school would not go away.

I had a paternal aunt (Kubra) who lived in another village who always encouraged me to go to school. She always taught me that there was no future in herding and that I should rebel against my family's choice and go to school. After the calf incident, her words rang and rang in my head. Her advice was reassuring for at least I had one adult who supported my new determination to go to school.

Days later, I was trekking with my animals as usual when in the distance I saw two young boys coming towards me. They were coming from the town of Tine and heading towards our village. I knew that the primary school was closing for the long

summer vacation and was soon to schedule a date for their new
first year intake. I was delighted to see my brothers coming back
home, for their presence gave the house a buzz that I missed
with their absence. As the boys came nearer, I realized that
they were not my brothers. Rather they were some cousins of
mine whom I also knew very well. Each was carrying a cloth
school bag similar to the bags that Europeans use for their daily
shopping. At the time, school children didn't have that much
belongings. So, in addition to the school bag, each one of them
carried a bundle containing one or two garments. That was all,
no extra shoes and no toys. When they arrived, we sat under
a tree for a chat. I offered them fresh milk but they settled for
water. I asked them about their ranking in the final exam. In
those years, schools had a dreadful system whereby pupils were
ranked according to their exam results and it was common to
ask a child about his rank in class. One of the boys didn't appreciate my question and responded rather sarcastically, "What do
you know about school ranking? You are only a herder boy". I
was taken aback by the vicious answer to what I thought was a
simple question. Their performance mattered little to me and I
was only trying to communicate. Nonetheless I felt humiliated
and immediately thought about the calf fiasco. As it transpired,
my cousins did not do well and were perhaps worried, for they
would be plagued by the same question later at home. I left the
issue of ranking aside and asked about the date of the impending new intake. They told me it would take place in a fortnight.
None of my cousins realised the importance of that date for me.
They were convinced I was destined to remain a herder for good.

As the boys left me on their journey home, I sat under my
tree hatching my own plans, or rather destiny. My mind was
already made up and I had an important date with my future:
in two weeks time, I would present myself to the school, with
or without the help of my family. Full stop. Later in the evening,

I arrived home, only to find my two brothers being fed. They walked a different route so we did not meet. For the first time, I listened to their stories about school with attentive interest. I asked so many questions about the school: number of teachers, pupils, guards, food, homework and everything I could think about. My brothers were delighted that I showed interest and passion in their experience and answered every question without insulting me like my cousins early on in the day. I wanted to tell them about my new plans but I held back. I was scared that my uncle, and particularly his wife, might stand in my way. Of course they would be right to be concerned. I was already too old for school and the animals had to be minded. I decided to keep my plans to myself and proceeded to learn more about school. And there was no shortage of questions to ask for I had never been inside a schoolyard up to that time.

On the school enrolment day, I arrived early at the school gate. The school was in Tine town that was not far from my village. My family didn't know about my school plans and thought I was visiting my relatives in the town. The school was packed with boys accompanied by their fathers. It was such a sad sight for me. As I came to notice, I was one of a few children who were not accompanied by their fathers. I was too young when my father died and I never knew him. Despite this, on that day, I was overcome by his loss. Fortunately, I had an in-law who worked as a school guard in the same place. His name was Ishaq and he was of great help to me on that day. To be precise, the man, who was also a relative, was engaged to my sister.

At around 10am, the gate of the school was opened and everybody was allowed in. Someone whom I later knew as the school Headmaster headed a committee of five men and presided over the business. It was easy to spot the Headmaster for he was older, louder and wore better clothes. He was also sitting on a chair that was bigger and higher than the other chairs around.

First they called for children who had birth certificates. Amazingly, there were five or six of those and they were all accepted in the school. I felt somewhat bemused as that was the first time in my life to hear about the 'birth certificate'. Those who had birth certificates never looked like me, the camel herder. They were clean and wore shiny garments. It was clear that their parents were government officials and they were born in cities where they could get those important papers, called birth certificates. As for my humble self, I looked rather rough and wore a short garment that was also of poor quality. It was made of the cheapest fabric, often used for shrouding the dead. Only herders and farmers wore garments made of this fabric. Traders, teachers and government officials never went near it.

Then the Headmaster called for the rest of the boys, including myself. Unfortunately, I was again pushed aside. The Headmaster looked at me and asked about my age. Like me, Ishaq was unsure about my age and suggested to the Headmaster that I was perhaps eight or nine or maybe ten. The Headmaster enquired about how long ago my front teeth broke and I told him that it happened two or three years before. He laughed and politely told me to wait under a tree near the office while he turned to deal with other children. I went to the tree and sat there, not knowing how my luck would turn. At the end of the session, I was called in. Ishaq was standing near the Headmaster and looked satisfied and I knew that things were going well. Then the Headmaster spoke and told me I was late coming to school by two to three years and that he would admit me into the school but there was no place for me in the hostels. He said I was too old for the boarding school and had to lodge with my relatives in town. I was delighted but before I could say anything, Ishaq thanked the Headmaster and the rest of the committee, saying he would take care of my upkeep. I left the school mesmerized about my achievement but with a few things to worry about. Not having a place in the boarding school was a nuisance but easy to overcome. As a school guard, Ishaq had a grass room right at the gate of the school and that was where I would be lodging. I was yet to find out how my family would respond to my school plans.

By the time I reached home, news had already broken that I was admitted to the school. To my utter satisfaction, both my mother and my uncle were very supportive and were quite impressed and equally perplexed at how I made up my mind and got myself into school. Of course they recognized that Ishaq's petition and assurance of accommodation also helped. My uncle's wife did not raise any objection and I was in no rush to seek her views on the matter. Needless to say, I was happy to continue with herding until the start of the academic year following the rather long summer vacation. My uncle immediately arranged for a hired herder to take my place and there were no shortage of interested boys for the job. Working as a hired herder was a good way of making money and establishing one's own herd, a good option for poor people who did not own animals to start with. Like today, hired herders were paid in animals, with cash reserved for their upkeep only.

Summer school break was a period of confusion and nostalgia for me. I resented abandoning herding, an experience that I perfected and took pride in. And yet, I was looking forward to what lay ahead at school. These incongruent passions were difficult to reconcile. My school brothers often dropped in and spent a night or two in the camp with us, only to run away to the village. It was extraordinary that the few years of schooling they experienced, had already separated them from us. They could no longer enjoy herding like myself and other herders with whom we often socialised. But their periodic stay with us was also rewarding. Unlike us, it was hard for them to sustain talking about animals for more than an hour in one go. That was somewhat awkward but it suited me very well for I wanted to learn more and more about school. As a result, their stay with us formed a period of intense coaching for me regarding everything I needed to know about school: food, homework, disciplinary measures, games and sport. They, in turn, were delighted with the ample opportunity I afforded them to boast about their experience and successes, and they obliged and opened their hearts for my naïve questions about schooling. By the time the summer vacation was over, I was well versed in everything the school had to offer and more. I knew the names of all the teachers and where they came from and I also learnt the names of their wives and children. More intriguingly, I paid particular attention to the disciplinary measures adopted in the school and the excesses of some teachers in punishing pupils who broke the rules. There were also some reassuring aspects of school that I liked in talking to my brothers. They were able to teach me how to recite or rather sing some of the patriotic poems schoolchildren had to learn in those days. To my delight, I also realised my study at the Maseed was not in total vain. At least for my first and second years, I would be required to learn the same Koranic chapters that I had already memorized in the Maseed. Well, it was a shame I did not learn to read or write a single Arabic letter in the Maseed. Nonetheless, I would surely be well ahead of my pals in our religious classes.

For better or for worse, the school summer vacation ended and I had to leave the animal world behind me and start my education drive. My last day of herding was tortuous and painful. Withdrawing from the only comfort zone I knew well was not easy. Yes, I was thrilled to go to school but I was apprehensive venturing into a life that I did not know much about. It took me years of diligent work to become an excellent herder, only to move on into a terrain with not even a single goat around.

A day before my departure to school, my uncle bought me a pair of shorts. I was delighted with my new acquisition, for prior to that, and like all herders of my age, I wore only a garment with nothing underneath. Altogether, my attire included two garments, one pair of shorts, a pair of shoes and a cotton throw-over sheet for sleeping. There were no books and no crayons but I had an empty handmade cotton school bag with me.

When I arrived with my brothers to the school gate, I went straight to Ishaq's room for that was where I would be staying. My fortunate brothers went into the school to be allocated places in the dormitories. It was evening and Ishaq was saying his prayers so I had to wait for him to finish before shaking hands with him by way of greetings. Instead of just waiting for Ishaq to be free, I took time to examine my new home. The grass room was flat and hence offered no protection against rain. The rainy season was nearly over so we were not expecting more than one or two showers before the year was gone. The room looked bare with almost no furniture in it. There was one thin bed, a mat made of palm leaves about the size of a single bed sheet, a goatskin prayer mat, a four-gallon clay water pot with a reused powder milk tin for scooping water and a clay washing vessel usually used for ablution. That was all the furniture in my abode for the next academic year, but I was neither worried nor disappointed. I was a herder boy and the room was far better than a tree shade in the open for that was what I was used to in the animal camps. There were no cooking facilities in the shelter at all, not even for making a cup of tea. Luckily, Ishaq's parents lived at the edge of the town and that was where we were to be fed. We went early in the morning for tea and later for breakfast. At sunset, we also went there for dinner. We never ate more than two meals a day. We were certainly never hungry and everybody in the village had two meals. Children in the boarding school were fortunate. They had tea in the morning and three meals during the day.

Ishaq wouldn't finish his prayers so I decided to visit the dormitories to see how my brothers were fairing compared to me, and I was jealous. To begin with, they had rain-proof grass rooms that would also be warmer than our room in winter. Each boy was issued two woollen blankets, one of which was folded to serve as a mattress. I saw the same blankets with some soldiers who visited our village during their holidays and I thought they were the best I ever saw in my life. My brothers also had a kerosene lamp each for studying and I had none. On top of that, my brothers would be served tea with milk and plenty of sugar in the morning and then they would call for breakfast after the first two classes. Later on, in the same day, they would also be given lunch after classes and super at sunset. No wonder schoolboys were healthy and fat while we, herder boys, looked scraggy and malnourished. I could not stand discovering any more goodies offered to my lucky brothers so I ran out to meet Ishaq who had finished his prayers and was looking for me. After some greetings, Ishaq offered me some water but that was all he had in the room. He then told me to accompany him to his parents' house for some food.

On the way, Ishaq passed by the school for some business and I took the liberty of asking some questions about the school layout. Ishaq obliged and we stood together right in the middle of the schoolyard to have a panoramic view of the whole compound. The school gate we left behind was at the eastern side of the school. A thick bush fence surrounded the school and our room sat at the only gate in the whole compound. Six or seven huts were located at the eastern side. Those were the dormitories with square walls built of red bricks. They had conical grass tops on metal frames. Each of these dormitories housed around 20 of the 120 or so pupils in the school. Just behind the dormitories but inside the fence sat the house of the school supervisor built of the same material. The house was small but quite adequate for an unmarried teacher. The other teachers, who were married and with families, lived outside the school. On the southern side was a row of four classrooms parallel to the fence. They were also built of red bricks with pitched grass roofs. They looked large and spacious, perhaps 4 X 8 or 5 X 8 metres in size. These rooms were the biggest I ever saw in my life. Attached to one side of the classrooms was the office where we went for enrolment. That was the office of the Headmaster and the teachers, all in one large room. On the western side of the school were a few rooms, built entirely of grass. One of them was a classroom and the other two were part of the hostels. The kitchen was located at the north-western corner of the compound. Next to it was the store that was of the exact design of the dormitories.

My first night in Ishaq's room was agitated. Ishaq took the bed and I slept on the mat near him. Well, it wasn't that much of a sleep. I was awake for most of the night, worried that I might over sleep and be late for my first day at school, or that the animals I used to herd would get harmed. I missed them very much and felt guilty about leaving them under the care of others who were not as good as me. I had nightmares of every danger that could befall them: camels snatched by thieves, cows going thirsty and goats being attacked by jackals and foxes. In the middle of my animal nightmares, I felt something like a goat licking gently at my right shoulder. As it turned out, it was not a goat at all. Rather, it was Ishaq waking me up at the crack of dawn. We had to go to his parents' house for a cup of tea. I got up and threw some water over my face before we sped off for tea. When we got there, Ishaq's father was sitting on his prayer mat with a pot of tea and a few glasses by his side. Ishaq served the tea for the three of us, starting with his dad. The tea tasted very much different from the tea we always made at the camp. In the camp, we used camel milk that was heavier and a bit salty. We also used plenty of milk. In fact, we never used water at all. We just boiled milk and added tea to it. The tea in Ishaq's home was different. It had goat's milk which was sweeter and a bit watery.

On top of that, they added only a mere drop of milk into loads of boiled water. Their tea was also much stronger than ours and looked as dark as coffee. But there was something nice in their tea. It had plenty of sugar. In the camp, we were a bit mean with sugar for there were no shops around the corner like in town. I did enjoy the tea but couldn't wait for Ishaq to finish his cup, for all that I wanted at the time was to go to school.

As we approached the school, a loud bell rang and I saw pupils rushing out of their dorms towards the classrooms. I did hear a school bell ringing before in my previous visits to the town. Also, sometimes we hung small bells on the necks of sheep because sheep had a dreadful habit of feeding at night and were often too stupid to find their way back to their herds. Bells alerted us to their whereabouts in darkness. But compared to all the bells I heard before, the sound of that morning bell was by far the sweetest. It seeped into my ears like music. Ishaq was too slow for me so I excused myself and rushed through the gate of the school. The pupils were forming four rows in the school courtyard with the Headmaster standing right in the middle. Other teachers stood in front of their offices but did not go near the Headmaster. I didn't know where to go so I made my way towards one of my brothers. Before I could reach him, a pompous child I knew shouted at me, 'Where are you going Hinain? You are only a first year pupil. Go to the other line over there.'

I must say, I didn't like the intervention of that stupid boy but I had to follow his direction. He couldn't even ride a horse, let alone a camel and he had the audacity to address me like that. Mind you, he was only in his second class and was not even good in his last exams. I joined the first year file and towered over them for I was much older than all of them. The Headmaster went from one class to another and appointed one pupil as a monitor for each class except us. We were to remain without one until much later in the year. Then we were ordered to proceed to our classrooms. It was such a strange sight for me. Pupils of higher classes knew what to do so they walked orderly and in lines like soldiers. As for us, the first years, we ran towards our classroom like a herd of thirsty goats running towards water for each one of us wanted to sit right at the front. Well, before we could make it to the classroom, the Headmaster gave us a sharp order to come back and stand in front of him. We were frightened because he had a cane in his hand and I thought we were about to taste our first punishment in the school. Surprisingly, the Headmaster and all senior pupils laughed with amusement at our disorderly behaviour. He made us stand in line and walk slowly into the classroom, one after another like camels in a caravan. The classroom was half full by the time I entered it. I had wanted to sit right in the front row so that I would not miss anything, but those places were already taken. I grudgingly settled for a place half way and sat with three other children on the same bench. When the Headmaster came in, I lost even that seat. Myself and a few other taller children were sent to sit on the last bench further at the back of the classroom. The smaller children were lucky and were moved to the front seats.

The appearance of the Headmaster in the class was very perplexing for us. We were busy giggling and making friends when he entered the class. We didn't know what to do so we went dead silent waiting for his instructions. He stood and looked at us as if we were a bunch of goats and we knew something went terribly wrong for he did not look happy at all. Then he ordered all of us to stand up and so we did and he gazed at us for a few moments. Then he snorted at us, 'Whenever a teacher comes in, you all stand up and remain standing until he tells you to sit down. All down now!' We were terrified. We sat down without a whisper coming from the class that was full of life only a second before. The place sounded like we had stopped breathing as well.

Then the Headmaster relaxed his face a bit, acknowledging our recognition of his authority and the emptiness of our little heads.

The Headmaster stood at a large desk at the front of the class. He was examining a file of loose papers. After a few seconds, the Headmaster ordered one of the children to bring him a chair. The child took a few steps and stopped in front of the Headmaster looking very confused. The Headmaster looked agitated and said to him, 'You little ass, I told you to get me a chair. What are you waiting for?' We were amused by the word, 'ass' but with the tone in which it was said, we were too frightened to laugh. The child looked at the Headmaster and asked with a petrified face, 'But from where sir?' The Headmaster, realising the dilemma of the child, managed to control his anger and said in a nicer way, 'Go to my office at the end of this row of buildings and get me one of the chairs you find in there.' The boy shot out of the office and within a few seconds, he came back with a chair for our bossy Headmaster.

I couldn't wait for the Headmaster to start showing me how to read and write. That was what brought me to school and at the time, I thought I would be able to read and write before the Headmaster left the classroom. But the Headmaster had a different plan that had nothing to do with teaching. He wanted to check all of us against a list of names he had in his file. What for? I could not tell. It did not take him long to come to me for he started right from the back of the class. When he came to me, I stood up facing him and struggled not to show I was shaking with fear. I was afraid he would fail to find my name in his list and send me out of the school altogether. To my surprise, the Headmaster was much nicer than I gave him credit for. He told me that he knew my family and asked me about some of them. I said nothing but kept nodding for I only had a vague idea about what he was saying. Then he scrutinized his list of names and my heart pounded. He looked at me again and then up at the ceiling as though he was meditating. I followed his eyes to the ceiling and wondered whether he was distracted by the cobwebs or the wasps' nests above us! Before I could find out anything worth looking at on the ceiling, the Headmaster interrupted my thoughts, saying, 'You are Hinain Ibrahim Mohamed.' I was thrilled that my name was finally located in the school official list and by none other than the Headmaster himself. I was so excited, for that was the first time for my name to be inscribed on a piece of paper. With great relief, I responded to the Headmaster with a huge grin, 'Yes sir.' In my naivety, I thought the Headmaster would nod and move on to the child next to me but I was wrong. He went back to his cobwebs, wasp nests or God knows what he had discovered on that dilapidated ceiling. Seconds later, the Headmaster said with extreme bossiness, 'From now on, your name is Khalil Ibrahim and no more of that Hinain business' and he walked away before I could recover from my shock. Wow, that was the power of the magical spells of our Headmaster for from that moment and until today, my name turned into 'Khalil' with 'Hinain' discarded and forgotten forever. My parents must have killed too few goats in the naming ceremony that gave me the name 'Hinain'. The Fekki too might have been present, bless-ing the naming ceremony with some passages from the Koran. What a waste! The Headmaster scrapped all that with a few words and a gaze or two at a dirty grass ceiling!

At that moment of my renaming, I spoke no Arabic at all. Of course I knew a few words, mostly from my school brothers but was not able to construct a single full correct sentence. Indeed, I could recite some Koranic chapters but had no idea what the words meant. I couldn't decide whether the name Khalil sounded nice or coarse and had to repeat it silently so that I would not forget it. I had to repeat and repeat that name for I had to make sure that I remembered my name. Imagine the situation if I were to forget my name and ask others or the Headmaster to tell me what it was. I would be the laughing stock of the whole school.

I had never come across the name Khalil before and none of my acquaintances bore the same name. As a name, Khalil sounded ok and I could just about live with it but it did not mean anything in particular. My Zaghawa name (Hinain) was certainly nicer. It meant something definite and was easier to pronounce, as I thought at the time. Having said that, I was not the only one in the class who came into the classroom with one name and emerged without it or with another. Worse than that, my former name was banned and became punishable by lashing. Hinain was a name but also a Zaghawa word and no school-child was to be permitted to utter even a single Zaghawa word without being reported and punished. That was one of the first rules we learnt at the school. Arabic was to be the only language allowed, for those who spoke it and those who did not alike. The Headmaster dictated that in no uncertain terms before he left our first class in school. 'From now on, no Zaghawa, no Masaleit, no Irigna and no Fur languages to be spoken. You shall speak only Arabic in this school,' he said.

On reflection, my name predicament was not unique. It was the order of the day and I was not the only one who lost his original or more precisely non-Arabic name on that day. The rule was devastating for me because my Arabic was non-existent or pretty close to zero. I must say we were already tuned to learning Arabic and looked at our non-Arabic language with apprehension and often contempt. The Zaghawa themselves colluded in this conspiracy against their language. When you uttered a Zaghawa word in big cities, your companions would order you not to speak Zaghawa and embarrass them. And that was the attitude towards all non-Arabic languages in Darfur and other parts of the Sudan.

Like in other schools in Darfur, ours devised its way of monitoring the ban of non-Arabic languages in the school vicinity. Our school was in the heart of Zaghawa land so almost all children in the school were Zaghawa. Unlike me, some of those children were lucky for they already spoke good Arabic. Those who did not, had to restrict themselves to using the handful of Arabic words they knew or simply shut up and avoid communication with other children. To monitor our conformity to the language rule, the school issued a leather ring to circulate among us. The leather ring was designed to be worn around the neck. The school monitor took this ring and slipped it over the head of the first child who spoke in Zaghawa. The poor child, guilty of uttering a Zaghawa word had to go around and hand the ring to the first child he could catch whispering a Zaghawa word.

Every morning, just before the start of classes we had to appear in the school courtyard. Each class would arrange themselves in two or three lines facing the teacher. That was when we were counted but it was also a time for instructions and the punishment of those who broke school rules the previous day. A guilty child would be brought forward and ordered to lie down on the sand and would be given five lashes or more on his bum and the more senior the pupil was, the harsher the punishment. But that was not all, for the child had to keep the ring until he succeeded to hand it over to another unfortunate child who was reported uttering a Zaghawa word. Surprisingly, we worked hard to make someone utter a non-Arabic word and reported that to the child with the ring. For that reason, the ring remained circulating long after we commanded Arabic and the language rule. What was perplexing to me was our Zaghawa teachers who were much more severe in discouraging us from speaking our language. In the school vicinity, the Zaghawa teachers stuck to the language rule and never spoke Zaghawa in front of us. Leaving the language rule aside, our teachers were very kind and worked exceptionally hard to make us learn and move forward. Their different backgrounds gave the school the feeling of a community that was above ethnic groups and tribal chauvinism. For me at least, the school was the first place where I shared the same space and experienced intense dealings with many people who were not Zaghawa. Our Headmaster Suleiman Nasur was from El Fashir and did not speak Zaghawa. He was a very kind man and was a father for all of us, including the teachers. There was also a senior teacher by the name Hassan Jalal Aldin from central Sudan. He too did not speak Zaghawa. In addition to those, there were two local teachers who were Zaghawa and we knew their relatives. They never spoke Zaghawa and were the worst when we broke the language rule.

I spent my first school year living with Ishag in his school lodge. There was little for me there so I spent most of my time playing and studying with other children in the dormitories. It helped that I already had two brothers in there. In general, my first year flew quickly and I enjoyed my new experience. It was true the language rule was difficult but I soon improved my Arabic vocabulary and did not mind when older children made fun about my bad Arabic. But one problem kept agonizing me a lot. It was the herd that I left behind and the freedom that went with it in the bush. I really missed my animals, particularly in my first few weeks. In the school, we were not allowed to stray far from the dormitories and we were literally banned from public places like the market and the water centres. I was not subject to dormitory rules but my brothers required permission from the teachers to visit those places.

Studying was not hard at all. Very often, we finished our homework even before we went home. In the first year we had little to read so everything was to be recited and that was the strength I brought with me from the Maseed. I had already learnt all the relevant Koranic verses in the Maseed and was therefore ahead of other children in my religious classes. There were a few poems to learn but those were ok and I had already picked up most of them from my brothers prior to my admission into the school. I was also older than almost all the children in my class and that helped. In some ways, I was also more disciplined, a quality that went with herding. All this experience paid off, judging from my performance at the end of year examination. I was top of the class. When the results were announced, I was exhilarated. The Headmaster called me in for special praise and my reward was even better. I was to be admitted into the dormitory with all that went with it: two wonderful blankets, food three times a day, morning tea with plenty of sugar and above all, shelter from rain.

Life in the Boarding School

At the end of my first year at school, I went straight back and caught up with my herding career. I missed my camels so much and I could even say they were delighted to see me back in the camp. When I arrived, I ran from camel to camel and was nearly in tears with happiness. That summer was particularly joyous; I was able to talk to schoolboys in the camp and the village holding my head high with pride and dignity. I was no longer a mere herder boy that other boys could look down on. Furthermore, my achievement in the school won me the admiration of my pals as well as my family. Yes, I was only a first year pupil but none of them could boast a performance like mine in the exam. My family was thrilled with the place I got in the dormitories. They appreciated the help of Ishaq and his family with my lodgings and upkeep but they also recognised that the situation was far from ideal.

Summer vacation turned out to be a great season for our education. My two brothers sat their final examinations of the primary school and were offered places in the Kabkabiya Intermediate School. That was a momentous achievement, for only a few pupils succeeded in continuing their education. With well over ten primary schools competing for seats in one or two intermediate schools, the majority of the pupils had either to abandon their education or repeat and try their luck a year later. I was delighted that my two brothers succeeded but was somewhat apprehensive of their departure from my school. Life in the dormitories was rough and it was always better to have your older brothers around for protection against bullying.

Those days, the teachers and headmaster were transferred from one school to another every few years. My worry at the time was to lose the Headmaster for it was he who promised me a place in the boarding school. When I arrived at the school for my second year, the same Headmaster was still there checking our arrival at the premises. I was delighted when I was checked in and sent to the store to receive my dormitory kit. I was issued two blankets, one metal cup for my tea, a bar of soap and a cube of blue bleach for washing my clothes. We were to keep the blankets and the teacup for the whole year while the bar of soap and the blue bleach were re-issued every fortnight. We were divided into rooms with 20 pupils in each and allocated places in strict order. At night, we were to fold one blanket as thinly as possible and use it as a mattress, while using the other one as a covering material.

Early in the morning before class, we were called to come and squat in rows in the dormitory courtyard, each with his cup in front of him. Big boys acting as monitors came with huge jugs of white tea and filled up our cups. That was our morning tea before our first two periods.

At around half past seven, the bell would ring and we had to go again to the courtyard and stand in file, each class forming a separate line. Day pupils who did not stay in the dorms also joined. The morning show was important and was supervised by at least one teacher. The teacher inspected attendance and gave instructions about extra-class duties like cleaning the courtyard, not leaving the school without permission and staying away from the kitchen and the fireplace. The teacher called forward the unfortunate children who broke school rules the previous day. The first one was always the child who carried the ring for uttering a non-Arabic word the previous day. His punishment depended on the class he was attending. First and Second Year pupils got away with five lashes but senior pupils got more. Other punishable offences included leaving the school without permission, inappropriate use of fire, fighting and wearing dirty clothes.

On Saturdays and Wednesdays, the teacher checked our clothes. We had to wash our clothes and iron them for these days. The teacher walked in front of the file and checked the pupils one by one. He looked at the neck and made sure that we bathed. Then he checked our garments and satisfied himself that we had washed and ironed them. Ironing was particularly important as it was used in an attempt to eradicate lice, common in dormitories. We also lifted our garments and exposed the lower rims of our shorts for examination. Our hair was scrutinised for louse eggs and general cleanliness. Children who appeared with dirty hair were punished and ordered to shave their heads. The latter was the worst punishment for only old people shaved their heads. It was not trendy and did not fit young boys.

After the courtyard demonstration, we were directed to proceed to our classrooms in an orderly manner like soldiers.

Each classroom had a monitor appointed by the teacher. The main duty of the monitor was to report attendance and to keep order in between classes. The monitor stood in front of the classrooms with a sheet of paper and read aloud the names of everybody in the classroom. Every time he mentioned a name, the relevant pupil shouted 'present' or simply 'yes'. Our monitor didn't have to read the names at all for he had memorized them in the order in which they appeared on the sheet of paper. He simply pretended to read but was actually reciting the names without looking at the sheet he held in his hand. We, on the other side, knew where our names were and we often responded the moment he started calling our names.

It took me quite some time to get used to the food in the school. I could not say the food was bad. It was simply not varied, compared to what I had in the animal camp or with Ishaq's family. The amount of food was certainly adequate and it was not unusual for us to return the dish with some porridge in it. But to say the food was repetitive would be an understatement. It was exactly the same, three times a day. We had our breakfast just after our first two classes. Then we had another meal after the final class, around 2.30 pm. Supper came later, around sunset.

For the purpose of eating, pupils in each dormitory were divided into groups of six or seven each. In line with the hierarchical school system, a monitor also headed each eating group. The monitor decided who was to bring the food from the kitchen, to go half way for extra sauce and who was to return the dish after eating. The last duty was always given to the youngest in the group for the empty dish was light enough for him to carry and if he tripped, we would not lose our entire meal. The food consisted of a large dish of millet porridge relished with sauce made of sundried ingredients: meat, okra, onion, oil and salt. The porridge sat in the middle of the dish with the sauce surrounding it. There were no fresh vegetables and so everything was sundried including the meat. We would sit around the dish, cut a mouthful of porridge and dip it in the sauce. The porridge and sauce remained exactly the same for the three meals, well almost. There were exceptions on market days, which were Mondays and Fridays, when the food was better and we relished it. The sauce on those days had yoghurt in it so it tasted much better. We also got meat twice a week on market days in the midday meal. It was stewed with tomatoes and brought in a separate dish. It was delicious, but it was a shame there was not enough of it. The monitor divided it into small portions for each pupil. As we came to learn, it was always wise to be on good terms with the monitor so that he would push a nice bone towards you. If you crossed him, you might end up with the leathery part of the meat that gave less energy than you spent chewing it.

We, the Zaghawa, always gravitated towards our relatives. In school, we made sure the eating group consisted of relatives who knew each other well. Although the amount of food given to us was adequate, it was a bit boring and required some extra relish. That we provided out of our own resources. In those years, we never had money to buy food in the market but our relatives sent us what we needed to improve our diet. On market days, our relatives came to the town and brought us things that went into the sauce like butter, yoghurt, chillies and kawal (processed Cassia leaves). Each group had its own stock of these ingredients and added it to the sauce. We also got other types of food that we used as snacks and shared among relatives and friends in the dormitories. We got dried pancake, peanuts, watermelon and cucumber seeds, Grewia, Ziziphus and Balanite fruits and many other things that I cannot remember.

There was one extra addition to our diet, and though it was minor, it is worth mentioning here. The schools of those days were well organised and had well trained teachers. In addition to learning in class, we were taught extra skills including gardening. Each dormitory was allocated a small plot of land by the wells. The plot was fenced with thorny branches for protection against animals. We planted watercress, spring onion and radish. Once or twice a week, we weeded the garden and watered the plot with the help of the men who supplied water to the school. Lifting up water from the well was dangerous and required some knowledge; the task had to be handled with care. Our gardens never produced that much. We ate the vegetables on the spot and never brought anything into the dormitories. Nonetheless, the experience acquired was worthwhile, particularly for those of us of nomadic background. We never ate fresh vegetables at home at all, not even spring onion and that was why the little produce of our plots was important for us. In addition to learning about gardening, the exercise gave us the opportunity for an outing, as we were otherwise rarely allowed to leave the school vicinity

Whenever you had a large number of children crowded in one place, you were bound to have a problem of hygiene. Our teachers did their best to maintain the school at a reasonable level of hygiene. Every now and then, the whole school was mobilized for cleaning. We roamed the schoolyard and collected dirt and took it to a rubbish heap outside the school to be later burnt by the town health workers. We also swept the dormitories and classrooms every single day. There was a timetable for that and each of us was a member of a cleaning team. We knew our days of the week and got up early for that purpose. The school courtyard itself was divided into small plots and assigned to us for cleaning. Each pupil had his own sweeper made of grass shoots that we collected in the wild and held together with a string.

Our school was in a dry zone so we did not have much problem with mosquitoes. We did have the odd ones in the rainy season but it was not that much of a problem. Our real problem was the periodic outbreaks of lice in the school. Whenever that happened, our teachers launched a campaign in which we all participated. We had to wash all our clothes and iron them. Each dormitory was issued with an iron and that was quite sufficient for we never had that much clothes. One or two garments and one or two boxer shorts were all we had. To heat the iron, all we needed was to get charcoal from the kitchen and we were ready for ironing. We took all the blankets and spread them under the sun heat for the whole day. That was enough to kill all lice and perhaps their eggs as well. As for our hair, we were all checked and ordered to shave if there was any trace of louse eggs. The campaign worked well but had to be repeated every few weeks.

By the time I got to the third class, I was well respected in school and was treated accordingly by the teachers as well as my pals. Because I came relatively late to school, I was rather big compared to most pupils and was hence entrusted with leadership positions in the dormitories. One of my first experiences of leadership happened when I was assigned to issue daily food ingredients to the cooks. The school had a contractor who delivered food items to the school store. My job was to go early in the morning and check that cooks got the full rations for the day. I kept the store keys with me and I was responsible for notifying the contractor to replenish the stock we had in the store. Every morning, I opened the store and checked out our daily rations. Using a scale we had in the store I gave an exact amount of sugar, tea, oil, sundried okra and tomatoes, salt and pepper. I also kept a check on the amount of water delivered to the school and notified the teacher of any discrepancy. It was an easy job but it required some discipline and care. There can be no doubt that the little management experience I earned in herding prepared me for the assignment. Nonetheless, it was the first time I experienced working for people who were not my relatives and that gave me tremendous pride and satisfaction.

Discovering My Age in El Fashir City

In hindsight, my years in primary school passed very quickly. In some ways, I had the best of both worlds for I was also able to go back to herding during all school vacations, a habit which I pursued throughout my education. The primary school years also coincided with pervasive change in the Sudanese educational system. For better or for worse, the primary school was upgraded from four to six years and both intermediate and secondary schools reduced to three, instead of four years each. Early in my sixth year, we were notified that we needed what was called the Birth Estimate Certificate if we were to proceed to intermediate schools. I was one of many Darfurians who had no birth certificate. In the peculiar bureaucratic system we inherited from the British, we had to start by obtaining a certificate from the Census Office in Khartoum indicating that they had no records of our birth. Fortunately, the Sudanese postal system was functioning at the time and the school was able to arrange that by mail. It did take three months but that was alright given the distance between Tina and Khartoum. In the following long summer vacation, I had to travel to El Fashir in order to complete the process of obtaining the Birth Estimate Certificate. On the journey, I was accompanied by other pupils who were in the same situation. The journey took a whole day on a truck but we were excited to see the capital of our Region. We knew that light in El Fashir was provided by electricity and we had never experienced this before. We learnt about electricity in the school but it was hard to imagine it and was good to experience it in real life. We knew that electricity connected with powerful light bulbs attached to walls and street lampposts. We were certain that electricity travelled in wires and that it provided light as powerful as that of the headlights of a big truck. We also wanted to taste the cold soft drinks which came in bottles and which we never had in Tina town. Much more, we wanted to visit the cinema that city children often talked about. Prior to that, we only saw fake films shown by government people who visited Tina town to talk politics. They showed moving pictures on a screen pitched to the back of a car. Those politicians were boring and nobody in Tina trusted them. They brought their cinemas to lure people into their meetings. We just couldn't wait to see El Fashir city.

Following the Final Primary school Examination, the school organised travel fairs for us to visit El Fashir and obtain Birth Estimate Certificates. We left Tina around 5pm on a truck. There were four children or rather young teenagers with me, all going to El Fashir for the first time. My family gave me some money and some food for the road. It was a long journey that took a whole day with a night's sleep halfway. Some adults from Tina town took the same truck and took care of us. They were to guide us in El Fashir and tell us where to go when we got there. We left Tina town around 5pm and headed east in the direction of Kutum town. The truck was so full that we had to sit on top of it together with around thirty other passengers. I always thought trucks were fast until I got on that one. My camel, Hasanain, would do twice the speed of that truck. To make matters worse, the truck got stuck in the sand twice and we had to stop once because the engine was overheating. At around one or two in the morning, we arrived at a village in the middle of nowhere by the name of Dore. We were to catch some sleep there and proceed early in the morning. There were two or three teashops open and some of the passengers went in there for tea and food. As for me, I just wanted to sleep so I threw myself on a mat provided by the shop and fell asleep. Early in the morning we got up and bought a cup of tea each. It did not take long to gulp the tea and we were soon hanging out of the top of the truck like monkeys. The travel was long and boring and the only interesting things were a few nomads with their camels on the way. These nomads brought back wonderful memories of my camels back home. Mind you, some of them were lousy and didn't deserve to own the camels they had. Their camels looked scraggy, sick and had not been given salt for weeks.

The sun hit us hard and dust mixed with the smell of diesel made us uncomfortable. But we persevered. At around 9 o'clock, we arrived at the town of Kutum, a fine town indeed and very much like Tina. Despite its beauty, there was something odd about it. It simply did not match the fame it had established in Darfur. During the colonial time, Kutum was the seat of the colonial governor of the whole of Darfur. Yet, Kutum was barely larger than Tina town. That was strange for I expected Kutum town to be nearly as large as El Fashir city and certainly nowhere close in size to Tina. We couldn't find porridge to buy for breakfast so we settled for wheat bread. That was the kind of food people ate in cities and I was yet to discover why anybody on earth would trade porridge for that horrible stuff. Hungry people had little choice so we ate the bread with salty beans. I was about to fall asleep when the truck driver started his engine for the resumption of our trip. I was tired but the thought of seeing El Fashir later on in the day gave me energy and I forgot about the fatigue. We had only one more stop at Kafout before the signs of El Fashir started emerging. Kafout was famous for tobacco growing and renowned for its excellent brand of snuff. When we stopped there for a short break, we were overpowered by the horrendous stench of snuff. Two trucks were being loaded with sacks of tobacco for El Fashir or maybe other cities. Some passengers dashed to the shops and came back with bundles of tobacco leaves. Those passengers knew how to process the tobacco and turn it into snuff and save some money. The Zaghawa were not very much into snuff but I knew how it was made. The leaves were pounded together with rock salt and a dash of water and that was it. Kafout also had beautiful orchards of every conceivable fruit tree—mangos, guava, bananas, oranges, papayas—but it was the tobacco farming that attracted the most industrious among the farmers.

The last lag of the journey was full of hope and expectation. As we moved forward, it became evident that we were approaching an important city. The tracks on the sand multiplied and trucks coming from the opposite direction became more frequent. Nomads disappeared but were replaced by scores of animal traders with sheep, cows and camels, clearly destined for El Fashir market. As I busied myself studying the landscape, someone shouted 'El Fashir' and my heart jumped. We all stuck out our heads to see El Fashir from a distance. To our disappointment, we saw nothing but a dark depot in the distance. Within a few minutes, we realised we were indeed approaching the city. Some buildings started emerging in the distance. I tried to murmur something to Mohamed, the youngest of my companions but he interrupted in a sharp whisper saying, 'Stop speaking Zaghawa. We are entering El Fashir'. I was taken aback by his comments but I conceded he was right and so I switched to Arabic instead. In El Fashir city, it was better to pretend not to know Zaghawa. Otherwise, people regarded you as primitive and looked down on you. No wonder we were not allowed to speak Zaghawa in the school.

As we gazed in the distance, a miserable residential cluster emerged on our left. I pitied those people because they justifiably claimed to be citizens of El Fashir and yet they lived in grass huts not dissimilar from what we had in our Kayra village. I thought everybody in El Fashir was rich and lived in a mud or red brick house, but to my disappointment, that was not the case. Behind the miserable village was a cluster of fine red brick buildings. I nearly fainted when someone said it was El Fashir Secondary School. That was where educated Darfurians went and no important government official from Darfur had made it to the top without going to that school. With luck, I would end up there as well. The mere thought of that gave me a tremendous fright. All of the Darfur intermediate school leavers had to compete for places in El Fashir Secondary School or its only other rival Darfur Secondary School. But El Fashir Secondary School was the favourite and attracted the cream of the cream of the Region and I was determined to be one of them.

Further away from the Secondary School was the airport, another landmark of El Fashir city. I couldn't wait to visit the airport and see the airplane, for up to that time I only saw airplanes high in the sky and barely bigger than a stork. Then we approached a flimsy bridge over a dry water valley. I was hoping that we would not drive over it but that was exactly what the foolish truck driver was doing. I held on hard to the truck railing, closed my eyes and prayed for the bridge not to collapse under the weight of our heavy truck. The sound coming from the engine changed and I knew we were exactly on the bridge. The few seconds on the bridge felt like ages but when the sound of the engine changed, I realised we had safely passed the bridge and I opened my eyes. We were on the tarmac road heading towards the centre of the city. The view was spectacular, with fine buildings on both sides of the road. I didn't know whether the buildings were the houses of rich people or government offices but I didn't care. All of a sudden we passed a huge building and a passenger told me it was the palace of Sultan Ali Dinar (1885-1916) and that was where the governor of Darfur had his residence as well as his office. The palace was majestic, dwarfing all the palaces of the Zaghawa sultans that I saw in Zaghawa land. Dinar's palace was indeed a real palace fit for real Sultans and the Zaghawa sultans should exercise some humility and stop calling themselves sultans. But there was something odd about that palace. It was heavily guarded and I wondered what the governor was afraid of. Our sultans kept their palaces open for visitors and no armed guards stood at their gates. Dinar's palace was different, with its occupants barricading themselves behind armed guards. They certainly had something to hide that I failed to understand at the time.

I was mesmerised when someone pointed to a building as the cinema house. It was a huge building with exceptionally high walls. I immediately knew the purpose of the high walls was to stop the people peeping at the screen for free from the outside. I asked about the price of a ticket to get in and was told it was four and a half piastres. I didn't know what the half piastre was for but the price was a lot of money for seeing one film. For four piastres, you could get 12 boiled eggs in Tina market. If you were interested in raw eggs, you couldn't carry them for you would get at least 5 or 6 eggs for a piastre. Well, I was hungry so I continued thinking about how much more that money could fetch out in Tina market. With half a piastre for roasted peanuts, I could get nine cups for the ticket price and perhaps one extra cup for free.

My thought about Tina market was interrupted by a sudden halt of the truck and the end of our journey. We were right in the centre of the truck station of El Fashir city. It was not the number of trucks around that attracted my attention. Rather, it was the number of people around for I had never before seen such a crowded place in my life. There were people of every conceivable complexion, shape, size and wealth. Some looked as poor and scraggy as myself and some looked healthy, wealthy and as fat as hogs. I was delighted to see nomads who reminded me of herding. I could spot a nomad from a mile away; the air of confusion they wore on their faces, the dirty garments they had on, the sleeping sheet they wrapped over themselves and the whip they carried, all disclosed their nomadic origins. Mind you,

I was tempted to ask them about the camel market of El Fashir city but I was embarrassed to do so for some city people didn't know or care about camels. I knew El Fashir city had one of the best camel markets in the world for El Fashir people were rich and would only buy the best of camels like Hasanain, Hore and Oriterr or even better. If there was any place where I would feel at home and comfortable in El Fashir city, that would be none other than the camel market.

I pushed the dream of visiting the camel market aside and focussed on the big crowd in front of me. The sight of the huge crowd took me back to my religious classes in our school. If the truck station didn't look like the Day of Judgement, it was pretty close to it. I wondered where all of those people would find food and water. The animal wealth of the entire Zaghawa land, their camels, cows, sheep, goats, chickens and all would never be sufficient to feed El Fashir city even for one day. No wonder there were so many beggars around.

I parted company with my school pals and was led to the house of my half brother, somewhere in the city. My half brother worked for the army with a rank of Corporal. He lived with his family in a government housing estate for soldiers and I knew him well for he visited us in Zaghawa land on his annual vacations and occasionally during the fasting month of Ramadan. In his house I felt really at home and was delighted to pair myself off with one of his visitors of my age by the name of Abdel Karim whose parents lived nearby in the same housing estate. I was also thrilled to discover the ban on Zaghawa language did not apply in the house. In fact, we only stopped speaking Zaghawa when we left the house. Inside the house, the Zaghawa language was spoken all through, although one of the children didn't respond to it. He spoke it well but he preferred to converse in Arabic. He certainly shared my teachers' perception that the Zaghawa language was not worth speaking, a view that I did not like but was content to follow.

My stay in El Fashir was very pleasant with plenty of new experiences every day. My half brother took me to the market and bought me new clothes. I was thrilled for it was the first time for me to wear shorts and shirts. Prior to that, I only wore traditional garments like everybody in the rural areas. Abdel Karim took me to the cinema, the airport and the market where I had a bottle of lemonade. The highlight of our city tours was the bicycle shop by the main market. That was where boys learnt how to ride a bicycle or simply hired one to ride around. There was a huge space in front of the bicycle shop and that was where you stayed when you hired one. They had four or five supervisors keeping an eye on customers. For half a piastre, you were given a bicycle for half an hour. You had to stay within sight of the supervisors who called you back when your time was over. It was a delightful experience for me, for I had never seen a bicycle before my visit to El Fashir. Abdel Karim showed me how to ride the bicycle and left me on my own. In the first half an hour, I might have fallen 20 times. I didn't mind, for there were at least ten other learners like myself and I was by far not the worst. Then I paid for an extra half an hour and I was slightly better after that but still had difficulty turning around without falling. Riding a bicycle was like riding a contrary camel that always swerved to the opposite of your guess. With a camel, you at least have a decent saddle to sit on. The bicycle seat was hardly bigger than my fist and I was curious how much had the mean bicycle designer saved by opting for such a small saddle. No wonder it was so hard to stay on it.

One afternoon, Abdel Karim asked me to go with him to view a soccer match between two local teams. I asked my half brother for permission and he was delighted because his team was playing that match. He even gave money for the tickets. But

Abdel Karim had another idea. I must say I wasn't into soccer. In the school, we never had proper soccer balls so we made them out of rags. The best ball we made was out of an old sock but I was certainly never good at playing soccer anyway. My best sport was to go hunting for rabbits and squirrels but it was hard to get permission from the school supervisor. Only occasionally did he say yes and only on Fridays after midday prayers.

There was a good soccer stadium in El Fashir but it was rarely used. It was too far away and people wouldn't spend money on transport. Instead, soccer matches were played in a field by the main market. They erected canvas walls around the pitch with two or three gates for collection of tickets. When we went there, Abdel Karim decided we sneak in for free and pocket the ticket fares. I didn't fancy the idea but had to follow. Because the walls were made of canvas, it was easy to lift the canvas, crawl under it and attend the match without paying. To stop us doing that, they had several policemen on horses to guard the wall. The policemen carried whips and were chasing away children who came near the wall. Abdel Karim was right, for the policemen were not doing a good job. You just walked behind the horse and before the police could turn his hose around, you were already in, mingling with the rowdy crowd inside. After several unsuccessful attempts and a narrow miss of the tip of the whip, we made it inside and with our money safe in our pockets.

On the day of getting my Birth Certificate, I got up early in the morning and put on my new clothes. First I had to pass by a studio to get my photograph taken. That was an easy job for I had all the information I needed for it. There wasn't that much of it. With luck the process wouldn't take long. I say with luck because it all depended on how much of the film was used at the time of your visit to the studio. The studio only processed the film when all the shots were taken. Otherwise, you might have to wait for the next day. When I got to the studio, the owner told me that I was lucky, for there were only just enough shots left in the camera and I would get the pictures within two hours.

I took the pictures with me to the hospital and could not stop looking at them. Of course I knew how I looked for I had seen my face in a mirror several times but I had never seen a picture of my face on a piece of paper up to that time. Every now and then, I took the photos out of my pockets and looked at them for a while and gave them to Abdel Karim to have a peep as well but he wasn't that much interested in them. There were four of them and I hoped the hospital wouldn't need all of them for the certificate. Abdel Karim said I could go back to the studio and get more of them made cheaply because they still had the negatives with them. I nodded, not knowing what a 'negative' was, but thinking that it probably meant a shadow of my picture was still there inside the camera.

When we got to the gate of the hospital, a guard directed us to an office. So we went there but the process wasn't as easy as I thought it would be. A nurse asked us to fill in a form, buy a stamp and put it on it. Realising our confusion, he told us to go and talk to a man sitting on a tea chest under a tree in front of the office. As it turned out, the man was friendly, humorous and knew his job very well. He worked as a scribe who helped people to fill out forms and most of his customers were either illiterate or like myself had never filled a government form before. When I handed him the letter I got from the Census Office, he said, 'My son, you do not exist, for the government has no record that you were born.' Then he proceeded in a fatherly way to ask every conceivable question about me: my village, my people, the school, exams and so forth. He then handed the form back to me saying in his funny way, 'Now you have to pay the government for that stamp and you pay my pen for the ink.' As I was getting out the money, he told me that the government required the use of stamps as a convenient way of retrieving fees we had to pay for the certificate.

We had to wait for a while in the medical office for attention. Suddenly, I was called to see someone inside. I knew the man was the doctor because he was full of himself and wore better clothes than everyone else. The doctor looked at the paper and then at me. He asked me to open my mouth to view my teeth but he continued talking to his staff scribbling on the form at the same time. I kept my mouth open until he handed the papers down to someone else. Within minutes I was handed a copy of my Estimate of Birth Certificate. I recalled the word of the friendly scribe and walked out satisfied I did exist and was indeed born on the first day of January, 1958. Like city people, not to mention prophet Mohamed, I even acquired a birthday date. I knew my new birth day date was fake, but it was nonetheless better than what Tina people had, for they had none at all. With luck, I would grow up and become a doctor empowered to decide who existed and who did not and authorised to grant birthday dates. Fortunately, the doctor didn't need all the photos I handed over to him. He left me one as a souvenir for that memorable first encounter with a real doctor in my life.

The Intermediate School

I spent the rest of my post exam vacation herding as usual. 1972-1973 was an exceptionally difficult time in herding due to the drought that hit the whole of Sub-Saharan Africa. For a year or so, social life came to a standstill in the whole of Zaghawa land: no wedding, circumcision or name-giving parties took place. Even funerals had to do without that elaborate mourning, gathering and feasting.

I was with the animals when news came that I did well in the exams and was allocated a place in Karnoi Intermediate School. Naturally I was thrilled for it was not easy to move from Primary School to the Intermediate. I received warm congratulations from my fellow herders but there was little opportunity for me to celebrate with them. Their genuine happiness for my success was no match for the level of elation and excitement that I had at the time. That was not because my herder friends begrudged my success. Neither was it because they didn't care. They simply didn't know the importance of the achievement I scored. I did not blame them for none of them knew the difference between primary and secondary school. Admittedly, their response gave me a feeling that the little education I had up to that time had already driven a wedge between us. Our world perspectives had already branched off in different directions.

The Intermediate School that I joined was around 60 kilometres away from Tina town where I visited the Primary School. Not that much of a special move I would say, but in social terms, it was a quantum leap, for the more you moved up the educational ladder, the further you left poverty behind. Or so I thought at the time. I was still within the Zaghawa land and was certainly not in a land of strangers. The Zaghawa ethnic group divided into several lineages and Karnoi people belonged to a different group compared to my people in Tina area. In Zaghawa lineage divisions, Tina town was dominated by Kobe while Karnoi was predominantly Gala. To my surprise when I got to Karnoi town, I discovered it was like a second hometown for me. Sultan Abderrahman Firti, a grandfather of one of my parents left a legacy of offspring behind. He was notorious for his multiple marriages that reeked havoc with Islamic nuptial rules, clocking a total of 49 wives. His callous disdain for Islamic matrimonial codes paid off, landing him with tentacle like connections to almost every lineage and ethnic group in Darfur. The people of Karnoi were no exception. Yes, Karnoi people were Gala branch of Zaghawa but they were offspring of a maternal grandmother of mine who was a daughter of Sultan Abderrahman. Not only that, my connections in Karnoi hosted some of the most influential families in the town, including the Head of Local Administration. It was in Karnoi that I learnt the Zaghawa dialect of Gala that was somewhat different compared to the Kobe version of my Tina people.

Karnoi was a beautiful town, better integrated into Darfur with a network of dirt tracks, but it was missing out on the benefits of border trade that Tina town enjoyed. Our school was built of grass, a feature of all new schools in Darfur. Almost every student was resident in the school and they came from many parts of Darfur. When I reflect on the years I spent in Karnoi Intermediate School, I cannot avoid describing it as a period of starvation. We very much missed the porridge we got in Tina Primary School. In Karnoi, we were fed on wheat bread with meat sauce, or something that vaguely resembled it. It was true they killed a couple of goats for us each day but there were simply too many of us around. The sauce was too watery with little nourishment in it. God help the Education Department because I can't. They utterly failed to realise we were teenagers at our prime growth age and we needed extra nourishment.

For the first time in our lives, we were forced to look for extra food to subsidise our diet and ward off hunger. In Tina, children got extra food in kind from their relatives. Karnoi was different and most students were away from their families. We therefore had to use cash for the first time and buy food in the market. We bought extra bread and a salad we made of onions, tomatoes, peanut butter and oil. We also bought various kinds of fruits and nuts like peanuts, dates, mangos and oranges. Students came from home well stocked with extra food. It was standard for each student to come from home with a small metal trunk of clothes and another one filled with dried millet pancakes. Students of sophisticated city mothers came with something called Khamees tawaira, which was dried millet pancakes ground with sesame seeds, peanuts and sugar. The pancakes were soaked in water and relished with either salt and oil or simply eaten with sugar. Industrious students took advantage of food shortages and made donuts to sell in the school. I was lucky that I had relatives in town. I was able to visit them at the weekend where I was well fed and they often gave me fruit and vegetables from their gardens to take with me to the boarding school.

By all means, life in Karnoi Intermediate School was very regimented. We started our classes after the morning tea just like in Tina School. Breakfast was served after the second period and then we had a short break later before the final two classes. Altogether, we had six classes each day of the week with the exception of Fridays. We finished classes at 2.30 pm and moved straight to lunch. Strangely enough, we had an official siesta period from three to four. During the siesta hour, we stayed quiet in our beds for the whole period. We were not allowed to talk, whisper or giggle. There were no desks or chairs in the dormitories so we lay on our beds. Some read while others took naps. At four o'clock, the bell rang and we had to stand in line at the courtyard for instructions and to be counted. Sport followed and lasted shortly before sunset. Our sport consisted of soccer, volleyball and basketball but facilities were only available for a few interested students at a time.

After sunset, we had to go to classes to study for two hours. There was no electricity in the town so we had to make do with light provided by Kerosene pressure lanterns. These were quite adequate for the purpose and are still used in all schools in rural

Sudan. Supper followed the evening study period and we went to bed at 10pm. In the dorms, students used cheap hurricane kerosene lamps for lighting. These were a precious procurement that every student had; no one could expect to do well in school without one.

The intermediate years were the turbulent adolescent time in our lives. It was a twilight that placed us somewhere between the innocence of childhood and wisdom of adult life. We rebelled against every rule and resented every code of practice we were ordered to follow. I now look back at some of our behaviour with regret and embarrassment. We pushed the School to the extreme when we were doing our final year and got away with it. One night, we left the dormitories after the sleeping bell and went to a traditional dance at the other end of town. When we came back to school we didn't know that the Headmaster knew about our adventure and was waiting for us at the gate of the school. Taking advantage of the darkness, we ran away and slipped into our beds, pretending to be fast asleep. But the Headmaster launched his years of wisdom against us. He came and checked every pair of shoes in the room where we went. If your shoes were warm, you were guilty. One by one, he tracked down every single one of us who were out in that night. The next day we were ordered to go home and bring our parents and that meant a travel of up to a few days. We thought that was unfair and refused to cooperate. The Headmaster stuck to his guns and ordered us out of the school. At the time, we were all senior students and the year was nearing its end. Worse than that for the Headmaster, we were already assigned code numbers for our Final Intermediate School Examinations and over which the Headmaster had no control. As a result I was actually dismissed when I sat my final exam. The Final Intermediate School Examinations were centralised at the time and were held in Kabkabi-yah town 250 kilometres away from Karnoi.

Following the Examinations in Kabkabiyah, I went back to herding. It was 1974 and was a bad year coinciding with the tail end of the drought. I had to take the animals hundreds of kilometres south-west to Gimir land for pasture. When I went back to the Tina area, I was given the good news. Despite my naughtiness, I did well in the Exam and was accepted in El Fashir Secondary School. In those years, Intermediate Final Exam results and placement in secondary schools were announced on the national radio. There was no radio in our house but someone in Tina who had one heard my name.

Radios were rare at the time and only rich and eccentric people had them. I still remember before I started school when an uncle of mine got one in El Fashir where he went to sell some animals. Someone with a sense of humour commented that the radio would make a good herder because it could tell you where good pasture was and inform you about other herds that had diseases so that you could avoid mixing your animals with them. The radio my uncle brought proved a disaster. The whole village, including strangers, flocked to the house every night to see and listen to the radio. My uncle's wife got fed up with unwanted guests in her house every night. One day, she took an axe and descended on the radio and battered it into small pieces. That was the first radio in my village and it took years until one appeared again.

The ABCs of Politics and Leadership

El Fashir Secondary School was a formative institution in my political career. The School was well organised with a tradition steeped in the history of education in Darfur. It was a melting pot for Darfur, if not for the whole of Sudan. It was true that most students as well as teachers were of Darfurian origin. Despite this, and for the first time in my life, I could not expect the student next to me in the class or the hostel to be a Zaghawa. As time passed, it gradually dawned on me that the globe did not rotate around the Zaghawa and that the Zaghawa formed a tiny constituent of a much larger world. That was hard for someone who once took Tina as the epicentre of the world and the Zaghawa as a racial reference point. The experience I had in El Fashir Secondary School was both enriching and challenging. Prior to the school, our world was limited. It was preoccupied with problems that besieged Tina town, Zaghawa people, the Kobe and Tuar lineages, their camels and cows and so forth. At El Fashir school there was no place for Kobe or Tuar, nor even for Tina and its sultans. Talking about camels or cows lost you company and invited ridicule. I had to reorient myself to assume a new perspective. A chain of new vocabulary started seeping into our language: central government, May Revolution, opposition parties, communism, socialism, development and Islam. There was no place for cover and I had to adapt. So alien were these terms to my Tina and Karnoi world that they did not even exist in the Zaghawa language. Despite this, I persevered and it did not take me long to comprehend them and conquer this new world.

The Secondary School was rich in extra-curriculum activities and there were vibrant debates among students about all of the issues facing our towns, cities and region. For the first time, the shortage of water was no longer a function of obstinate wells, and the failure of our friends to continue their schooling was no longer due to recklessness or lack of intelligence. All of our problems were summarily hurled at the gate of the government and particularly at Khartoum. It was a relief, for we finally discovered what was wrong in our society and where the solutions resided. To be honest, blaming Khartoum was much more appealing than blaming our people or even Allah for what went wrong in our communities. We were ready for a revolution but where was the starting point?

Our options as political neophytes were severely limited. Only one party was allowed to operate in the land, providing training, offering avenues for political work as well as agitation. It was the Sudanese Socialist Union (SSU), the ruling party of the May Revolution Government. The term 'socialism', and its twin 'communism', were somewhat off-putting for many of us with our various cultural backgrounds but we had to take advantage of what was available. Darfur society was deeply religious and anything remotely connected with communists was suspect, if not out-rightly stigmatic. Government propaganda with arts, music and nationalist songs and funds gradually broke the stigma and made the government party appealing, at least to the youth like ourselves. In my first year at the school, I joined the SSU. We knew nothing about socialism as an ideology but we fully identified with its broad and highly publicised mundane philosophies: equality, cooperation, freedom, development and a total break away from the deplorable past with its poverty, illiteracy, hunger, disease and servitudes to 'fake' imams masquerading as politicians. I swiftly rose through the ranks of the student branch of the SSU and became the Head of the North Western Sector of Darfur, not a modest achievement for a Kayra boy. Joining the SSU was meant to give us access to government departments where we could agitate for services like schools, clinics, water and jobs. Access was indeed given and the promises were mesmerising. However, the promises of the SSU simply failed to translate well on the ground. The student branch of the SSU was like a scout and it paid in terms of training, travel and camping but that was it. Our naïve commitment to the SSU did not take long to fizzle out.

Going to Egypt

I fell sick towards the end of my first year at the Secondary School. I suffered irregular heartbeats, diagnosed as palpitations. The school did its best and presented me to several doctors in El Fashir city. My connections with the ruling party in the city and later in Khartoum also helped. At the end, I was advised to go to Egypt for treatment, a daunting task for a young man who had never even seen Khartoum before. Travelling to Egypt for treatment involved a large amount of funds, way beyond the means of an ordinary Darfur family. Fortunately, my brother was working in Libya as an engineer and was doing well at the time. He offered help and advised me to waste no time and to proceed immediately to Khartoum where he sent the first consignment of money for travel. I travelled to Khartoum by road, a rough trip that took three days and spent a few days there organising a passport. While in Khartoum, I used every connection I had—relatives, neighbours and politicians to organise my travel. As luck would have it, I could not find any acquaintance visiting Cairo so I prepared myself to go on the trip on my own. The information I gathered about the journey was pervasive and assuring. I knew how to get there, where to lodge and whom to contact in Cairo. Most importantly, I discovered that Egypt was under a strict import rule and there was a dearth of foreign goods in the shops. I also found out what sold in Egypt and at the same time did not attract the attention of Egyptian custom officials. Using almost all the money I had, I packed my suitcase with European razorblades, Colgate toothpaste, English loose tea, Sudanese hibiscus petals and watermelon seeds. These things sold in Cairo like good camels, I was informed, and it was damn right.

The journey to Cairo took four days. First of all, I had to board a train to Aswan Dam at the Egyptian border. That took a day and a half. Then we took a boat on Lake Nasser of Aswan Dam for an overnight trip. From Aswan to Cairo, the trip was much easier on a relatively comfortable and fast train. I was mesmerised by Cairo, thought Cairo was extremely developed and wondered how useless our politicians were. As I moved around the city, the more I saw, the more I got angry with our government. I was fooled by what I was told to bring from the Sudan and sell in Cairo for it gave me the impression that Sudan was a country of abundance compared to Egypt. Well, in Egypt they had manufactured most of what they needed while we in Sudan imported them all. That was my judgement at the time and I never stopped thinking about how far behind we were.

When I arrived in Cairo, I asked someone to tell me how to get to Baghdad Hotel at 62th Street, Al Ataba Quarter. That hotel was famous for Zaghawa traders who visited Egypt to sell camels. When I got to the hotel, I felt sort of at home for there were indeed some Zaghawa traders lodging in the Hotel, although not all of them were camel traders. Some of them referred to themselves as 'suitcase' traders and they shuttled between Egypt and Libya selling on whatever sold at both sides of the border. Libya was under an economic embargo at the time and dependent on petty traders for filling an important gap in the market. Traders dealt in electrical appliances, light bulbs, dry cell batteries, cosmetics and even antibiotics. The Zaghawa I met there knew Cairo well and were helpful in finding a suitable doctor to deal with my medical condition. My brother in Libya remained in contact and was able to organise payment for my treatment. After a few weeks, my doctor gave me extra medicine and told me he did not need to see me anymore. I had indeed recovered and was fit to travel. As I did in Khartoum, it was time to stock up with what sold in Khartoum and there was no shortage of that. Egypt produced good quality cotton fabrics, sandals, perfumes, honey and many other things that were far too heavy to take. I had no shortage of money for my brother sent me money to take back to the family and it was good to make some profit on the way back. I knew exactly what to buy and had a customer ready for me in Khartoum, the same shopkeeper who supplied some of the goods I sold in Cairo.

My trip back to Sudan was botched as it coincided with the 1976 abortive coup in Khartoum or to use its racist term, the 'Mercenaries' Coup'. The term 'mercenaries' was used with reference to the soldiers who were used to topple the government, recruited predominantly from Darfur. They were trained in Libya by Sadiq Almahdi of the Umma Party with the help of Ghadafi and ferried across the desert to Khartoum. The coup unleashed apocalyptic hatred against Darfur people and was followed by persecution similar to what followed the abortive JEM invasion of the capital in May 2008. Following the coup, Sudan's border was briefly closed and we were stranded at Aswan port for a while. When we finally crossed the border into the Halfa Port of Sudan, irate soldiers received us and were checking all passengers landing at the port. The soldiers targeted passengers from Darfur in particular and I had to devise a way so that I did not attract attention and be labelled as a mercenary. I had a substantial amount of money with me belonging to my brother and I was afraid it might cause some suspicion. As I judged at the time, it was risky for a Darfur citizen to appear with a substantial amount of money. To say the money was mine did not tally well with my status as a student and might make me a suspect in financing the plotters against the government. To avoid this, I distributed the money among several acquaintances on the boat, arranging to get it later after passing the checkpoint. Well, things didn't go as planned. At the port, only students and foreign visitors were allowed while the rest were kept on the boat. As a result, I landed without enough money for a train ticket to Khartoum. When the rather infrequent Khartoum train appeared and was leaving, the soldiers ordered us to board the train leaving the other passengers stranded on the boat. I got on the train without a ticket and no money for I had no other choice but to obey the soldiers.

The train was chaotic and it carried nearly twice its capacity. The moment we left the station, some adventuresome passengers left the cabins, climbed up and sat on the roofs of the carriages. They obviously had no tickets and were escaping the train conductor; a wise move as I later discovered. There were not enough seats for us so I sat on the floor like many other passengers. The afternoon and the evening passed well and nobody checked on me for a ticket. In the middle of the night, the ticket conductor appeared and was accompanied by a policeman. Discovering I had neither a ticket nor money to pay for one, the policeman took me to a separate carriage at the back of the train. The carriage served as a detention room and had a dozen or so ticketless passengers like myself. An hour later, the conductor came and demanded that we pay or be ejected at the next stop, at Abu Hamad, over 300 miles north of Khartoum which translated into a nine to ten hour journey on the train. My appeal for clemency did not help and I was no exception in that. Every single one in the room offered a good reason for not having money but to no avail. The conductor gave me one last chance and that was to go around in the train and find someone to lend me money for the trip. That seemed a logical proposition but only for passengers who came from that part of the Sudan. It was unlikely for me, a Darfuri man, to find someone I knew in the train but I took my chances.

With the policeman closely behind me, I walked the carriages of the long train looking for anybody that I could recognise. Unfortunately, it was late at night and passengers were asleep. They were either wrapped in blankets or covering their faces with their sleeves. To make matters worse, it was dark and I had to make do with light provided by a torch carried by the policeman. Half way in the train, I decided to try my luck with someone fast asleep on the floor. I had no idea why I opted for him for he was hardly distinguishable from other passengers. I woke up the man and narrated my predicament. The man, barely awake, looked at me for a while then asked me about the cost of a ticket. At the time, trousers had a small finger pocket at the front just below the belt. The man stuck his fingers inside that pocket, got out sufficient banknotes, handed them over to me and went straight back to sleep. He did not even give me a chance to thank him, let alone to discuss how I could pay him back. And the policeman had no time for niceties. When I reached my final destination at Khartoum, I went around looking for the man who bailed me out. The station was crowded and I had to drag my luggage behind me. The nice man disappeared and I could not track him down. That was in June 1976.

Seven year later, in 1983, I was a senior medical student at the University of Gezira in central Sudan. In the fifth year of medical school, students had to do a Rural Residency Internship in any convenient hospital in the country. I chose El Fashir hospital for my Internship so that I would be able to connect with my family in Darfur. While working in El Fashir, a classmate who was also on an internship in the same hospital asked me to accompany him to a party organised by a relative of his in the city. The party house was busy, crowded with around fifty men squatting under a temporary canvas shade constructed for the day. In the middle of the crowd sat a man with a familiar face. I was intrigued and struggled to recall where I came across that face before. Suddenly, I remembered. He was the mystery man who paid for my ticket on the train in northern Sudan. I approached the man and asked whether he took a northern train to Khartoum in 1976 where he paid for a student who had no money for a ticket. The gamble paid and I was dead right for he was the mystery man himself. I told the story in the gathering and he and everybody were amazed by my memory. The man's name was Tigani and he worked as a teacher in El Fashir at the time. Obviously, Tigani would not let me pay back my debt. He graciously declared it was not simply a loan—end of story. I was delighted my herding career never failed to come to my assistance. That strong recollection was unmistakably nomadic. If I could recall exact features of a camel I saw several years before, I could surely remember the face of a man who saved my life seven years before, even if that face was barely visible under the light of a torch.

Joining the Muslim Brotherhood

In my second year of El Fashir School, I was still an active member of the SSU. The Addis Ababa Peace Accord between the rebels of southern Sudan and the May Revolution Government of President Nimeiri of 1972 was still holding, with only minor breaches here and there. However, the fortunes of the government had turned sour on all other fronts. The violence of the government against its people reached worrying records. Corruption reigned among cadres of the government party. The Socialist Union and its wonderful promises that attracted us to the government, failed to materialise on the ground. As a result, people turned against the government and its ruling party and started agitating for change. The government became more paranoid and crackdown on government opponents reached an unprecedented level. Oppression and persecution of government opponents unleashed an unprecedented sense of humour and sarcasm against the once 'beloved' and 'divinely gifted leader and father of the nation'. People entertained themselves by making jokes about Nimeiri, portraying him as 'stupid' 'deranged' and 'poorly educated'. The once highly visible President withdrew from the public and surrounded himself with corrupt puppets and incompetent stooges. Instead of venturing out of his office and seeing for himself what he had made out of his nation, Nimeiri restricted his public appearances to carefully stage-managed rallies and a monthly media programme of public response to letters he allegedly received from aggrieved supporters. His monthly response to letters, broadcast on public radio and TV backfired and turned into an entertainment show that provided further ammunition for ridiculing him. In a highly befitting sarcasm, the President's monthly occasion was renamed 'the President's menses'. The popularity of the government sank and it became stigmatising for many of us to claim affiliation to the SSU. Those of us who joined the Union for non-ideological motivation and who were driven by the illusion of bringing public services to the people were exposed as having nothing to show for it. Our affiliation to the party became untenable and I partially withdrew from the activities of the SSU.

In my third year at the school, my infatuation with the Revolution dissipated. I went into a period of soul searching but I didn't have to go that far. The head of our hostel, by the name of de Gaulle, invited me for a chat about joining his group. De Gaulle belonged to a Chadian Arab ethnic group and had started his education in Chad prior to his move to Sudan. He excelled in French classes in the School and that earned him the nickname 'de Gaulle'.

I admired de Gaulle a lot because he was friendly, orderly and knowledgeable and I saw him as a model for other students. He was the head of our hostel and was also the unofficial imam of the School. De Gaulle also headed the Muslim Brotherhood that was a mixture between a reading group and a political front. As a member of the SSU, I had my dislikes for the group but still admired certain qualities in their members. They were disciplined, serious and well organised. They also formed a close-knit community that cajoled and cared for its members and protected them against other students. Those were the exact qualities we lacked in the SSU. We were undisciplined, disorganised and disunited. When it came to competing for new membership, a prime mission of any political group, the Muslim Brotherhood simply outshone the SSU. As a politico-religious group, the Muslim Brothers did not have to call for meetings. The mosque provided a meeting hall with a captive audience that came together up to five times a day. Disguising themselves as a religious study group, the Muslim Brothers used the mosque to expand its membership and keep its followers abreast of the progress of the organisation. It was true that the study of the Koran was one of the activities that took place in the mosque but that did not distinguish the Muslim Brotherhood from other Muslims who studied the Koran in the same place. For the Muslim Brothers, the mosque operated as a public library for the Koran as well as numerous other books authored by founders of the group. Those books were discussed alongside the Koran in the mosque and exchanged among members of the group. Bad or lazy readers needn't worry; the contents of those books were discussed and analysed for the benefit of all members in mosque meetings.

I must say, it was not its political ideology that drove me into the hands of the Muslim Brotherhood. It was true that the May Revolution lost its appeal to us, but not because of its ideology as such. Rather, it was because of its failure to meet our development dreams. The schools, clinics, roads, finance and many other services promised, simply dissipated. When I joined the Muslim Brotherhood, I was neither looking for services nor for a new ideology. I wanted to learn more about Islam, its theology and history. Of course I was also attracted by the character of members of the group. Chief among them, was de Gaulle, the caring Head of my hostel. As a relatively avid reader, my new membership exposed me to many books written by pivotal godfathers of the Muslim Brotherhood like Sayed Qutb, Mohamed Qutb, Hameeda Qutb, Al Mawdoodi, Al Ghazali and many other authors whom I cannot recall now. Not surprisingly, my membership of the Brotherhood influenced the little political perspective I had at the time and made me contemplate drawing on Islam as a possible path for the development of my society. The choice made perfect sense at the time. If I could draw on socialism to deliver development, why not use Islam for the same purpose. At least Islam was part of our culture and was readily acceptable to the people. Socialism was not. It was alien to our people, harder to sell and the problem was further confounded by the mere fact that the term itself neither existed in the local vernacular Arabic nor in the non-Arabic languages like Zaghawa, Fur and Masaleit.

On the academic front, Third Year was certainly the toughest for it was the final leading to the Sudanese School Certificate, or Leaving Cert as it was known. The intensity of the competition was obvious for all of us in School. The whole of Darfur had only six schools for boys and three for girls, vying for places in six universities and a similar number of technical colleges in the country. In the best years, the entire Darfur region of secondary schools sent less than 50 students to universities. That was precisely why young people resented Khartoum government and agitated for change. I knew the challenge ahead and took every opportunity to prepare for it. I was determined to make it to the university, full stop. Difficult as it was, the prospect did not seem unrealistic, for while I was preparing for my Leaving Cert, two of my brothers were already university students and I was an excellent performer in the school. But there was no room for complacency.

El Fashir School had electricity provided by a generator, confined to service from 6 to 11 o'clock at night. We already had a study period between 7 and 9 o'clock in the evening but that was not enough for Leaving Cert students. My hurricane kerosene lamp provided a backup in the early morning when I got up for extra study. My beloved camels too had to do their bit for my Leaving Cert and endure abandonment for a while. When the School closed for the mid year break, I stayed behind in El Fashir city to study. That was the first extended break I spent without herding since the start of my education 12 years before. I missed the animals so much during that break but studying took precedence over everything else.

The Leaving Cert Exam passed with relief and apprehension as well. Not every paper I sat was satisfactory but I reconciled myself to the inevitable; that I did my best and my destiny lay with the examiners, and stipulated by the will of Allah. There was nothing else I could do but to go where I found peace and joy, in other words, the camel camp. The season was good and the drought years were gone. The landscape rejuvenated its vegetation and regained its beauty. At last, nature redeemed itself, at least in the Zaghawa land for a while.

On the day of the radio broadcast of the Leaving Cert results, I left the camp early on one of my favourite camels to head for Tina town as we had no radio in the camp. I also needed the support of my family for handling the results, for better or for worse. My colleagues in the animal camp had no appreciation of education and probably had never heard of something called 'university'. Most of them spoke only Zaghawa, a language that had yet to concoct a term for 'university'. Of course they had alternative expressions for 'big school', 'important school' or simply a 'school for adults/old people'. The latter had an equally large mouthful of a translation in Zaghawa for it read: 'o bettae ke geryle taw'. Either way, I did not expect them to show pertinent rejoicing or empathy, as the case may be, when the result came. The best way for me was to abandon them and go to the town. Transistor radios were still rare in Tina but fortunately my brother in-law Sulaiman Siro had a good one. To be on the safe side, I bought extra dry cell batteries to make sure that we did not run short of power for the transmission. Mind you, the airing of the results took two days and Darfur schools were among the last to be broadcast. We knew that well but we had to prepare for all eventualities and listen to the whole list.

The first day of the broadcast was disappointing as it focussed on Khartoum, north Sudan and the central region. There were too many schools over there and most of them were well provided for. Their students scored well in the Leaving Cert so it took a long while to go over all of them. We were demoralised and thought those schools left no space for the likes of us in the available universities. As the broadcaster moved away from elite regions to the likes of eastern, kordofan, south and Darfur regions, he suddenly moved into high gear and went on faster and faster. Cities like Port Sudan, El Obeid and Juba passed so quickly. Our demoralisation reached its zenith and we were ready to take arms and go to war. We perfectly understood the broadcaster was only meant to read the names of those who made it to one of the public universities, together with the statistics of how many students obtained the Leaving Cert. Fair enough, we graciously accepted that. But as he came to those impoverished zones, we found that entire cities only merited minutes if not seconds in the broadcast. More often than not, the broadcaster simply mentioned the name of the secondary school and added, 'no candidate succeeded' and then moved on to another school. Those were good schools, with reputations not dissimilar to that of El Fashir Secondary School.

On day two, we came early and surrounded the radio set, with pens and papers ready as on the previous day. Members of my family were all close by, putting me under immense pressure. The female members of the company sharpened their voices for the characteristic Zaghawa ululation usually heard during celebrations. My sister Husnia was particularly good at ululation for she had the highest voice pitch among all my female relatives and was gifted for singing.

By midday the broadcaster came to the neighbouring region of Kordofan and we knew Darfur would be next. Kordofan was only slightly better in its number of secondary schools so it did not take long. Then Darfur came and we held our breath. I was the only one in the company who was doing my Leaving Cert and the only one who mattered for the crowd. But I also had other schoolmates, of whose success I wished to hear. I hissed to everybody to remain quiet throughout the broadcast.

Well, all hell broke loose and everybody in the village, near and far knew that my moment of success had come. The ululation screeched through the sky, long before the broadcaster reached my middle name. Other creatures too joined in marking the celebration in their own way. The storks on a tree nearby flew around squawking, the chickens ran away in a circle and a couple of dogs in the neighbourhood went off barking. Despite my excitement, I stuck the radio set to my ear and finished listening for the rest of my El Fashir schoolmates. Myself and another student by the name of Malik were offered places in the University of Al Gezira (UoG) in central Sudan. I had wanted to go to the University of Khartoum but I obviously did not score its slightly higher entry points and Al Gezira was not a bad achievement. In that year, the entire area of Darfur sent only two students to study medicine. A dozen other students were offered places in other faculties.

I still think about why I ended up doing medicine. It was true the Kobe branch of the Zaghawa gravitated towards science and biology while the Tuar branch mixed math with social sciences. Among my Kobe relatives, eight doctors graduated before me while the Tuar had an equal number of engineers and a handful of social science graduates. Earlier in the schooling, my brother Gibriel, who did economics, advised me to do biology and go into medicine. I think that was bad advice for I made little use of my medical profession and ended up as a politician. I regret that I did not study social sciences for that would have been more useful for what I do now. When we were young we had no advice on what subject to do. Many of us followed in the footsteps of successful relatives and never thought about what line matched our capabilities. That was a task to which our teachers did not give attention. No wonder many of us wasted valuable time and resources on subjects ill suited to our aptitudes.

The University of Gezira (UoG)

When I went to the UoG, in 1978, I was already a seasoned politician or at least more experienced than many of my classmates. The university was new, we were the first batch and that meant we did not have senior students on the campus to guide us. It was a miracle that I graduated, considering the extent of my involvement in politics and other public works. The term Islamic Front came into much use by the public, replacing the archaic and gender unfriendly term 'Muslim Brothers'. The government was still under Nimeiri who shifted ideology and masqueraded as an imam of Sudan. Like all dictators in the Muslim world, religion was always a dormant power to be used and abused when other causes for rallying support failed. Nimeiri's move towards religion came as a blessing for us and opened the doors and windows for us to campaign and promote the Islamic Front.

Because the University was new, there were no student organisations when I started my first year. We had to experiment with things and create everything afresh. Thus we established a student committee for social affairs and I became its first president. I also became the president of the Association of Medical Students, UoG, when it was formed.

With the Islamic Front, I had two portfolios during my study at the UoG. Firstly, I took over as Head of the branch of the Islamic Front that dealt with secondary schools in the central region. My job was to visit various schools and help establish Islamic Front units. The portfolio gave me a wonderful opportunity to visit almost all schools in the region and meet with prospective members.

Secondly, I was also elected president of Youth for Construction, which was an affiliate of the Islamic Front. My job was to mobilise young people and volunteer labour to help in the construction of public and private amenities. We helped in building roads, schools, houses of poor people, cleaning streets, etc. The job was worthwhile for it taught me how to mobilise young people for work and exposed me to problems of poverty and lack of services at both private and public levels.

At a different level, I also collaborated in one of the regional TV programmes. I worked with Dr Majzoub, who was my classmate at the time, in presenting a series of TV programmes called 'Your Health in Your Hands'. The aim of the programme was self-explanatory: to show people they could do certain things to improve their heath and at the same time inform them how to deal with diseases that were endemic in the area.

But things didn't always go well in my leadership and there were occasional times when my leadership did not resonate with the views of my friends and party members alike. I was a stubborn man and was always prepared to follow my conscience even if that labelled me as, so to speak, a 'consensus breaker'. Sudanese culture valued consensus and those who were unfortunate to be labelled as consensus breakers were subjected to severe ostracising and social isolation. In our Second Year at the UoG, the University experienced budgetary problems and had to undergo certain measures to remain solvent. One of the measures taken was to introduce a self-service system in our dining hall instead of us being served while seated at our tables. The students didn't like the change and decided to go on strike. To be frank, I thought it was silly to go on strike just because of that. We would still be served provided that we collected our food and later returned the tray to the clearance counter—big deal and what a sacrifice for a camel herder. That was precisely the elitist mentality that squandered the limited wealth of a poor nation and left so many people in abject poverty. Of course I was ridiculed by fellow students and ostracised, but I persevered.

The second time when I got into trouble with my colleagues was when I was doing my medical training in Medani Hospital, following my graduation in 1984. The doctor who was in charge of my training was an orthopaedic surgeon by the name Attalmannan, or Mr Attalmannan to use his medical title. Attalmannan was my indisputable archetypal model in my medical career. He was from the Jaliyeen ethnic group of northern Sudan and commanded his job very well. I loved and admired him very much for he taught me a great deal, not only in medicine, but equally other skills that were no less important in the profession. Attalmannan taught us orthopaedics in the medical school and oversaw our practical training in hospital. He knew his competence and displayed it with a stunning level of arrogance that we humbly accepted. We used to walk behind him from ward to ward, a view that intrigued passersby and patients in the hospital. He used to wear white shoes that went tap, tap, tap, tap and provided a rhythm for us to follow, two or three feet behind him. When you saw the 20 or so disciples behind Attalmannan, you knew you were looking at a professional prophet, not simply a surgeon. When our procession moved from one ward to another, we walked on hospital roads and met cars coming from the opposite direction. Guess who had to give way? Attalmannan would just walk on and all cars had to leave the tarmac road for us as we passed by, while waiting drivers gazed at Attalmannan with admiration.

Attalmannan kept a meticulous file for every staff member in his office. When someone made a mistake, he called him to his office and pulled the file out and it was like a Day of Judgement for the offending staff. No wonder no staff, senior or otherwise wanted to be called to Attalmannan's office.

One day I had a patient with a prostate problem that needed an emergency operation that required administration of local anaesthesia. The anaesthesia required for the operation was quite simple but medicine had its rule. As a doctor, I was obliged to commission the assistance of medical backup to help me with anaesthesia. Because I was a junior doctor at the time, the staff refused to cooperate with me and I had to do the anaesthesia myself. The operation went well. The anaesthetist didn't know that I had already secured permission to administer the anaesthesia in such conditions. For him, I was too inexperienced to do the operation and far too junior to give him instructions. Attalmannan was a practical and realistic surgeon. He realised the shortage of staff and told me that the interest of the patient came first and that I should never wait for absentee staff and risk a patient's health. When I discussed the operation with Attalmannan, he was furious about the anaesthetist and called him. He then pulled out the man's file and went on and on: 'on such and such a day, you failed to show up for work. On day such and such, you didn't do this or that. On such and such a date, you committed an error in such and such'. The anaesthetist was shaking with fear but had to listen to a full narrative of his shortcomings in the file. Then Attalmannan enquired why the man did not cooperate with me. The anaesthetist totally surrendered, but in a rather uncharacteristic way, saying, 'Your Excellency, I am just an ignorant (unwise) and undisciplined man. I promise never to act like this again'. Attalmannan let the man off but I was sorry for him for I had never before come across a person who would say 'I am ignorant and undisciplined'. I thought he would invoke some rules from somewhere and defend himself but he did not.

Despite his might and brilliance, Attalmannan too had his bad time at Medani Hospital. In 1985, the powerful Sudanese Medical Union took an industrial action that later brought down the government. The Union declared lack of cooperation with any member who was affiliated to Nimeiri's government and Attalmannan happened to be one of them for he was the Head of the Medical Union's Office in the city. Among others, Attalmannan was stigmatized and labelled as a crony of Nimeiri's May Revolution or even more derogatively 'May Cronies'—without the 'Revolution'. The once powerful surgeon was demonised and all his trainees deserted him in line with the Union call for lack of cooperation. But I objected. In his walk around the hospital wards, I remained a lone marcher behind him. Attalmannan looked like a hen that used to waddle with 20 chicks and then an eagle snatched 19 of them and left only one to walk behind her. That one chick was me, walking behind Attalmannan in Medani hospital with his white shoes sounding tap, tap, tap. The man taught me a lot and I decided not to abandon him because of his political views. Of course, my colleagues persecuted me for crossing the line of the industrial action. I ended up, yet again, a despised consensus breaker but I persevered.

I knew exactly what I thought about Attalmannan: an excellent teacher, a competent professional, a man of integrity and an exemplary model to follow. Yet, I never knew what he thought of me. In one of my solo walks behind him, Attalmannan said to me, 'You will never stay for long in the medical profession but I advise you to hurry and do your medical specialisation even if in one finger' and he raised his finger to show me what he meant. He never said more and to this day, I contemplate what prompted him to say so. Years proved him right, for I never stayed in medicine for long, but I did not specialise in the one finger either.

The strike of the Medical Union galvanised the whole nation against the government and President Nimeiri was ousted in a popular uprising, in April 1985. A few weeks later, Attalmannan left Sudan for Saudi Arabia where he worked and died a few years later.

Following my medical internship in Medani Hospital, I registered with the Sudanese Medical Council and was posted at Alnur Hospital in Omdurman. I must say my experience in Omdurman was most rewarding but equally frustrating. My work exposed me to patients of different levels of income and I have never seen so much poverty right in the capital of the country. Like any other doctor, I remained focussed and concerned with the survival of the patient. But Alnur Hospital presented a different demand. It was the doctor who faced the challenge of survival, and not the patient as such. What was the point of prescribing medicine for someone whom you surely know cannot afford to procure it? That is what I mean by survival of the doctor, for it was so hard for any doctor to continue working while seeing their patients dying of the lack of medicine and nothing that he/she could do about it. As a young doctor driven by idealism, I found the experience simply crushing and left for Saudi Arabia.

Getting Married

When I was a student at the UoG, I met my wife Zeenat. She was a student in Omdurman Islamic University and was also active in student politics like myself. Her father was a chief of the Arakiyeen ethnic group and was related to the family of the well-known Sheikh and saint Abdel Bagui of Tayba town, near Medani city. Shortly after my graduation, we decided to get married. As it turned out, the decision was hardly in our hands. Her father, and indeed most of her guardians, refused to marry their daughter to a stranger from Darfur. As if that was not enough, my family too rejected my marriage proposal. My mother saw no reason for me to marry an Arab woman from central Sudan and instead she wanted me to choose from among her Zaghawa nieces or any other Zaghawa women I preferred. It was a stalemate that had to be fought on two fronts.

My battle for Zeenat followed typical Zaghawa tactics whereby I deployed all human resources available to me to achieve my objective. I talked to all Zeenat's uncles and other influential relatives assuring them that I would take good care of their daughter and would never isolate her and her future children from the family. Sheikh Abdel Bagui headed a religious sect with a wide web of followers, many of whom belonged to other ethnic groups and who were in turn bound with Zeenat's family as members of the same sect. I was fortunate to locate an influential Darfur merchant in Medani who was friendly with the Sheikh's family. That man was instrumental in persuading Zeenat's family to allow the marriage to take place.

My work with Zeenat's family went hand in hand with similar activities on my mother's side. I sent mediator after mediator to talk to my mother and eventually secured her consent about the marriage. In the end she gave me her blessing and I got married to Zeenat. I still feel guilty that I was not able to follow my mother's original advice. I know she has already forgotten it but I have not, and still ask for forgiveness at every opportunity. It is not good to go against a parent's wish for they always have the interest of their children at heart. To further appease my mother, I sent her to Mecca for she always wanted to perform the hajj. Up to the present moment, my mother has made the pilgrimage to Mecca four times; an important achievement for her generation. I would like to believe that she has forgiven me and is enjoying her relationship with her daughter-in-law and her seven grandchildren. I pray my judgement is right.

Saudi Arabia:
From Medicine To Politics

It is true that I was driven into Saudi Arabia by adverse health policies that crippled Sudan's medical system. However, by the mid 1980s, an economic decline coupled by Sudanese social commitments, made working abroad an inescapable duty across all professions. Physicians were no exception. Spending at least a few years in the diaspora became institutionalised into Sudanese culture and was necessary to help build a house, secure a pension and sustain needy members of the extended family.

The period I spent in Saudi Arabia evoked a memory of my early nomadic experience. I was working as a physician but was by all means as mobile as a nomad. In the four years that I spent in the Saudi Kingdom, I served in numerous hospitals, sometimes moving twice a year. I also worked with Saudi nomads whom I visited regularly in camps in the catchment area. My wife, who worked as a teacher, had to move with me and keep the family together. Overall, I can still say our life in the Saudi Kingdom was exceptionally fulfilling. My family and I loved the people around us and I would like to think the feeling was mutual. Everybody we knew was sad and disappointed when we decided to leave. An influential superior of mine tried to persuade me to change my mind and stay, but he did not succeed. At the end, he gave me a glowing letter of reference, strongly recommending my immediate re-employment in the Kingdom, should I wish, anytime in the future.

In 1989, the Islamists took over in Khartoum, toppling the legitimately elected regime of Sadiq Almahdi and forming the 'Government of National Salvation' (GNS). Shortly after the takeover, the GNS launched a pervasive policy change, intended to rejuvenate the delivery of services across the country. In the health sector, they initiated what was codenamed 'Health Revolution'. A shortage of doctors and a lack of cooperation of the Sudanese Medical Union derailed the Health Revolution initiative. In response, the new government dispatched envoys abroad to encourage workers in the diaspora, and particularly potential sympathizers, to repatriate and participate in rebuilding the country. At the time, Turabi was detained with many other politicians and the new regime was in denial regarding its Islamic connection, a smart ploy in which many of us believed.

Realising the shortage of staff for the implementation of its 'Health Revolution', the government dispatched a medical doctor by the name of Jimayabi to us in Saudi Arabia. Dr Jimayabi convened a meeting of physicians and persuaded us to go back home and participate in the Health Revolution to move the country forward. The meeting steered clear of any Islamic references but was steeped in nationalism and the necessity of participating in the development of the Sudan through contributing to the provision of basic services for the average citizen. The 15 of us who attended the meeting, all men, agreed to be repatriated to Sudan. After all, living abroad was never ideal and most people would rather stay at home if things were right, a concern strongly emphasised in the meeting. However, things didn't work out exactly as planned. Most of those who agreed to repatriate changed their minds. Their wives put pressure on them to stay longer in order to build a house back home, buy furniture or simply save money for future security. Our relatives in the Sudan also subjected us to tremendous pressure to stay, for fear of losing their financial support. These were the harsh realities that every worker abroad had to take into account. In the end, only two of us who attended the meeting left for the Sudan. My wife also left her job and has never worked outside the home since. When we arrived in the Sudan, I was appointed as Medical Director of Omdurman Hospital and participated in other activities of the 'Health Revolution Initiative'.

Karnoi Conference in Darfur

My stay in Khartoum was relatively short and equally uneventful. Although I was very much committed to the ideals of the Islamic Front, I still envisaged my future to lie squarely in the medical profession. After less than two years, I was relocated to Darfur and away from medicine. The move was a Party decision and was not instigated by myself. Of course I was delighted to work among my own people and since I was moving away from medicine, being away from Khartoum had no adverse effect on my future.

In Darfur, I seemed to have once again approached my work portfolio with a stunning nomadic pattern moving from one job to another, some formally and some not. In the seven years that I spent in Darfur, I worked as an informal Head of the Red Crescent, Minister for Education, Minister for Health, Deputy Minister of Finance and as Darfur Political Advisor.

My relocation to Darfur was prompted by a realisation in Khartoum that Darfur was agitated and close to rebellion against the government. In particular, the relationship between the Zaghawa and the government had reached a stalemate and many Zaghawa traditional leaders became openly antagonistic to the regime. A lack of security encouraged bandits to thrive and camel theft evolved into an institutionalised cottage industry in the area. The bandits grew too powerful to contain by the local system of administration, which in any case was emasculated by the government itself. In some instances, the local administration colluded with the bandits due to their frustration with the government. At the same time, the camel thieves too struck at local chiefs who tried to reign over them and bring them to justice. Our role was to convene a conference in Karnoi town, the heartland of the Zaghawa, and find ways of containing the situation. Needless to say, the government wanted to win over the Zaghawa and establish a workable relationship with them. These were the stated objectives and they looked sound and agreeable to many of the parties involved.

I travelled to Darfur together with many others to hold what later became known as the Karnoi Conference, 1992. Our mission was two faceted: to heal the rift between the Zaghawa and the government and to secure the cooperation of local chiefs in the maintenance of law and order. But the security agents, who were pulling the strings behind the scenes, had another motive, namely to pre-empt an open rebellion in Zaghawa land. Due to my poor knowledge of Darfur, coupled with my commitment to the government, I missed out on that other motive. With some naivety on my side, I followed government propaganda that Darfur was facing a lack of security due to internally generated ethnic conflicts. That was only half of the story, as I later learned.

Shortly before the Conference, camel thieves assassinated King Musa Khamees of the Artaj. King Khamees strongly opposed the camel thieves and had taken bold measures to disrupt their operations and bring them to justice. King Khamees gave his life while the camel thieves remained at large.

The Conference was well provided for and all prominent Zaghawa leaders in Khartoum and particularly those, like myself, who were allied to the government were flown in. A contentious issue to be raised was that of bandits and camel theft. This is a sensitive issue as the Zaghawa were often stereotyped in Darfur as camel thieves. Prior to the Conference deliberations, we agreed that Abu Bakar Hamid, Mohamed Bishara Dousa and myself would raise this issue and in this order. The first two spoke before me and omitted any reference to the issue of camel theft. When I climbed on the platform, I raised the issue in total oblivion to its sensitivity and all hell broke loose. Chief after chief hammered me with frantic accusations and frenzied denunciations. When we broke for the night, rumours abounded that my assassination was imminent and that I would not survive the night. The entire area was marred by lawlessness and the assassination of a junior and young man like myself was not an unlikely prospect. However, I survived the night and tempers cooled down a bit.

In the morning sessions following my speech, the mood of the Conference changed a bit and we were able to debate the contentious issue of camel theft in a less tempestuous manner. The shift came when chief Basi Salem Tegel took the stage and redirected his anger against the government. In an uncompromising speech, he castigated government policy that eroded the authority of the local administration in favour of a corrupt and cowardly police force. To make his point in a forceful way, chief Tegel deviated into an apt but unconventional metaphor saying his senior wife was more manly than all the policemen of the area. He then launched into a forceful rebuke of the government, cloaked in an appeal to increase the authority of the local administration and help in the confiscation of firearms, otherwise legally-held by the public. Government officials present in the conference swiftly seized this opportunity and agreed to take immediate steps to augment the authority of the local administration to launch a rigorous collection of firearms in the area. The campaign for the decommissioning of firearms started even before we concluded the conference and the first person to hand over his gun was Ali Shammar, who was the Regional Minister for Engineering. Within weeks, 5,000 pieces of firearms were collected and there was a marked improvement in the security situation in the area, lasting for nearly a decade after that.

There was no doubt that the Karnoi Conference was worthwhile for the government but not so much for the people of Darfur. Paradoxically speaking, and I humbly muster my courage to say so, we colluded to delay a Darfur uprising. We were part of the system and we backed it with stunning resolve. At the time of the Conference, Darfur was at the brink of revolution but needed some work on the ground. The treatment of many ethnic groups in the region and the utter deprivation of services to them, including justice, paved the way for a rebellion. But there was a dearth of leaders able to seize the opportunity. To combat the rising spirit of rebellion in the region, and instead of reflecting on the causes of discontent, the government classified the whole region as a fifth column and unleashed the security agencies to deal with the matter. The outcome was obvious: the government army and its flourishing official intelligence industry got a blank check for pillaging the people and humiliating them with utter contempt for the legal, and ironically, the constitutional rights of their victims. In 1991, the army took an interest in nine Zaghawa merchants in the town of Shearia, South Darfur. Having classified them as anti-government, they ordered them at gunpoint to supply ropes from their shops with which they were subsequently bound. They later ordered them to dig a mass grave in which they buried them alive. The incident created a colossal level of discontent leading to the decision of Dr Sharif Harir, a relative of some of the victims, to leave Sudan and rebel against the government. Along with Dreig, Dr Harir later co-founded the anti-government Federal Alliance Party. They joined the resistance coalition of the National Democratic Alliance and Harir is now a prominent leader of Darfur armed movements, commanding a litany of rebellions against al-Bashir's regime.

Harir was not the only Zaghawa who dissented against the Khartoum government. Around the same time, Ahmed Togot and Adam Ali Shogar, both now prominent leaders of JEM, crossed the Sudan border into Chad looking for help to start a revolt against their government. Because of the entrenchment of the Zaghawa ethnic group in the Chadian ruling elite, Togot and Shogar assumed help would be forthcoming. Little did they

know that President Deby, a Zaghawa himself was all too pleased
to pay back Khartoum for catapulting him into power in Chad
and was in no mood to betray Khartoum. Far from it, President Deby had no intention of seeing his ethnic brothers rise to
power in Khartoum. Discovering that their flight amounted to
a near fatal miscalculation, Togot escaped into exile in the UK
while Shogar fled to Nigeria.

Other ethnic groups in Darfur also shared similar discontent with government policies in the region. Abdel Aziz Alhilo
of the Masaleit ethnic group defected and joined the Sudanese
People's Liberation Army/Movement (SPLA) of the predominantly Christian South which was waging war against the Khartoum Government. But the biggest revolt in Darfur was yet to
come. That was the catastrophic invasion by Bolad, indisputably
a prominent father figure of the present Darfur uprising.

Dawoud Yahia Bolad Movement in Darfur

I was not party to Bolad's brief war in Darfur but at the time,
1991, I was a supporter of the system that treated him as a
rebel and dealt with him as such. Darfur was indeed ready for
revolt and Bolad accurately recognised it but failed to undertake
the necessary groundwork for it. By the time Bolad's potential
supporters heard about his rebellion in Darfur, he was already
defeated and dead. Bolad did send letters to many leaders in
Darfur, including myself. However, he miscalculated his channels and as a result, many of his letters either arrived too late or

fell into the hands of government security agents. I knew about my own letter a year after the event.

Bolad left the South with 1,000 troops, almost all of whom were southerners recruited by the SPLA. His army was badly provisioned, resulting in a phenomenal loss of 30% of its troops even before he made it to Darfur. As it was planned, the Fur and Masaleit, the ethnic groups of Bolad and his commander Alhilo respectively, were to mobilise 10,000 fighters to back the SPLA fighters. When the hungry and dilapidated survivors of Bolad's army reached Darfur, the plan disintegrated into utter farce. The only contact that responded to Bolad's call was Omer Zarroug, the Mayor of Mukjar town, in West Darfur. Chief Zarroug failed to provide fighters but killed several bulls and fed the fighters.

The slow progress of Bolad's march into Darfur gave the government intelligence forces ample time to gauge his movements and prepare for total annihilation of his army. Taking advantage of the ethnic composition of Bolad's army, the government played its usual ethnic card and presented the invading army as racist and anti-Arab in nature. The government also spread absurd demonising rumours inciting hatred against Southerners, such as that they fed on donkeys and that they were antisocial and devoid of ethics. Having turned the Arab population against Bolad, the government proceeded to recruit dangerous criminals freshly released from jail for the purpose. This strategy was later employed against us.

When the engagement took place, it wasn't that much of a battle. Two Darfur Arab groups, Beni Halba and Salamat, well armed by the government and aided by bandits did the job. Bolad's army was nearly wiped out. The Arabs lost just over a hundred fighters while most of Bolad's army were either killed or forced to flee the battlefield. Bolad's only means of communication, a solar powered radio, was destroyed. His troops were reduced from solar power technology to word of mouth and face to face communication; a pitiful state for a revolutionary army. Alhilo, who commanded the force managed to escape with a few others and made it to the South and is now a prominent leader of the SPLM. Bolad and a handful of others scattered around in the area.

Although Bolad belonged to the Fur ethnic groups, he grew up somewhere else, with the misfortune of not speaking Fur. When he eventually managed to track down some relatives, things took a course for the worst. As it was narrated, Bolad gave money to a relative to fetch fresh clothes for him for a disguise. Instead, the messenger brought back the police and Bolad was arrested. His appeal to be flown to Khartoum and for council with Turabi did not succeed and he was executed. He was not even honoured with a kangaroo trial. Later in the year, around 40 of his men, all Southerners were found working in orchards of Mukjar town. They were captured and taken to Shala Prison of El Fashir, the then capital of Darfur Region.

Bolad's revolt and his subsequent treatment left a legacy of discontent and humiliation in Darfur. Across Darfur, the incident inspired reflection among many on the state of the region, and paved the ground for the present uprising.

Bucking Them Off Our Backs

My work in Darfur coincided with the dubious World Bank-IMF informed policies of making the government leaner, if not anorexic altogether. In the early 1990s, the central government devolved service delivery and ordered all localities to bear the costs of all services, including security and policing. The country was reorganised into 26 States, housing 666 administrative zones. Each State was to raise its own revenue with little or no assistance from the central government. At the same time, the government hiked up its tax collection across the country. Taking advantage of the civil wars in the country, and the alleged global embargo on the Sudan, government officials flaunted their innovative skills in devising new tax levies: the martyrs tax, Jihadist sustenance tax, defence of the nation tax, popular defence tax, Highway tax, secured road tax, and so on. The result is colossal but obvious, particularly in the already over-impoverished zones like Darfur. Not surprisingly, most of the revenue collected departed to the northern region leaving local markets paralysed due to shortage of cash. That was what I discovered when I visited a town in Wadi Saleh. The market was full of donkeys laden with agricultural produce, most of which was reloaded for home due to lack of interested buyers. In the market, a sack of hibiscus sold for a mere £s500, roughly the price of two cups of coffee at a modest Khartoum coffee shop. Innovative local traders went back to a non-monetary barter system for lack of cash. Grain, peanuts, hibiscus, leather bags, sugar and tea were bartered in small measures. Wadi Saleh was a rich area by all means. Gum Arabic produced in the area was exported through Central Africa, not Sudan. But a cash shortage, all sucked out by the central government, crippled the production process in the area and brought normal trade to a halt. In the absence of local markets, people had to abandon their farms and migrate, just to procure cash. When I raised this issue with Turabi at a later date and told him about the misery visited on the region, his response was naïve and unsympathetic. He advised us to 'not talk about food and drinks and to fill people up with faith'. It was the most callous and bizarre advice considering Darfur had the highest concentration of devout scholars in the Sudan who had managed to commit the entire Koran to memory, a cherished achievement in Muslim countries. In collaboration with the Red Crescent at the time, I was able to organise a credit fund to ease the liquidity problem in Darfur but our effort was a drop in the ocean.

My first lesson of rebellion was given in a social gathering I attended at the house of Abu Bakar Hamid, now a prominent JEM leader, in El Fashir city. An old man who shared the mat on which we sat, narrated his experience. He worked as a school guard in the city. He himself had no education but knew its value over the years and was committed to it. Realising that I was the Regional Minister for Education, the man launched into a scathing attack on the destructive policies visited on the educational system. Then all of sudden the man broke into tears. Not knowing how to handle his pain, I asked him to tell us what to do. I wish I did not say that. The man gave me, or rather us, a scornful look and said: 'Listen, our children; we did not send you to school to come back and ask us what you should do; you ought to know'. Drawing on his nomadic origin, for he was from a nomadic Arab ethnic group, he added: 'If a man is contemptuous enough to ride on your back, do not hesitate to buck him off'. Well, the audience, many of whom were prominent Darfur politicians, went numb for a while. The statement was a forceful and challenging invitation for an open revolt against a system that ravaged the Region and its people with poverty, neglect and injustice. Little did I know that I would shed similar tears at least three times in my experience in Darfur. Admittedly, we knew things were going terribly wrong and that the system required a drastic change. However, we were inexperienced and naïve and still had the illusion that change could take place via debate and persuasion.

In my work with the Regional Ministry of Education, I visited a substantial number of schools across Darfur. During these tours, the man's statement haunted me and his grief about the education system was by all means justified. A return to government-sponsored schools, backed by free and adequate dormitory services is what we now call for in JEM. In some of my school visits in Darfur, I was horrified to find pupils squatting on the bare sand in their classrooms. Desks had disappeared for a lack of maintenance or simply had not been provided at all in the first place. Some pupils had to lean on the backs of their classmates to write. Still worse, at other schools, pupils were too poor even to obtain pens and paper. Instead, they simply learned their lessons by writing on the sand. The absence of pen and paper created a problem in monitoring homework. Teachers had to be content with the scribbles their pupils inscribed on sand in class. But the most formidable problem was yet to come. For the final Primary School Certificate, the Ministry of Education issued a random Exam Code Number for each candidate. The teachers then notified students of their Code Numbers. In order for students to remember their respective Numbers, they had to carve them on a piece of wood or stone. The practice amounted to a degeneration of the Sudanese 'modern school' into a pathetic state that lagged behind the traditional Koranic schools where pupils used rudimentary and yet far superior wooden slates for writing.

The policy of devolution adopted by government, backed by skyrocketing taxation, brought public services to a near collapse. States too failed to raise enough revenue to pay the salaries of staff, with some of them in more than a year's arrear. As a result, public service officials had to turn to other jobs to make ends meet. In the educational sector across Darfur, many schools closed down, leading to a drop of 50% of primary school attendance. Veterinary clinics were abandoned by their staff and became homes to bats, crows and stray animals. This pitiful state spanned across public service institutions.

Institutionalised Injustice

My early years in Darfur coincided with what the government controlled media portrayed as tribal conflicts between the Fur and their Arab neighbours. Bolad's unsuccessful invasion of Darfur created an alliance with Darfur Arabs and provided legitimacy for giving the army and other security organs free reign to maintain law and order. As head of the Red Crescent in Darfur, I launched a campaign, mobilising resources to help the Fur in particular who were most devastated by the conflict. In Kabkabiyah and Wadi Saleh areas, we were able to help reconstruct 647 villages destroyed in the conflict. But it was during this work I grew suspicious about the nature of the conflict, and my conviction that it was entirely tribal became somewhat shaky. It was undeniable that the government had armed the Arabs and disarmed their Fur neighbours to help squash Bolad's rebellion. However, the Fur continued to be victimised long after the defeat of Bolad, and the tribal conflict thesis I once subscribed to, became difficult to sustain. The possibility that the so-called tribal conflicts were instigated by the central government and that certain ethnic groups were deliberately targeted in the process became more and more plausible.

During my work in Darfur, I noticed that most senior government officials were reluctant to leave their comfortable offices and travel in the hinterlands. Whether it was because of my nomadic experience or not, I was different and was more comfortable in the rural areas than inside government offices. I remember in 1992 we got intelligence that government officials in the Fur West Darfur city of Zalingei were abusing women who were applying for Identity cards. These Cards were important for official business but equally so for the issuance of Sudanese Nationality Cards. The latter was very similar to passports in the west. At the same time, we also received complaints about a bandit by the name of Abu Jalajil who was accused of terrorising the local inhabitants, killing nomads and seizing their cattle. Further information pointed to the failure of the law enforcement authority to intervene and investigate into the matter or even visit the alleged victims.

It was a hot day, well over 40 degrees, in the Muslim fasting month of Ramadan when I approached a wooded land in the vicinity of Zalingei. We stumbled across an unusual sight of around 15 men axing down trees and burning them to make charcoal. The men were clearly prisoners, as evident from their prison uniforms. The day was exceptionally hot and we were all dehydrating in our fast and so of course were the wretched prisoners. A few prison guards were resting with guns in their hands under a tree, keeping a watchful eye on the prisoners and ensuring that they were working. I stopped my convoy and approached the prisoners and their guards. I was serving as Assistant Governor at the time but none of the prisoners and their guards would have recognised me. The convoy of government vehicles would have indicated I was speaking with authority. The prisoners informed me they were making charcoal for their Prison Manager in Zalingei and that other prisoners were minding his herd of cows and tobacco farms without pay. I listened intently and when I was satisfied, I informed them that no prisoner was to work under such heat while fasting and that it was illegal to employ them without pay. The prisoners were frightened to go back and demanded I give them my ruling in writing. That I did, while adding a message to the Prison Manager to report to me at the government guesthouse in the city.

The Prison Officer called at the guesthouse. He did acknowledge his mistake of employing the prisoners but insisted that he was paying for their services. When I asked to see evidence for that, the Manager requested time to furnish me with the records.

176

In that night the records were compiled showing payments made for the previous three months. I knew the records were backdated but allowed it to pass when I checked and found out payment was fully made a few hours before my meeting with the Manager.

I travelled then to Wadi Ayour and attended to the victims of Abu Jalajil, whom I referred to earlier, and worked out security arrangements to the satisfaction of the victims. Later in the guesthouse, I received another notorious government official. It was Ali Mageit, the Commissioner of Zalingei city. I raised with him a new concern brought to my attention about a few people who died of starvation in Jiddu of Zalingei district. The Commissioner dismissed the report as unfounded and urged me to ignore the matter. He was able to bring some Fur leaders who testified to me in the guesthouse, confirming that the reported deaths were due to natural causes and had nothing to do with starvation. But I was not convinced for I knew all too well how local leaders could be threatened, bribed or otherwise simply manipulated. Despite evidence presented to me, I had a strong inclination that the Commissioner and the local leaders were not truthful and hence I decided to go and hear from the people concerned.

During the following morning, I travelled to Jiddu, the site of the starvation claim. I met some men in the village and asked them to show me the graves of their recent relatives. They did and confirmed the starvation claim clearly in a different way. As a doctor, it was easy for me to identity evidence of a food shortage by a mere glance at children in the compound. I asked the chief of the village to show me their communal eating-place. Before he could respond, tears started running down his cheeks; it was such a heart breaking sight. I could not control my tears and neither did my tour companions. The man said he was ashamed to say nobody shared food in his village anymore for people simply did not have any to share. Following this depressing encounter, I asked for permission to visit their houses and examine their kitchens. With the chief leading me into different houses, I entered 53 cottages altogether. In the wretched villages, I was able to see many children and elderly who could barely walk. It was such a traumatic tearful tour that was extremely difficult to complete but I persevered. I swear by Allah that I had never seen such poor people in my life and it had never dawned on me that such poverty could exist in Darfur. Not a single house had enough food for even one day. Most of the houses did not even have a single rag of a garment hanging down their walls. There were no straw mats, no blankets, no beds and not a single metal pot was in sight. Apparently, every piece of household equipment that could fetch out a penny had long been traded for food.

The kitchens in these houses told a dismal story altogether. There wasn't a single bowl, let alone a bag or a sack of grain in any of the kitchens we visited. The only food we saw, if you could call it such, was wild seeds, husk and chaff of grain and piles of stones of palm. These stones, entirely inedible under normal circumstances, became the staple diet. As I was told, in order to convert these stones into edible form, they had to bury them in wet ground for several days to soften them. Then they were boiled and then mashed to make some sort of a gruel or porridge.

I did not know whether to describe the Commissioner who was insisting on denying such a self-evident truth as incompetent, inhumane or an outright perpetrator of genocide. Surprisingly, the Commissioner came from the Eastern Sudan and belonged to an ethnic group that was all too familiar with periodic starvation. One would have expected such an official to be sympathetic to the poor and an expert in detecting famine symptoms. But there was no limit to the cruelty of that Commissioner. At the time of the events described above, Mr Mageit had 20,000 sacks of grain stored as strategic reserve and with full authorisation for its free distribution should the need arise. Needless to say, we were able to use the strategic reserve grain to assist the people of

Jiddu and many others who were experiencing similar hardship. I was aware that those people could not subsist on grain alone and that they had no cash to obtain other food items. For that reason, I radioed the Governor, El Tayib Mohamed Kheir, who was my boss in El Fashir, to come to our help. Mr Kheir was popularly known as El Tayib Sikha due to his early habit of wielding an iron bar (Sikha) in political student debates at the University of Khartoum. When I contacted him, he was gracious enough to oblige and within three days, I received truckloads of edible oil, sugar, salt, flour and other items that I cannot recall now.

The callousness of Commissioner Mageit and the Prison Manager we referred to earlier was no exception among top officials in Darfur, particularly those who came from outside the region. More often than not, those officials remained a separate caste, very much disconnected from the people they were supposed to serve. At the same time, they ruthlessly squashed any advice that might have alerted them to grievances of the average Darfuri. My frustration with those officials in Darfur reached its peak in 1996. I was then Health Minister for North Darfur. We were flown in a tour to Kabkabiyah with Governor Younis and a man from north Sudan who was the National State Minister for Defence. While in Kabkabiyah, the chief of the security came with a request to the Governor. The Governor was about to grant the request when I intervened. To tell the truth, I overheard some of the problem presented to the Governor. So I asked the security man to show me the document he wanted the Governor to sign and he did, interrupting the process. Apparently a member of the Regional Parliament, by the name of Mohamed Saleh Jiddo, wrote a letter to the Regional Government appealing for intervention regarding injustice visited by some officials in his constituency. The Security Office intercepted the letter but could not approach him because of his constitutional immunity as a Member of Parliament. The Chief of Security wanted the Governor to sign a document to authorise removing the immunity of Jiddo so that they could arrest him. I immediately intervened in defence of MP Jiddo. I told the Governor the MP did nothing wrong, meriting loss of immunity against arrest, and that he, in fact, acted correctly and legally by approaching the government with his complaint. As a result of my intervention, there was a stand-off and the Governor did not sign the document. The situation became tense between me, the Governor and the Chief of Security. We flew all the way back without talking to each other. The following day, the Governor flew to Khartoum for some duties. As it later transpired, accompanied by some of his security staff, he approached the then powerful Vice President Zibeir Mohamed Saleh regarding my performance in Kabkabiyah. They argued that my intervention was racially motivated as both the Minister for Defence and the Chief of Security happened to be from north Sudan, from where the Vice President hailed. The Governor insisted he could not work with me and it was a case of either himself or myself remaining in Darfur. Needless to say, he was more important for Khartoum. Days later, I was transferred to the Blue Nile Region; in effect, an exile.

Revamping The Health Service in North Darfur

When I left Darfur, I was nagged by one thing, a job that I did not last to see completed. The health system was ruined by devolution polices of the central government, coupled by poor vision of my predecessors in Darfur. The State was dotted with

Primary Health Care Units (PHCUs) run by poorly trained staff, many of whom deserted their jobs for lack of pay. At the time, each PHCU was managed by a Primary Care Assistant whose training was a mere four to six months. Such training grounded the personnel in nothing but the bare fundamentals of medicine. It was a poor lot for poor people. I decided to do something and provide a model for others to follow but funding remained a formidable constraint. My view was to replace the PHCUs with rural hospitals of some sort, each headed by a trained physician. In order to overcome the funding hurdle, I decided to resource the project in an unconventional way, leaving the usual government channels out.

North Darfur was divided into 23 localities, each one was to serve as a base for one rural hospital. Local people were enthusiastic about the project and they were ready to shoulder the costs of premises to house planned hospitals. Most localities had hospitals or dressing stations that could be promoted into premises to house the new rural hospitals. On a few occasions, people had to construct new premises from scratch. Either way, premises became the manageable part of the project. The main problem was how to organise obtaining adequate medical equipment, a responsibility I vowed to personally take care of.

In order to equip these hospitals, I used every available source of finance to raise funding. I was fully aware that if I were to rely on funding from the Ministry of Health or Ministry of Finance, the whole project would simply collapse. I decided not to ask for a penny from normal government channels, not even for my ticket expenses. I used every source of funding available to me: private enterprises, individual donations, national and international NGOs and government Ministries that had a stake in the project. The Ministry of Defence, led by Lieutenant General Ibrahim Suleiman alone donated $100,000 for the project. Zibeir Philanthropic Organisation also offered a substantial help. At the end I had enough funds to proceed, and China was my choice for the modest price of its medical equipment.

I arrived in China and commissioned the help of the Sudanese Embassy to procure the medical equipment I needed. We ended up in a medical equipment store that sold everything I needed and within prices that I could handle. When I had everything that I required on the list, priced and ready to pack for shipment, the sales person asked me a final question by way of settling the account. Working through a rather awkward translation medium, the question came to me like 'And how much is yours?'. I got a bit confused and asked the Embassy aid what he meant by this. As it transpired, the store allocated 10% for corrupt government officials who visited their stores. Of course the bribe or 'commission' was computed in their pricing index and it would be stupid of me to decline the offer so I said 10%. After working out the amount in money terms, I requested a short break to find out what I could buy for the 'commission' and went back and ordered more equipment. The Chinese sales person looked surprised but was happy to oblige. Well, I left Darfur before we received the consignment. When it arrived, it was put to good use but not in accordance with my original plan.

Fighting A Jihad War

My work in Darfur also coincided with my involvement in wars against the SPLA in the South. Many of us accepted the much-hyped propaganda portraying participation in the war as 'jihad'. All senior government officials had to fight and I happened to be one of them. In 1993, my name appeared on the list of those ordered to serve on the war front in the South. At the time, I was an active supporter of the government and had no objection to fighting for its survival. Thus, when I was called for action, I did not hesitate and I must admit that my war experience had a lot to do with my current rebellion against the system.

My 1993 war experience did not involve any fighting. I was part of the medical Corp and had acted as Manager of the Mujahideen Hospital in Juba. Our Hospital was well provided compared to Juba Military Hospital. Unlike the Military Hospital, ours was open to the public and we treated everybody, including the rebels, who found their way through our doors. Being a senior official from Darfur, my work also attracted many from that region who contacted me for help or for usual sociability. I must say I enjoyed being a magnet for Darfur people and there was no shortage of them in the different armies operating there as well as in non-government domains. In the range of Darfur people I met, there was a particular young man by the name Mohamed Shakir (not his real name) who was a driver of the controversial southern rebel leader William Nyuon Bany, a southern rebel who switched sides and reconciled himself with the government against the SPLA.

Shakir was originally from Darfur but he grew up in Gezira Abba in central Sudan. His family remained connected with Darfur and that was why he was interested in meeting me. Shakir was indeed an interesting man in many ways. He was a member of the Sudanese Communist Party (SCP) and a university graduate. Having found the SCP too pacifist for the realisation of his socialist ideals, he abandoned his family and went to fight with the SPLA. Things however went wrong with his relationship with the SPLA and he defected with Nyuon, his commander, and joined the very enemy he was fighting before. But the treatment he received from his new allies was far from cordial. When he appeared at my house in a private visit, his looks told it all:

he was barefooted, dressed in rags and looked destitute, on the verge of starvation. He certainly did not look like a driver of an important commander whose defection to the government was celebrated across the national media. Given his miserable appearance, I thought for a while that he must have fallen foul with the commander, been sacked and left to his own devices. To my surprise, Shakir told me he was still working as a driver for Commander Nyuon but that all the forces he belonged to were in that miserable state. They were badly treated by their new allies and rarely received any benefits like other government soldiers.

Shakir stayed in my house for few days and I supplied him with fresh clothes and a pair of shoes. While in the house, Shakir was able to make a phone call to his family after a long time of separation. I also told him that Commander Nyuon himself would be welcome in my house and that if they needed any medication, they could contact me at the Mujahideen Hospital.

A few days later, I received Nyuon's wife who was experiencing pregnancy difficulties in the hospital. The treatment she received from us created a bond between us and she brought a stream of relatives and fighters with different kinds of ailments. It was much later when Commander Nyuon himself appeared at my door and he became a good friend of mine. Commander Nyuon was an honest and determined man who fought hard for the rights of his own people. He was a formidable member of the SPLM but things went wrong between him and John Garang. When he defected to the government side, he expected to be treated with dignity and worth, commensurate with his status. That simply did not happen and he felt treated like a rebel on the government side. Maltreatment of Commander Nyuon was not intentional but there was an ethnic dimension to it that the northerners did not understand. Nyuon was from the Upper Nile but upon his defection, he was placed under a Commander from the Equatorial zone and there was historic enmity between the two peoples. As a result, Nyuon and his forces were badly treated and they later defected back to the SPLM. Unfortunately, things did not go well for Commander Nyuon in his new move. He was assassinated in mysterious circumstances, possibly by a rival group of the SPLM, the South Sudan Liberation Movement (SSLM) of Riek Machar.

My contact with Shakir was instigated by a sense of comradeship between people joined by one region, Darfur. We were both interested in exploring how Darfur people were fairing. The trust I was able to build with Shakir and the debates we had about his struggle intrigued me to meet his Commander Nyuon, who became a regular visitor to my house. Prior to meeting Nyuon, my contacts with the local people were confined to what my hospital duties allowed. After all, I was there as part of the government and my relationship with locals was, to say the least, precarious. But it was Commander Nyuon who enriched my knowledge about the people we were fighting against and the legitimate grievances they had against the north. For the first time, Nyuon challenged me to consider their war as just, while ours was lacking a moral base. There can be no doubt that Commander Nyuon awakened my sense of rebellion and was a forceful landmark along my own path towards the armed struggle against Khartoum.

Fighting for the Nation

In 1995-1996 I left Darfur again for a fighting mission in the South. Unlike the previous mission, the second one was a real war; a vicious one I may say. 1995 was a turbulent year for government. All major opposition parties came together and formed the National Democratic Alliance (NDA) and allied themselves with the SPLM/A. With the assistance of neighbouring countries, the SPLA made tremendous military gains that brought the government to its knees. I was working as the Regional Minister for health (1995) when I got a disturbing radio call from El Tayib Mohamed Kheir, popularly known as Sikha, who was then the National Minister for Internal Affairs in Khartoum. I worked with Kheir before in Darfur and we were still good friends. Kheir was panic-stricken, almost at the brink of a nervous breakdown when he called. His message was prompt and desperately urgent. Kheir told me they needed Darfur to come to the rescue of the government. He thought Juba would fall under the SPLM within a week without our help and that Sudan was facing an invasion by three countries—Ethiopia, Eritrea and Uganda. He further added that over 40% of Sudan's army was in Juba and with its fall, they would have no exit. I told Kheir that I needed 10 to 12 days to mobilise assistance but he thought that might be too late. I left him with a promise to do what I could.

That night, I did not sleep. A substantial proportion of the army in the South were from Darfur and other marginalised areas of the country. Losing Juba would lead to a massacre of many people, particularly from Darfur. But the event also had another dimension. The Jihad thesis of the early days of the government almost collapsed but the involvement of foreign troops in the war ignited my deep sense of nationalism and I was ready for action. In that night, I toured south Darfur and ended up in El Dein. The nomadic Arab ethnic groups in that area traditionally gravitated towards working for the army. The possible fall of Juba meant a disaster, for many of their members were posted with the army in the South. El Dein people were particularly responsive to the mobilisation but I was also successful in other towns as well. I continued my tour in the morning and when I was confident about my progress, I radioed Minister Kheir. I told him to organise a shuttle airlift of 10 planes with a capacity of 120 each. Altogether, I had over 1,500, all volunteers who pledged their readiness to board the planes to Khartoum and then the South. Kheir didn't believe me and sent only one plane that did four trips on that day to Khartoum.

I arrived in Khartoum with the first 480 volunteers. Awad El Jaz, the current Minister for Finance received us at the airport and we drove straight to the Army HQ to receive our arms and prepare for the South. I remember all Ministers used to carry walking sticks. So when I got my machine gun, I gave my walking stick to Minister El Jaz to keep it as a souvenir. I spent the rest of the day preparing for departure and gathering information about my new mission.

During the following morning, I landed at Juba. Ironically, we lodged at the residence of Mujahideen Hospital where I was three years earlier. The shuttle planes continued arriving and I was told the President himself was receiving their flights from Darfur at Khartoum Airport. That showed me how desperate the situation was and how appreciative was the government of our efforts.

My first important duty in Juba was to visit the injured soldiers in the Hospital to gather information about the enemy. In the Hospital, I found many relatives I knew including my brother Ushar who was later sentenced to death following our invasion of Omdurman, 2008. The injured soldiers lost the last major battle against the SPLM, leaving Juba totally exposed for occupation. The defeated army consisted of 6,000 soldiers while I had just over 900 at that moment. The matter was serious and I was determined to rise to it. Ushar and other soldiers around him gave me a full briefing about the SPLA, their number, armament, discipline, motivation, tactics and the terrain in which they operated. In short, I had almost all the information I needed.

Following the military intelligence work, I dashed about working out logistics like fuel, vehicles and food. At the time, I was assisted by Jammali Hasan Jallal El Din, whom we subsequently lost in the invasion of Omdurman. I gave him money to buy red fabrics which we used as head bands to avoid friendly fire. Surprisingly and shortly after that, the SPLA also started using red bands in imitation of our practice. A day later, we were ready to move and Ibrahim Shams El Din, the prominent member of the Revolutionary Command Council came to attend our final orientation and give us some encouragement. We crawled slowly to the South of Juba and towards the battlefield. We took no chance on our march and were fully prepared for all eventualities. When we arrived at Kit River Bridge, 60 miles south of Juba, we saw the retreating army coming towards us from the opposite direction. I ordered my troops to cross the Bridge on foot and move past the retreating army, very much slowed by the large number of injured soldiers among their force. There was always resentment between our force known as Popular Defence Forces (PDFs) and the regular Sudan army. Moreover, I did not want my soldiers to meet with a retreating army for fear of unnecessary demoralisation. When the two armies were well separated, I went back for a meeting with the Commander of the retreating force. After exchanging some military intelligence, I requested certain kinds of rockets that his force used. The man laughed at me, saying he would not waste these weapons on us. He wondered if his force of 6,000 soldiers could not defeat the enemy, what chance was there for 900 'Apache' soldiers, meaning my own army. I left him there and resumed marching with my army. We moved forward to around 70 miles from Juba and landed in a wooded wetland. We immediately recognised it as the site of the lost battle. The evidence was clear from the broken tree branches and the occasional bloodstain on the ground. In the middle of the battle site were two armoured vehicles stuck in the mud. They were clearly left there because the army had no time to dig them out in their hurried retreat. The SPLM hesitated to approach them at the time just in case they were booby-trapped. We were certain that they would come back for them when it was safe enough to do so and after disappearance of the government army. We made a square around the two armoured vehicles and used the site as our camp.

Early morning the next day, we were attacked by the SPLA and a fierce battle ensued. The SPLA did not know there was a new army in place and their mission was just to complete what they had started well the day before. They were able to advance and two of their tanks broke into our square. I still remember with extreme vividness how one of the tanks rolled with its chains over a fine soldier and an acquaintance of mine. His name was Mohamed Abdalla and he was from Gadariff city of Eastern Sudan. The poor man was literally minced by the monster, the military tank. My men fought hard and it was a battle of wills between two bitter enemies. Eventually, the SPLA caved in and we held the upper hand. We chased them for a few miles and never left them until we scattered them in the jungle. It was a wonderful victory of the few against the many. The victory left us much better provided with ammunition, armoured vehicles, tanks and fuel. Our site became a strategic defence line and spearheaded the fending off of the SPLA. When news spread about the defeat of the SPLA, the Commander of the retreating army was the first one to deliver his congratulations and apologies about describing us as Apache soldiers.

I remained in the same site for seven months. There were a few skirmishes here and there but no serious attack as such. The SPLA was demoralised and turned its attention to other war zones away from Juba. In the seventh month after our arrival to the site, I packed my troops and went home and another force came to replace us. A month later, the SPLA came back with a vengeance. They defeated our replacement army and occupied the site. I was already in Darfur then, occupied with civilian duties.

That was all my experience in wars in the South. At the time, I believed that foreign countries had invaded the Sudan and it was my national duty to defend the nation. It just so happened it was in the South and had nothing to do with any religious sentiment. I did not fight that war under any illusion of Jihad and I would have fought that war had it been anywhere in the Sudan.

With the Poor in the Blue Nile State

The government used me like the Joker of a pack of cards. Every time I settled in a job, found my way through it and started a serious project, they moved me to somewhere else. In 1997, I ended up in the Blue Nile State as a minister in the Regional Government. Given the way I was moved out of Darfur, it was hard not to look at my transfer as exile by another name. As a matter of fact, from 1994, I started drifting away from the Islamic Front and my heart simply ceased to remain with the government. I was getting somewhat impatient and increasingly agitated but still retained a glimmer of hope that the system could be reformed.

The Blue Nile State was indeed the most wretched place in Sudan. Extreme poverty existed in some spots in Darfur, but in general, Darfur was a haven compared to the Blue Nile State. I have had the opportunity to roam almost every part of the Sudan and have seen spots of extreme poverty even in comfortable areas of the country like central Sudan. One of the most visible indicators of poverty is the number of beggars found in towns. In that regard, the Blue Nile State baffled me for I had never seen so many beggars as I saw in the Blue Nile towns. Every morning we woke up to a score of them besieging our house and those of our neighbours. We did our best to distribute remnants of food, grain, sugar, clothes and anything that we could part with. The scale of need around us dwarfed our capacity for help; our means were very limited. What was most disturbing in the Blue Nile was not simply the sheer number of beggars. The beggars I had seen in other parts of the Sudan came from destitute sectors of society: the disabled, the crippled, the aged and their children; not so in the Blue Nile State. Its beggars were men and women in the prime of their lives, who, given the opportunity, could be productive and self-reliant. Most of them needed only a small amount of capital and a bit of other kinds of assistance to stand on their own feet. The poverty I saw in the Blue Nile State haunted my mind and disturbed my sleep and I felt compelled to do something about it.

I spent only one year in the Blue Nile State, first as a Minister of Health and later as a Minister for Social Affairs. At the time, I was developing my ideas about how to help the needy people in Sudan through an initiative that we called the Poverty Alleviation Project (PAP). Unlike many of my government colleagues, I believed Sudan had enough resources to play a substantial role in tackling poverty in the country. I did not accept the usual shortage of funds thesis that was often used as an excuse for a lack of action. On the contrary, I thought Sudan had substantial misused resources. For example, Sudan's Savings Bank was originally founded to raise funds for development initiatives, particularly for the small to medium projects. Instead of focusing on that tranche of investors, the Bank was monopolised by the elite and as a result its contribution to the poor remained negligible.

The Islamic Tax Chamber, or Zakat Chamber as it was popularly known, was a formidable source of funding that was vastly underused. The very essence of the Islamic Tax was on our side, for it was intended to be for philanthropic use, privileging the poor in the first place. However, that had never been the case in Sudan. Tax collected by that Chamber became a lucrative source of capital for the better off instead. I must concede that nobody knew how the collected Islamic tax revenue was allocated but we were certain there was little evidence that it went to the poor.

When I moved from the Ministry of Health to that of Social Affairs, a golden opportunity obtained whereby I could upgrade my Poverty Alleviation Project from a mere concept to actual work on the ground. I must say, the idea found some listening ears among my colleagues and was also blessed by some top officials in Khartoum. Despite apathy and a lack of political will, government officials wanted to be seen to be doing something. Thus I was able to find some seed money, if only for the experimental phase of the project.

It was my conviction that a person's thinking, dreams and ambition were commensurate with what he or she had by way of means. A hungry person, with a meal sufficient for a single day never thought beyond the limit of that food. The poor farmers in the Blue Nile State cultivated small plots adjacent to their houses barely enough to keep them alive for one year. A slight tilt downwards in their production and they had to supplement their diet through begging. Their thinking, dreams and energy were trapped within a parameter of a harvest that lasted them for a year. That was what I thought I could challenge and change through the Project. I wanted to stretch the ambition of these farmers by giving them the opportunity to experience having a food supply exceeding a year's need.

Using the seed fund I got for the Project, I bought tractors, secured land and started the work. That particular Project was code-named Seedling (Nabta) and was set to be part of the bigger Poverty Alleviation Project. In Seedling, we divided the land into five acre plots, split evenly between the two popular crops—Sorghum and Sesame. The first was the staple diet in the area while the second was mainly a cash crop. These crops were known to the farmers and suitable for the ecology. Seedling took over early work in the plots. When the crops were around six inches high, we handed the plots to the farmers; a five acre plot to each one. The farmers' work consisted of weeding, protecting and finally harvesting the farms. To circumvent any possibility of exploitation by grain dealers when the harvest was ready, Seedling offered them the option of buying their produce at market price. The project was a stunning success. Even before the crops were harvested, the farmers campaigned to have their allotments increased to 10 acres while new farmers arrived on the scene, demanding to be included in the project. These were the same farmers who never cultivated more than one or two acres a year in their lives. Of course we understood the difference between obtaining a subsidized farm and starting one from scratch. Nonetheless, we were happy to have raised their ambition and made them think much bigger than they ever had prior to this initiative.

As we planned, the next phase—the implementation of which I did not last to oversee—was to hand over all Seedling agricultural machinery to the farmers. A farmers' cooperative was to be formed with Seedling confining its role to the provision of extension work and the limited credit facilities. Planning of the second phase was interrupted by my sudden departure from the Blue Nile State and I did not have the opportunity to follow the progress of Seedling afterwards. According to limited information that I had at the time, Seedling lasted for a few more years before it finally collapsed.

The Recalcitrant Advisor

After just a year in the Blue Nile State, I was hit again by a reshuffle ending with my transfer to Juba, the capital of Bahr El Jabal State. Given the rebellion in the South at the time, Bahr El Jabal was much more important for Khartoum than the Blue Nile and hence my move could be seen as a step up the political ladder. In Juba, I was supposed to serve as Advisor to the government; a job that I undertook once before in Darfur. Prior to my transfer to Juba, a man from Darfur by the name of Habeeb Hamdoun occupied the post. When Hamdoun nominated me for his replacement, Vice President El Zibeir expressed his embarrassment at the prospect of transferring me twice within one year. He implemented this directive and I ended up in Juba replacing Hamdoun as Government Advisor.

My role as a State Government Advisor, whatever that meant, was rather perplexing. In Sudan, the job of an advisor was coined to enable the authority to push an official to the margin of power and yet retain him or her in the club. The position reduced the possibility of dissent and kept the official in check. It was a temporary portfolio with the presumed intention that with good behaviour, the official could be brought in from the margin or otherwise sacked. In any case, the post came with a vague job description. I was there to offer advice to the Governor but I could only do so when asked. Worse than that, neither the Governor nor the Ministers were obliged to take my advice on board. There was, however, another dimension that bestowed disguised power on the post. As in all totalitarian systems, Sudan's central government often used the advisors to keep an eye on State governments. I was fully aware of this fact and equally recognised the precarious nature of my position. In most marginalised parts of the Sudan, hegemonic elites of the River Nile reserved the posts of Governors and Ministers to augment their control over these areas. But the South had always been an exception, for they never accepted northerners as ministers or governors. For that reason, Khartoum settled for a post of advisor. Paradoxically, I was regarded as a northerner in the south, a term which we in Darfur reserved for those coming from River Nile parts of Sudan. As a matter of fact, the necessity for such a role pointed to worrying aspects of governance in the country, namely a lack of sound institutions with checks and balances and within which government officials operated. Regional ministers were never trusted and had to be supervised and spied on and hence the position of an advisor. In developed countries with mature institutions, the position of advisor attracts personnel with competence in a specific sphere. This was not the case in the Sudan. Commitment to the policies of the central government and loyalty to the dictator qualified one for the post.

By sheer accident, my office in the Government complex became a breakfast room. Every day at around ten, the 15 Ministers and the Commissioners came and shared breakfast in my office. The breakfast served a dual purpose—sociability and business combined in one venue. My portfolio as an advisor became a regular issue for debate. The unconventional nature of the venue facilitated a relaxed atmosphere and enabled us to couch serious issues in a friendly and unofficial cloak. Being the only non-southerner in the group, I was often challenged about my qualifications for they all knew more about the south and its people than me. They argued passionately that it was me who should be at the receiving end of the advice and they were right in many ways. Recognising and pragmatically accepting my dubious position as the Khartoum 'eye in their midst', they made the best of my presence among them. Many of the Ministers earned their position out of their excellent performance as rebel fighters. They came straight from the jungle with no civilian work experience. My own relatively lengthy experience in government corridors gave me an edge over them and those who recognised that, sought my counsel in their work. But there was another area where I proved indispensible and that was when they visited Khartoum. Sudan was a capital centred country and State Ministers often had to shuttle to Khartoum to lobby for their work and obtain legitimate resources. It was a sad fact that in Khartoum, southerners were often treated as foreigners even when they were Ministers. They needed somebody like me to accompany them and help in their endless lobby for resources. There was nothing odd in that, for we too in Darfur used the same tactics to get by. State Ministers who came from the River Nile basin were key to corridors of power in Khartoum and we often used them as such. There was simply no way out of it, for the River Nile elite controlled all key positions in the country and the best way to approach them was through their friends and kin.

Despite my dubious status as an outsider Advisor, I was able to build trust and form cordial relationships with all cabinet members. It did not take me long to detect the paternalistic, racist and exploitative attitudes with which the northerners approached the local inhabitants, irrespective of their importance. The northerners in the south were simply unwilling to differentiate between the rebels in the jungle and their allies in the government-controlled zone. Not surprisingly little trust was built and the community remained divided in a near apartheid style. As an Advisor to a cabinet, entirely consisting of southerners, I found myself straddled between two worlds. I may say though, that I always felt closer to the southerners, since their grievances resonated very well with our own in Darfur.

My wife recently reminded me of what I said while we were travelling to El Damazin, capital of Blue Nile State where I was based in 1997. In the car we were listening to a speech given by Colonel Younis, noted for a speech he gave daily, following 3pm Omdurman National Radio news in the 1990s. Colonel Younis was nicknamed 'the barking dog' because his frenzied speech demonized almost everybody and every country with a scant disagreement with the government. His victims ranged from Kings of Saudi Arabia, gulf Emirs, opposition parties and, of course John Garang of the SPLM/A. There was no limit to the choice of offensive words Colonel Younis used in his speech; it was vulgar, coarse and designed for the sheer aim of degrading and demonizing his victims. Garang was a regular target of Younis' attacks, whom he approached with venomous and openly racist fervour. According to my wife, after listening to a hurled attack on Garang, I said to her, 'A day will come when this same radio will label me as a rebel like Garang and will demonise me in a similar manner'.

I remember an event that stirred a staunch debate at our breakfast table. Khartoum—represented by northerners who were almost entirely Muslim—strongly controlled the security organs of the State of Bahr EL Jabal. They controlled the army, the police and intelligence. They also controlled strategic sectors that influenced security like finance, trade and transport. One day, the Governor asked me to replace him in addressing a gathering of security agents in Juba. The venue attracted top security personnel in the State and was dominated by northerners. In my speech, I told the audience that we, the northerners, had grave misgivings in the south. We opted not to differentiate between rebels and allies, enemies and friends, supporters and renegades and that we had turned Juba into a huge prison of 40 miles diameter besieged by the SPLA. I told them our behaviour and policies were squandering the dream of building a united country and would soon lead to a loss of the south altogether.

Naturally, my speech was loved by the southerners but did not go down well with the rest. Some northern officials castigated my speech and I felt that my post hung in the balance. The meeting was confidential and confined to top security officials and in such venues, self-criticism was allowed. Nonetheless, my speech breached a taboo and touched on a sensitive nerve. It tainted perception of my loyalty to the central authority. The criticism that followed, and the dangers cloaked behind it, did not agitate me. My mind was already made up and it was only a matter of time before I would depart and declare my open rebellion against the system.

It was doubtful whether any northerners working in the south were unaware of the unjust treatment visited on the local people. Being posted in the south was so popular in the north and many government officials saw it as a better alternative than migration to the oil rich Gulf countries. I may have been the only top northern government official who had worked in the south and failed to build a fine house or Villa in Khartoum out of savings made during the posting. The security organ of the government controlled transport to the south, and hence trade in general, and opened an avenue for trading on almost everything coming from the north. All top government officials were, in effect traders, either on goods transported on barges commissioned by the security forces or military planes shuttling between Khartoum and the south. They also traded on inflated rations they received at cost price to government officials that included grain, fuel, sugar, oil, rice, lentils and even salt. The NGOs, national or otherwise, joined in the feast and the Islamic ones were no exception. They certainly assisted the needy for free, but they raised substantial money for their institutions as well, for private use, out of semi illicit trade. A sack of grain would be bought in Khartoum for £s5,000, arrive at Juba at a total cost of £s20,000 and then be sold in Juba market for £s100,000. A 400 to 500% profit was standard for other imported goods as well. A reverse trade also obtained, whereby timber, ivory and even alcohol found their way to Khartoum and lined the pockets of government officials and army officers alike.

Juba, as a trade city, was certainly a lucrative hub arising out of its important strategic military position. The transient nature of the tranche that monopolized trade in the city dictated the continuous flight of wealth towards the north. It consisted of government personnel who were posted in the south for a short period and had no enduring relationship with the place as such. Thus the city remained impoverished with little investment of wealth made within its borders. The northerners lived as wealthy and privileged racketeers turning the entire place into a venue of cheap labour and an aid-dependent depot. It was such a humiliating existence for the locals who were forced to endure a subservient position vis-à-vis the wealthy exploitative class of northerners. The houses of top officials from the north were filled with servants, cooks, guards, cleaners, child minders and even masseurs. Southerners, who were not fortunate enough to avail of these posts, had to be content with reliance on food aid, an undignified source of sustenance. I remember once that I received one of the Sultans who sought my assistance looking for food for his own people. I was dismayed to learn that he, the Sultan, had to queue with a bucket in hand to obtain a few kilograms of grain by way of food aid. The sight of a Sultan given grain in a bucket haunted my mind for a long time and if the motive of the NGO was to humiliate the Sultan and his people by such an action, they couldn't have done it any better.

While I was in Juba, things were not going well in Darfur. Far from it, they were getting worse, with the near collapse of public services, lack of security, ethnic conflicts and a drastic shortage of food. After the Juba assignment, I started seriously thinking of doing something, not only for Darfur but for the whole country including the south. I resigned my post and left for Khartoum. For nearly a decade that I served with the government, I did not come across a single individual who wilfully gave up a ministerial position, but that was exactly what I did.

From the Poverty Alleviation Project (PAP), to the Black Book of Sudan

While I was in the Blue Nile State (1997), we conceived the Seedling venture as part of the broader initiative of PAP. Following my transfer to the Bhar El Jabal State, we continued developing our views of PAP. My work as an Advisor involved frequent travels to Khartoum where I was able to debate PAP and galvanise support among other likeminded colleagues and top government officials. When I left Bahr El Jabal, I continued my work with PAP until I left the Sudan, a year or so later.

A major problem that we faced at the very conception of PAP was the absence of reliable data on the nature of poverty and its distribution in the country. The government and its various bodies that dealt with poverty had to depend on unreliable anecdotal information. At another level, the government established numerous institutions to address poverty in the country but nobody knew where the funds went and what impact they made. For example, there was the Islamic Tax Office with its annual receipts of £s23 billion. There was also Sudan's Savings Bank and the Family Bank; both of which had substantial funds earmarked for income generation projects, cottage industries and other related activities. At the charity level there were many official institutions led by the Martyr's Organisation and so forth.

Though not by design, PAP struck a cord at the highest governmental level. Foolhardy economic polices adopted by the government created havoc, with poverty now infringing on a substantial sector of the hitherto comfortable middle class. The popularity of the government sank and there was a genuine need to assure the public that something was being done; there was no better slogan for this than 'poverty alleviation'. Government propaganda forces jumped on the bandwagon and 'poverty alleviation' became a dominant catch phrase. From our own side, we needed legitimacy to operate. After all, we lived under a totalitarian system where a government mandate was essential for any worthwhile task. Among PAP activists, I was the only one with an executive position and access to government ministers. I used that position to secure a mandate, register the organisation and obtain finance to launch the work in earnest. Seizing on the opportunity, I persuaded some influential government officials to enable me to proceed with the task and offer a comprehensive report complete with recommendations to the National Council of Ministers.

We appointed a team consisting of a handful of administrators and research personnel led by Abu Bakar Hamid of Darfur and Seif El Dowla Kuku of Omdurman. It was true that the PAP was driven by intellectuals from Darfur or western Sudan in general. Nonetheless, poverty spanned through all parts of the Sudan, including the hegemonic north. As such, the initiative galvanized so many people, young and old, Islamists and otherwise from every corner of the country. Activists in PAP belonged to the so-called elite class of the country and yet, they either rose from impoverished backgrounds or otherwise grew up within extended families ill-served by successive governments and ravished with poverty. Hence, most of them were passionate about the cause they were fighting for and ready for a selfless sacrifice for realising the ideals of the Project.

Like a magic wand, the mandate we obtained from the government opened closed doors for us, and we stretched the power we got to its outermost limit. Our staff proceeded to execute their job with firm confidence, often exceeding their mandate and pretending they had access to the highest authority in the land, including the President himself. The scope of contacts they made, showed just that, for they were able to visit 23 States, storming into a whopping 28 Ministries and 56 Institutions and semi-state bodies. Some managers even initiated contact with them, protesting their lack of inclusion. We knew their weaknesses and we made full use of them. Some saw PAP as an opportunity to publicize their achievements, some wanted to be vindicated and some thought we had money and wanted to pursue their insatiable appetite for embezzling public funds. We obliged them all and made good use of our opportunities. We had no money to spare and certainly none to be embezzled in any way.

The result of the investigation was startling. Poverty was indeed rampant and had posed a serious threat even within the middle class bracket. Wealth was concentrated in the hands of the few and systematically siphoned off to the River Nile States of northern Sudan. Five per cent of Sudan's population controlled almost every avenue of power in the country from culture to capital, music to security and cuisine to religion. Within the north itself, a mere three ethnic groups dominated the theatre while others were sidelined like the rest of us. Control of these ethnic groups was hegemonic. It metamorphosed into an enduring pattern that remained the same, irrespective of the nature of the government in Khartoum: democratic, socialist, theocratic, military or otherwise. In a nutshell, that was the thesis of the Black Book.

It would be a mistake to assume PAP's team was coterminous to that which later produced the Black Book. In reality, the Black Book group was established much earlier and had used PAP's team to realise its objectives. In 1993, a clandestine unit of seven disenfranchised individuals were formed in Darfur but later grew to provide personnel for the Black Book. PAP's group was motivated by discerning what was wrong with the country in the hope that other leaders would take action and set things right. The Black Book group had a different motive. It wanted to provide scientific evidence that a minority of northern elite controlled the whole of Sudan. More importantly, it wanted to instigate and lead the change, by force, if necessary.

The Birth of JEM

Anybody searching for a specific date forming the birthday of JEM will certainly be disappointed. JEM's emanation was a lengthy process involving a decade of arduous debates and actions. However, there were landmarks along the road that laid the foundation for establishing the organisation.

In 1993, seven of us came together in El Fashir to convene a meeting and establish a clandestine cell to look into ways of articulating our grievances and galvanise likeminded people behind a cause that was yet to be fully defined. The Darfur cell was followed by another cell, established in Kordofan in 1994. The Khartoum cell was not established until 1997. Many of those who formed the earlier cells were alienated Islamists but Islamism was not the unifying factor. As such, the cells included others who had no connection to the Islamic ideology and propaganda of the government but were motivated by a genuine need for change.

We joined the Islamic Front because of its wonderful ideals of justice, care, freedom, inclusiveness and the rule of law that applied to shepherds and flock alike. These were the propagated ideals that attracted us to the party when we were in opposition. We members of the impoverished parts of Sudan tried other traditional parties but drifted away from them because of their utter failure to realise these same cherished ideals. Well, it didn't take the Islamic government long to prove it was no more than the same institution under a different banner. We soon discovered the affinity between the Islamic government and all previous regimes. Even in kinship terms, our new leaders were siblings and cousins of their predecessors and were united by their dedication to the preservation of the hegemony of River Nile Sudan, north of Khartoum, over the rest of the country at all costs. They were the legitimate members of the government while we were caretakers mandated to act in total subordination to them. They continued to control the banks, defence, security, finance, culture and even religion. They appointed us, the Darfuris, as ministers and yet we could not achieve anything worthwhile without their blessing and acquiescence. I worked in several service ministries and had experienced first hand how the central government was failing them. It starved them of the most rudimentary services that any decent government on earth would be expected to provide. It showed an unbelievable capacity for lack of mercy on the very people it was meant to lead and care for.

My work with the poor also taught me something else: that poverty was not due to a lack of ingenuity, poor aptitude for work or a dearth of natural resources. Far from it, Darfuri people, as indeed many others in the disenfranchised parts of the Sudan, were hard working citizens. Over the years, they sustained the State, fed the urban elite and boosted the export sector with meat, sesame, peanuts, gum Arabic, hibiscus, fruit, etc. But there was no limit to the greed of the ruling class of Sudan. Taxation continued to rise while government input in terms of services declined at the same pace. In the end, the government decided to go for the kill and offered nothing at all by way of services. That was the motive behind the policy of devolution of public services. No matter how you looked at it, it was hard to avoid compelling evidence that the resulting poverty was neither a product of accident nor of incompetence. It was simply an insidious and deliberate plan for the impoverishment of the many and the enrichment of the few. Had those few been distributed fairly across disparate regions, ethnic groups and classes in the nation, the story and the result would have been different. Indeed, the few had come from a specific geographical zone and had to be members of elite ethnic groups of the Sudan.

People who did not understand the history of the Darfur uprisings often accused us of rushing to war. They thought we could have addressed our cause and settled our grievances through peaceful debate and campaigns. That was precisely what we naively thought and did in the past and got nowhere. We were part of the system and had worked within every conceivable party and regime for half a century. As early as 1992, we initiated intense debate within the Islamic movements with our colleagues of the River Nile ruling elite. The response was, to say the least, unfortunate. Like all oppressors, our northern friends were in no mood for listening. In fact, to use a medical metaphor, they suffered from verbal diarrhoea. They insisted on lecturing us and expected us to remain obedient and compliant listeners. When we raised the issue of injustice we were accused of being racists, ethnic chauvinists and ungrateful with regard to what they had offered us. Some took our complaints as evidence of weakness in our faith and an obsession with earthly material gains. More often than not, we were told that River Nile States too were impoverished and the whole of Sudan was poor anyway and there was nothing we could do about it. To begin with, I did not believe that the Sudan, or for that matter Darfur, was poor. But even if we assumed the country was poor, we wanted to see the weight of poverty shared equally. We pointed out to them that certain regions shouldered the weight of poverty while others simply did not. That was the problem.

Perhaps the most compelling defence put forward by some of our northern opponents was the absence of hard evidence proving western Sudan was systematically pillaged in favour of the north. The powerful northern elite in full control of the production of knowledge seized on the argument and challenged us to prove we were marginalised. Unfortunately, some members of our support were intimidated and started demanding statistical evidence to bolster their case. As a consequence we launched our data gathering programme which gradually evolved into PAP. With the firm backing of an enthusiastic government, we were able to tap into every important source of data, ending up with an impressive array of information.

In 1999, our core group within PAP launched our seminal publication; 'The Black Book: Imbalance of Power and Wealth in Sudan'. It was a bombshell for the government and a last ditch endeavour for us; a turning point between debate and machine guns. The publication exposed not only the Islamic government of the day, but all Sudan's successive regimes since independence. The spectacular once off distribution designed to beat the tight government intelligence added to the mastery of the Publication. In the history of Sudan's literate realms, no publication ever, with the exception of the Koran and the Bible, surpassed the popularity of the Black Book. Literally speaking, the Book distributed itself through spontaneous photocopying; its thesis becoming a topical issue in every social setting across the nation, debated even by non-literate people. In as much as PAP was a national project involving activists from across the Sudan, so too was the Black Book but admittedly to a lesser extent. By the time the Book was prepared, JEM's core group in PAP had attracted membership from all over the country. Ironically, and in order to outmanoeuvre the national security organs, the Book was stored in the house of someone from north of Sudan, who came from one of the hegemonic elite ethnic groups of north Sudan.

Instead of re-examining its policies in the light of information contained in the publication, the government panicked and channelled its energy into frenzied denialist tactics. President al-Bashir also entered the fray and ordered publication of the White Book of Sudan to debunk the Black Book and bolster the contribution of his government. Needless to say, the White Book was stillborn and failed to capture the attention of the public, including supporters of the regime.

The refusal of the government to take the Black Book seriously and initiate a responsible debate on its thesis was the final straw that broke the camel's back. It sent a clear message to all, that dialogue would never shake the status quo and that debate was a sterile channel for reform. The ferociousness of the attacks on the Darfur authors was astounding and galvanised Darfur activists to unite. Why not, since al-Bashir unleashed all his racist thugs who used their position in government media to override every rule of rational debate. Authors of the Black Book were labelled as racists—ignorant, tribalist, regionalist, treasonous and agents of western and Zionist imperialism. That sad response shifted the debate into a cleavage between the Gharraba (westerners) and the northern Jallaba (procurers of goods). Both of these two terms were derogatory, the first referred to inhabitants of western Sudan while the latter referred historically to a slave owning class, primarily from River Nile Sudan. That was not the purpose of the Black Book but whether it was or not was immaterial. The weeks that followed the release of the Black Book witnessed widespread harassment of Darfuri citizens in the capital. Many of them were detained by government security agents, tortured in the so-called Ghost Houses and had their businesses ruined for their alleged connection with the Black Book.

Callous response to the Black Book and victimisation of Darfur citizens intensified an already unprecedented resentment against the northern-based ruling elite. In some ways, the main thesis of the Black Book was hardly new. The Book simply added statistical evidence to the marginalisation thesis that everybody experienced. That knowledge was bolstered by a preceding political event which the northern ruling elite botched in 1996. In that year, the ruling Islamic party went through a process of electing its Secretary General. Members of the marginalised regions of Darfur, Kordofan and southern

Sudan formed a block to secure the election of El Shafey Ahmed Mohamed, a prominent politician from Darfur. The centre, led by a northern-based block opted for Ghazi Salah El Din, the current Envoy for Darfur who was also the choice of the northern dominated Political Bureau of the Party. The bloc of the marginalised regions had an absolute numerical edge and the election of their candidate was thought to be guaranteed. But was it? To the utter dismay of most members of the Party, Majzoub El Khalifa, the head of the election committee reversed the result and announced Salah El Din the winner. There was nothing Ahmed and his marginalised supporters could do except to sulk in their resentment. The status quo had to be preserved, election or otherwise. There was no point soliciting Turabi's help for he was the one behind the selection of Salah El Din over Ahmed and for obvious reasons. The former would shower him with praise while the latter would swamp him with the problems of rural Sudan: poverty, illiteracy, disease, thirst, injustice and so forth, and hence the choosing of Salah El Din made sense for the arch imam of the Party.

In 1999, I resigned my post and obtained a WHO scholarship for the University of Maastricht where I studied for a Master's Degree in Public Health. My presence in Europe enabled me to continue debating the issue of injustice in Sudan with a wide range of Sudanese in Europe. At the time, we had already abandoned dialogue with the ruling elite and started preparing for an armed struggle. The response I got in Europe was reasonable and we were able to set up a network of activists to compliment our work inside Sudan. In December 2000, I returned to Sudan where we continued our preparation for the uprising. There was no going back and it was only a matter of time before discharging the first bullet.

Discharging The First Bullet

My return to Sudan was brief, lasting only two months and was focussed on putting the final touches on the plan. Finance presented us with a formidable challenge, for which I was deemed responsible. Thanks to the Black Book, our ground-work was almost complete and we had no shortage of volunteers at both levels, political and military. We were fortunate to have come along after Bolad's aborted uprising and had the advantage of learning from his mistakes.

Just days before my departure from Sudan again, my uncle Sultan Dosa of the Zaghawa died and I was attending his mourning at his house in El Fashir. Due to the high profile of the deceased, President al-Bashir flew to El Fashir to offer his condolences to his family. He arrived at the family house accompanied by his two cabinet Ministers, Abdel Rahim Husain and Tigani Adam Tahir. The latter was also a Zaghawa like myself and a relative as well. Just before they left, Tahir took me aside and informed me with a mixture of excitement and benevolence that al-Bashir wanted me for a ministerial post somewhere. Tahir then said his responsibility was to take me to the President, a task he was to organise soon. I thanked Tahir for his help and left it at that. My mind was already made up and I had no interest in taking up another post with the government. However, I was delighted our plot did not come to the attention of al-Bashir or to his companion, Husain who was the Minister for Defence. I had no contact with Tahir again until I left Sudan.

In March 6th, 2001, I crossed Sudan's border into Chad and arrived later at N'Djamena. I was on my way to Europe looking for finance. The Chadian intelligence under the same President Deby of today, detected our plot and offered to hand me over to the Sudanese government. The Chadian government knew exactly what I was looking for but their Sudanese counterpart did not. Kheir, the then Presidential Advisor for National Security refused the Chadian offer, stating that I was not classified as 'wanted' in their intelligence list and there was no need to repatriate me to Khartoum. It was true that Kheir was a friend but that was not a determinant of his response. He was simply unaware of my motives.

A few days later, Sudan government sent a small delegation to look me up in N'Djamena with an offer of a post. The delegation included Minister Tahir who contacted me in Khartoum and businessman Jar El Nabi from Kordofan. The latter was also a good acquaintance of mine. As I detected, part of their mission was to gauge the accuracy of the Chadian intelligence report, assess the level of danger I posed to the government, and perhaps bribe me with a post, in line with the wishes of the President. When the delegation located me, they were far from impressed. They expected to find me in a decent hotel suite complete with a meeting room suitable for a confidential gathering. Instead, they located me lodging with a relative in the city. Like all houses around impoverished sub-Saharan Africa, I shared a guest room with numerous male relatives. The guest room was all encompassing and was used for sleeping, sitting and entertaining visitors including my eminent visitors from the Khartoum government. It was a pathetic scene for someone trying to stage a revolution and my visitors made no attempt to disguise their pity and sympathy for me. I think they arrived at the 'intelligent' conclusion that I was too destitute to start a rebellion. Whatever the case, the delegation left me and went back, perhaps with a report that I was harmless, had no resources, and hence the government needed not worry about me.

It was strange the government did not contemplate an armed struggle in Darfur. We had debated our anger and discontent very widely with several top government leaders like Majzoub El

Khalifa, Ghazi Salah El Din and others though of course we did not mention the possibility of an armed struggle. As for Turabi, we never discussed the issue with him. We knew his views for he already told us prior to this to ignore earthly material gains and focus on the Islamisation of the Darfur people. Vice President Taha, who was a disciple of Turabi, came closer to cracking our plan. According to some reports, El Shafey Ahmed warned him that an impending armed struggle would ensue unless the government moved fast and addressed the rising discontent among Darfur's politicians. Taha's response evoked his characteristic contempt of the marginalised in Sudan. He summarily dismissed Ahmed's revelation stating, 'Darfur people were too hungry to stage an armed revolution.'

In April, 2001, while in Chad, I made the first appointment in JEM. I appointed Adam Hasan (false name) as Commander of our force, with Abdalla Abdel Karim Abbaker as Deputy Commander. I also assigned a finance portfolio to another person. At the time, we did not yet declare our revolution. With an unsympathetic government in Chad, it was not possible for us to launch the revolution there and of course it was inconceivable to announce it inside Sudan either. The only possible venue would be in Europe, which then became my second destination. My departure for Europe was also necessitated by another factor. We needed finance and I had to tap into the resources of our sympathizers in Europe and the rest of the Diaspora. I arrived at Charles de Gaulle Airport on the night of July 31st 2001 and ended up in the Netherlands three days later. In August 31st of the same year, I announced the birth of our new organisation in Den Haag in the Netherlands.

The announcement of the birth of JEM went almost unnoticed in government circles as well as among top politicians in Sudan. There was also confusion regarding who was heading the new organisation. Some government circles seized on my previous connection with the Islamists and labelled JEM as a mere extension of Turabi's Party that later came to be known as the Popular Congress Party. A tight grip over media outlets in Khartoum also meant that no accurate information would seep to the public at home. To add further to the confusion, no clearly structured political leadership was formed. In Sudan, Tawir Abdeen (not his real name) was acting as Secretary General for JEM. In Europe, I was doing everything, acting as de facto president, secretary general, spokesperson and treasurer. These were to change following an important conference we attended in the German town of Vlotho in July 2002.

The Vlotho Conference or rather its fringe was the first foundational gathering for JEM. The name JEM was little known at the time and the gathering was couched under the rubric of discussing the multifaceted problems that besieged the country at the time. The Conference was truly national and multiethnic and befitting for its main theme: 'Marginalisation'. Every single region in the country was represented and so were all major political parties. Leaders of Sudan's political parties who attended, included Nur El Dayem for the Umma Party, El Shafey Khidir for the Sudanese Communist Party, Ali El Haj for the Popular Congress Party and Khalid El Mubarak from the Democratic Unionist Party. Dreig of the Federal Alliance Party and Abu Fatna of the Beja Party were invited but were not able to attend. A number of delegates represented different factions of southern Sudan including the SPLM. Among others, the Vlotho Conference bolstered JEM as an organisation determined to be national and open to all activists from every corner of the country.

As envisaged by the JEM delegation, the Vlotho Conference offered a formidable opportunity to realise certain defined objectives: to debate Sudan's problems, publicise JEM, gain new members and endorse the leadership of JEM. To a varying extent, all of these objectives were realised. More importantly, it was during Vlotho that I got some sort of a mandate to act as President of JEM. However, my Presidency remained tenuous until I was later elected as President in the General Congress of JEM in Libya, 2005. Unlike what transpired in Vlotho, the 2005 General Congress in Libya operated under clearly endorsed rules and regulations that JEM did not have in 2002. Finance remained the most daunting problem with which I left Vlotho.

My search for finance did not take long to expose my naivety and poor knowledge of our Diaspora supporters in Europe. To be fair to them, they showered me with advice, moral support and good will but failed to provide any finance. As I came to understand, almost all of them were struggling to survive and were saddled by formidable extended family obligations at home. As a result, I found myself stranded with difficulty in paying for my upkeep, let alone having the capacity to send money back home. My stay permit expired and I had to apply for asylum in the Netherlands.

The staff I appointed in Darfur were getting agitated. They had their expensive satellite Thuraya phones, which were far too costly for me to ring, particularly from a public pay phone. Every time I phoned, they gave out about my audacity in staging a revolution with not a penny in my pocket. I was simply broke and their patience was running out. I had nothing but Allah with me and when I say so, you (the author) keep telling me 'He is with everybody!'. Well, as I was sitting commiserating on my destitution, some money passed my way. But don't hold your breath, my treasurer lost it and we were back to an organisation with zero in its coffers.

Of course, part of my problem was lack of experience. I would never handle scarce money in that way today. The post of a Treasurer is now reserved for people vetted for honesty and integrity. Passion for the cause of Darfur is not enough. It took us some time to recover from that and find some more funds from other wealthy sympathisers. To be exact, our callous treasurer delayed the commencement of the first engagement from September 2002 to the beginning of 2003. However it was, we obtained some resources and were back on track. Commander Hasan went on the offensive against the government early in 2003, thus ushering in the real birth of the Darfur revolution. Since then, JEM has gone from strength to strength. It is now the biggest armed Movement in Darfur, a mover and shaker of Sudan's present and future politics and a regional player that cannot be ignored. Despite this, few people know the provenance of Commander Hasan. His name is rarely mentioned in the literature on JEM and many prominent members of JEM who joined us later cannot recall his name. That is understandable because Hasan fought only one battle, in which he was injured, and then left us and disappeared. I salute ex-Commander Hasan for starting our revolution, a momentous act that should never be underestimated. Before his discharge of the first bullet against the authorities, we were no more than a coalition of aggrieved citizens. Sudan was full of aggrieved citizens, including cabinet ministers like myself prior to my resignation. The first battle that Commander Hasan launched, transformed our organisation into an armed movement with all the corollaries that this entails. We became rebels and had to live up to our new status. The government too of course shifted its strategy towards dealing with us. I am grateful to Commander Hasan and have no regrets that he had to leave. I did not pick him up to continue with us. Rather, I appointed him because I knew he had the quality and audacity to perform that first and most difficult task, which he accomplished to the fullest. Think about our traditional dance Hajouri and how it starts. An initiator goes to the middle of the village in the evening and starts clapping his hands and singing, by way of invitation for others to join in for a dance. Young men and women arrive minutes later and commence the dance proper. The initiator of the dance finds himself surrounded by far better dancers, feels intimidated and withdraws. As an initiator of the dance, his job is to bring everybody out for a dance and whether he remains in the dance or not is a separate matter. Commander Hasan had the ability to start the process but not the stamina to remain with us. That was all right and he was to be commended for it. Many good people joined the Movement along the way, did an excellent job and vanished.

The Battle For Omdurman, May 2008

The invasion of Omdurman of May 10th 2008, codenamed Operation Long Arm (OLA) was a momentous event in the history of our struggle for justice in Sudan. It is true that the battle did not achieve its ultimate goal of unseating the government. However, it certainly brought the ruling regime to its knees and reduced it to a pathetic state, forced to rely on ethnic based defenders against JEM. OLA transformed JEM into a national and regional power, humiliating al-Bashir and exposing his unpopularity in the country and his inability to trust the government army to defend the capital. Since the Mahdi's revolution and the fall of Khartoum in 1885 at the hands of the British Forces, no force had been able to invade the capital. The SPLM, with its decades of experience and ample military might did not make any attempt to come near the capital. In 1976, Sadiq Al Mahdi staged an armed botched attempt to topple the government. His troops, labelled 'mercenaries' in the usual racist style did not invade the capital. They were infiltrated over time and lived for a while as sleepers waiting for the order. JEM invaded the capital in broad daylight. It was an achievement worthy of being taught in military colleges. In the days following the invasion, an American army General whom I had never met, sent a message and saluted me for the operation.

OLA was not a gamble. It was a necessity. The continuous onslaught and genocides that ravaged the south of Sudan, the Nuba Mountains, Darfur and many other corners of the Sudan were all planned and ordered in the capital. The capital was the centre where these eugenic decisions took place and that was why OLA moved the battle to Khartoum. For years and years the ruling elite remained in comfort in the capital and sent members of the marginalised people to fight and die for them in the hinterlands. OLA was staged to take the battle to Khartoum and fight face to face against those depraved and cowardly warmongers who were addicted to having others fight their wars. No wonder when we reached the capital, several ministers fled the city, while others gathered in the VIP lounge at Khartoum airport ready to be airlifted out into exile. As for their vile President al-Bashir, he sat meditating in his jet in Kinana town, near Kosti at the white Nile, 300 kilometres away from his palace.

The decision to take the battle to Khartoum was taken at our Annual General Congress in the liberated Zone in October, 2007. However, preparation for it was not completed until May 2008. It was a complex task. It involved crossing 1,500 kilometres in three days. Each vehicle carried 4,000 kilograms of food, water, fuel, sleeping kits, and ammunitions and of course the soldiers as well. Tankers were ruled out as they were too slow for such a rapid trip. We were guided by the satellite GPS system but aided by conventional knowledge of the terrain and clues provided by stars at night.

OLA was not a surprise attack on the capital. You, yourself (the author), had relayed a message from the US State Department warning us not to proceed into Omdurman. The government knew about our advance and were bombing us on the way with Antonov planes, Mig fighters and a helicopter gunship, but we persevered. Despite information available to the government, they simply refused to believe we were heading towards the capital. At first they assumed we were heading towards Kordofan. When we got to Wadi Al Malik, about 350 kilometres away from Khartoum, their communications reflected some confusion between Kordofan or Khartoum as possible destinations. Then we advanced towards Wadi Muqaddam, and they settled for either Khartoum or the Northern Region. In Wadi Muqaddam, we were around 100 kilometres from Al Dabba city of the Northern Region. We were also not too far from Dunqulah which led some of them to think with some relief that our target was the Northern Region and not Khartoum. We were tracking down their communications and were fully aware of their intentions. Darkness engulfed us as we progressed beyond Wadi Muqaddam. Our original OLA plan was designed to take advantage of moonlight and travel by night. Unfortunately, our logistical arrangement ran behind schedule, forcing us to lose bright nights of the lunar cycle. Delaying OLA for another lunar month would have divulged our plan so we opted for going ahead with it. That was a costly mistake as it transpired to be. It deprived us of entering Khartoum early in the morning and the enemy took advantage of darkness against us.

We spent the night exactly 190 kilometres away from Khartoum. Government planes flew over us but mistook us for a nomadic camp. In the morning we progressed and were a bit confused about the fastest route to our destination. We met two Ford trucks and commissioned them to lead us for a while and they did. When we got close to the western side of Omdurman, we swerved north in a deceptive way and ended up 44 kilometres north of Khartoum where we joined the tarmac road coming from the north. Government intelligence expected us to approach Omdurman from the west. We entered it from the north instead and that threw their defence into disarray. It was a fierce battle and a historic day to remember. By the afternoon, we controlled the whole of Omdurman and some of our forces crossed into Khartoum. Darkness constituted a problem for us with many of our commanders unable to find their way in Omdurman and Khartoum cities. In the morning of the second day, we lost control and evacuated.

Despite the impeccable execution of OLA, we were forced to retreat. A major problem was our late arrival into the capital due to lack of moonlight on the last night of the journey. That robbed us of valuable daylight and as a result we were not able to accomplish our planned work for the first day. To make matters worse, one of our battalions was delayed by a battle near Omdurman and it took them some time to deal with the enemy and march into the town.

It was true that some of our soldiers did not know the city well and wasted time looking for targets. Some of their vehicles were well and good in the desert but hardly suitable for city traffic. Those were the vehicles we replaced in Khartoum by captured government ones and were later displayed in the media as bootie from JEM. We certainly failed to forecast how difficult it would be for a soldier from the desert to manoeuvre a vehicle in a city and to handle a roundabout at fast speed without flipping it, with brakes adjusted to the terrain of sand dunes.

Our communication system was also faulty. Prior to entering Khartoum, we confiscated all Thuraya satellite phones and relied on radio communications. The Thuraya phones were wonderful but they came with their problems. Their GPS system betrayed the position of the speaker. Furthermore, JEM troops spoke every conceivable language on earth: German, Chinese, Russian,

French, Persian, not to mention a host of local languages. For security reasons and just in case we were infiltrated, we planned not to use Thuraya phones in the operation. Thuraya phones also required an open space and performed badly near city buildings. Our problem was that our radio communications system also failed to operate satisfactorily in the city. As a result, different units were disconnected from each other. Inappropriate communication severely damaged our evacuation process. We left behind many fine men who did not know about the evacuation and continued fighting until the last bullet.

The organisation of the army also proved problematic. It was divided into much bigger divisions. Our army should have been organised in smaller units while retaining the possibility of joint operations. Bigger divisions were not cost effective, leading to small jobs being handled by too much power.

We entered Omdurman with strict orders not to harm innocent civilians. Those orders were well adhered to and we say that with extreme pride. However, we expected to be fighting against the government army with their distinctive uniform. We were mistaken. The government kept the army away and defended the capital with fighters belonging to security divisions, most of whom were in plain clothes. It was a daunting task for us to differentiate between targets and civilians at a quick first glance. In combat, a fraction of a second of delay in opening fire could be fatal.

Critiques of OLA often argued that the operation was a costly gamble that should not have been executed. Well, to begin with, freedom does not come cheap and freedom fighters have to be prepared to pay for it. The death of a dozen, or so, of people in the capital, almost all of whom were combatants, outraged the very people who expressed only a modest protest about the half million people who prematurely and unjustly perished in Darfur, five folds of whom met their death in the south of Sudan and numerous others in different parts of the Sudan. It was as though the death of scores of inhabitants in the capital rated much higher than that of hundreds of thousands in Darfur and other marginalised parts of the country. In fact, JEM soldiers had long ago decided they would rather die in the streets of Khartoum than the desert of Darfur, as the ruling elite would have it. The war of Darfur had certainly led to the death of far too many. However, like all marginalised people in Sudan, they had been dying of poverty, disease and famine on a much larger scale and for far too many decades. OLA was a bold and courageous move to put a stop to just that.

But what was the actual cost of OLA in human lives to JEM and others, defending justice and injustice alike? We certainly lost fine men in the invasion but to our surprise, the overall number of those who died in the engagement itself was bewilderingly low. In our firm knowledge, 26 of our fighters were either killed or injured in the battle but many more were killed later in the so-called ghost houses of the government security organs. Not all those who were tortured to death were our men but were simply targeted either because they were from Darfur and/or bore the complexions of Darfuri people. Sudanese army and security agents have a long history of killing their captives without any effort to investigate their incrimination and with total disregard for international norms and conventions regarding rules of engagement and treatment of war prisoners. So institutionalised is this culture of extra-judicial killings that they even coined a term for it: 'Licking' (lahis) is the term they use for the physical liquidation of captives and any junior officer can easily authorise the 'licking' of captors. Over 60 of our captured soldiers died through this insidious practice of 'licking'.

The assault on innocent citizens just because they looked Darfurian or westerners also happened with regard to the alleged JEM prisoners in Khartoum, some of whom were later pardoned by al-Bashir following the Doha Framework Agreement of February, 2010. In general, the number of casualties sustained in OLA was not dissimilar from casualties we had in many other battles we fought along the way. Reports later told of over 4,500 people being arrested in a security crackdown on Darfur citizens in the capital and many other major cities across the country. Many of those arrested were subjected to horrific abuse and some perished under the hands of their interrogators. As for the government side, their loss was estimated to be as high as 2,500 but that remained a rough guess we could not verify. These were the estimates of Sudan's official armed forces and not ours.

Despite its failure to achieve its prime objective of unseating the government, OLA has been a miraculous event. For years and years, the government, mimicked by some international circles, argued that JEM was a politically strong movement but had little to show in terms of military might. Overnight, OLA settled that debate and the military supremacy of JEM became a reality even for its staunchest opponents. Omdurman afforded JEM an opportunity to stock up on military hardware and to replenish its dilapidated fleet with superior captured vehicles.

The defamatory image of JEM and other Darfur Movements as steeped in savagery and banditry was also destroyed. OLA showed to all in the Capital that JEM was the most disciplined rebel force Africa had ever seen. There wasn't a single case of JEM soldiers targeting civilians, stealing their properties or attacking non-military amenities. JEM soldiers marched through the famous Libyan Market in Omdurman without a single break-in to a single shop or a hint of attack on pedlars. The soldiers bought tea, coffee, soda water and food with their own money, a practice virtually unknown for Sudan's Armed Force when in action. Citizens in Omdurman streets welcomed JEM rebels with their distinctive celebratory cheers, clapping and ululation. Terms like 'owners of the land have finally arrived', 'you deserve to rule the country' and 'we are tired of the monkey in the Presidential Palace' were shouted at the rebels.

OLA raised the ceiling for our fellow movements in Darfur. Though not by design, the invasion threw other Darfur movements into total disarray and ushered in negative consequences lasting to this day. Almost all other movements went in the direction of recriminations, desertion of members and multiplications into smaller units. JEM emerged as the ultimate beneficiary and had attracted high calibre figures from many of the other movements. At least 27 groups and movements flocked to join JEM and some of the newcomers like Jamous, Mansour Arbab and Shogar have risen to the top of JEM leadership. Their arrival enriched JEM and boosted its national and international profile.

OLA did not only attract rebels to JEM. It also brought in new ethnic groups that were traditionally mistrustful of the rebel movements. The Arab groups, in particular, flocked to JEM and the list included: the Aggrieved Soldiers Group, Tergem, Beni Halba, Misseriya, Slamat, Awlad Zeid, Ireigat and even the Mahameed of Musa Hilal. Many of those groups and particularly the latter, provided a source of Janjaweed recruitment before. The arrival of the new groups changed the political address used by JEM beyond recognition. All of a sudden, JEM had new members who resented the use of the term Janjaweed and openly declared: 'no more of that word please, we are now members of JEM, full stop'. Perhaps 85% of the Arab ethnic groups of Darfur are now represented in JEM. OLA put an end to the very division of Darfur into Arabs and Africans.

OLA also boosted membership of JEM beyond Darfur borders and copper fastened its essence as a national organisation. Kordofan, in particular, took the lead with strong representation at the highest level with fine Commanders like Mohamed Bahr of Misseriya and Mohamed Bilail of the Hamar ethnic groups. Our membership increased sharply in other parts of the

Sudan as well, such as the Northern, the Eastern and Central Sudan. Of course JEM always had a small but fine contingent from South Sudan, with commanders like Almaz and Thong Thong, both from the Dinka ethnic group. Last year, JEM celebrated Christmas with drums, dances, bible prayers and the slaughtering of camels and sheep in acknowledgement of the multi-religious aspect of JEM. It was a wonderful experience that gave our Muslim soldiers a great taste of sharing Christmas with their Christian comrades for the first time in their lives.

Remaining within national circles, OLA presented Sudan's political parties with a perplexing situation. All of them were caught off guard as they were duped by the powerful government media and were of the opinion that JEM was impotent to reach their den in Khartoum. The SPLM in particular found itself in difficult circumstances. It was a member of a coalition of the Government of National Unity and yet it sold itself as a champion of the very marginalised people who were invading Khartoum. It was a difficult situation particularly in light of the SPLM's strategy to sustain the Comprehensive Peace Agreement at almost any cost. If that meant sacrificing non-southern marginalised people, so be it. Kiir, First Vice President and President of Government of Southern Sudan issued a feeble statement indicating his readiness to defend Khartoum. Well, he wasn't tested in that but his position was understandable given the constitution of the Government of National Unity. Subsequent revelations, relayed in meetings with JEM, offered sympathetic but equally non-committal messages. It was true that the SPLM wanted to retain the status quo until the Referendum scheduled for January 2011. The SPLM was certainly a beneficiary of OLA. The act of humbling the Government gave the SPLM much latitude for challenging al-Bashir's foot dragging in the implementation of the CPA.

OLA threw the northern-based parties into utter confusion, steeped in fear and apprehension. With the exception of the Popular Congress Party, the Umma Party of Al Mahdi, the Democratic Unionist Party (DUP) and the Sudanese Communist Party buried their differences and closed ranks behind al-Bashir to varying degrees. Every single one of them saw Khartoum as their safe garrison against the people of the margin and had used it in a similar fashion in the past. However, the humbling of al-Bashir came as a blessing to all of them. It encouraged them to crawl out of their holes and expanded the space al-Bashir allowed them in the past. After all, OLA revealed the nakedness of their emperor. It exposed the fallacy of al-Bashir's invincibility and laid bare the alleged tight security he had put in place. OLA ended their years of hibernation and pushed them to muster their courage and act as opposition parties per se.

The Arab world was particularly incensed by OLA in the first few days. Egypt expelled our senior officials and Libya showed its displeasure with the operation. However, their negative response soon abated and they resumed their relationship with JEM and not without some sort of quiet admiration. Both Egypt and Libya had little other choice. The stability of Sudan affected them and they needed to play a role in the resolution of Darfur conflicts. OLA affirmed the centrality of JEM to any resolution in Darfur and there was no way for these neighbouring countries but to maintain the channels of communication with JEM.

The USA have always approached JEM with contempt. Since the start of the conflict, the USA adamantly refused to allow JEM a fair hearing, suffocated its voice and employed every strategy to strangle it. OLA forced the superpower to review its strategy, at least to some extent. As a testimony to that, OLA opened the doors of the US State Department and the Pentagon to JEM. For the first time in the history of our organisation, these two iconic departments received our delegation in their offices in Washington. That was one of the miracles of OLA.

Our revolution is very successful. It has raised the level of consciousness to its highest position in the land. OLA has taught all the oppressed people in the Sudan that, if necessary, the struggle can be taken to Khartoum, the heart of power and decision-making. If we decide today to halt our revolution and disband JEM, I will still be very satisfied. The struggle has been firmly placed on the right path towards democracy, rule of law and respect of human rights and dignity. The march of the marginalised people towards justice and equality has begun and is simply irreversible. Al-Bashir will be relegated to the dustbin of history, marked 'last dictator to rule Sudan.'"

Appendix

The Black Book: Imbalance of Power and Wealth in Sudan

Authors: Seekers of Truth and Justice
Translator: Abdullahi Osman El-Tom, Ph.D.

MARCH 2004

General Translator's Introduction

In 2000, a mysterious book appeared in the streets of Khartoum under the title, *The Black Book: Imbalance of Power and Wealth in the Sudan*. The mystery of the book was strengthened by its impeccable method of distribution necessitated by the regime's firm grip over information in the country. The launch of the work consisted of a once-off distribution at gates of major mosques, following Friday prayers. Soon after, the circulation of the book gained momentum. Spontaneous photocopying made the book available all over the country and abroad. The book soon became the most talked about document in the country. It was the envy of any writer, the world over. Most readers had never seen the original copy of the book. Illiterate people too became familiar with the book as it was debated in every gathering.

The thesis of the book is simple but disturbing. Using statistics, the authors claim that Sudan is controlled by only one region (the Northern Region) with just over 5% of Sudan's population. Within this hegemonic region, power is monopolised by only three ethnic groups. The book then gave detailed statistics about the hegemony of the Northern Region over the whole country. All of Sudan's Presidents and Prime Ministers came from this region. Members of this region also controlled all key positions in the country ranging from ministerial posts to heads of banks, developmental schemes, army, police, etc.

Part Two of the Black Book did not appear until August 2002. Unlike Part One, this one joined the global world and appeared in a website (Sudanjem.com). Part Two has less text but more statistics. Altogether, there are more than 200 Tables in it.

As of last year (March 2003), some of the activists involved in the preparation of the book took up arms against the government. The armed uprising, referred to as the Darfur Conflict, constitutes Africa's youngest civil war. To date, this war has resulted in 800,000 displaced, 120,000 refugees and no less than 100,000 fatalities.

In translating the Book from Arabic, I did my best to remain faithful to the text. Passages that are of no value for the English reader have been eliminated. These passages are either steeped in Arabic metaphors, or elsewhere presuppose some knowledge that is particular to Sudan's history, folklore and traditions. Retaining them in the text would require substantial explanation that lies beyond my role as a translator.

March 22, 2004
Translator

DEDICATION

To those who filled themselves with haughtiness, arrogance and feelings of superiority, wishing to silence our Black Book or elsewhere replace it with their White Book.

To the Sudanese people who have endured oppression, injustice and tyranny.

To the majority of the Sudanese people who still suffer marginalization of power and wealth

To those, who work for justice and equality with extreme honesty and self-denial.

Introduction to Part 1

We present our work, *The Black Book; Imbalance of Power and Wealth in the Sudan*, as a document that exposes the performance of successive governments which ruled the Sudan in its recent history. This book is not driven by narrow motives that seek to incriminate or blame certain circles in the country. Rather, it is a critical work that documents objective facts that are hard to overlook.

This book is an exposé of the injustice that was visited on the Sudan by successive governments that ruled it since independence −1956. The pattern of injustice remained almost the same throughout, irrespective of the political orientation of the incumbent government: secular, theocratic, dictatorial or - presumed - democratic. They all displayed the blatant favouritism of one particular circle in the Sudan to the detriment of all others. The favoured part of the Sudan attracted disproportionate attention, care, services and developmental resources from those successive governments. That favoured part of the Sudan is the Northern Region where most of the ruling elite come from.

For the purpose of this Book, we have divided the Sudan into five Regions:

1. Northern Region: Current River Nile and Northern States.
2. Eastern Region: Gadharif, Kasala and Red Sea States
3. Central Region: Gezira, Sinnar, Blue Nile and Khartoum States
4. Southern Region: Upper Nile, Bahr Alghazal and Equatorial States
5. Western Region; Kordofan and Darfur States

In its blatant favouritism for the Northern Region, successive governments in the Sudan have systematically breached the rights of its other citizens. They deviated from the principle of treating all citizens as equal. They have accused others of racism, a crime that they have themselves practised every single day of their reign.

Successive governments of the Sudan have thus lost their credibility and have, therefore, disqualified themselves in so far as support of the Sudanese citizens is concerned.

In presenting this Book, we intend to shed light on this unfortunate reality and make it crystal clear for all.

The new Millennium is now approaching, full of hope and optimism. Due to its recent history, Sudan meets the new Millennium steeped in poverty, illiteracy, disease and lack of development. Despite this, the Sudanese citizens are invited to rise to the challenge by appropriating the same powers that have so far crippled them. Let them do that in collaboration with other global citizens whose rulers have delivered and prepared them for the new area.

INTRODUCING SUDAN

Sudan lies between lines 14 and 38 Latitudes East, and 4 and 22 longitudes North of Equator. It occupies 968,000 square miles. The White Nile, the Blue Nile and River Nile zigzag their way through it and provide a rich source of water and food. Sudan is surrounded by nine countries: Chad, Central African Republic, the Democratic Republic of Congo, Uganda, Kenya, Ethiopia, Eritrea, Egypt and Libya. The position of Sudan between these countries is a source of wealth but equally of trouble. Sudan also touches the Red Sea with a shore that extends to 309km. Sudan has three distinctive geographical zones. North of Latitude 16 is barren desert. Below Latitude 16 is a region rich in equatorial climate. In between is a savannah belt that gets drier the further you move to the north. These distinctive climatic variations have their impact on Sudan's populations and their cultures.

The last National Census, 1993, put Sudan's population at 24,940,703 with an annual growth of 2.6. For the purpose of this document, we divide Sudan into five regions. Each of these Regions has its historical, cultural and administrative particularities. Furthermore, each Region consists of a number of provinces – see Table 1.

TABLE 1: POPULATIONS OF SUDAN REGIONS

REGION	STATES	POPULATION	%
Eastern	Kasala, Gadharif, Red Sea	3,051,958	12.2%
Northern Region	Northern, River Nile	1,291,620	5.3%
Central Region	Gezira, Sinnar, White Nile Blue Nile, Khartoum	8,829,367	35.4%
Western Region	Kordofan, Darfur	7,912,285	31,7%
Southern Region	Upper Nile, Bahr Alghazal Equatorial	2,845,480	11.4%
TOTAL	-	24,940,703	100%

Khartoum, the capital, which we include within the Central Region has a population of 3,413,034. More than half of this population come from deprived regions of the West and the South, primarily fleeing lack of development and war.

NATURAL RESOURCES

Sudan is rich in natural resources, particularly agriculture and forestry. It has no less than 120,000,000 acres suitable for agriculture. Only 16,000,000 of that are currently under use. Agriculture is still dependent on rainfalls despite ample underground water. The economy of Sudan now rests on rain-fed agriculture. Major products include peanuts, hibiscus, sesame seeds, watermelon seeds and gum Arabic. Animal resources, like camels, sheep and cattle also feature in Sudan's export economy.

Recently, petrol and gold have been added to the export wealth while the country still awaits exploitation of other minerals such as copper and natural gas.

ADMINISTRATIVE DIVISION OF THE COUNTRY

A recent constitutional Decree, 1996, divided the Sudan into 26 States. These are then grouped into five Regions: three in the East, two in the north, five in the centre including the capital Khartoum, six in the west and ten in the south. Each State has its government and its legislative council. If we exclude the South that is still a war zone, whatever development we can find in the country has been confined to the north, Khartoum, part of the Central Region and an even smaller part of the Eastern Region. The entire Western Region now lacks a single developmental scheme that could support one province for a single week. The oil refinery in Alobeid, Western Region is now classified as a national project. As such, its proceeds are controlled by the central government in Khartoum. The oil wells at Abu Jabra and Maglad, also in the Western Region have also come under a similar strategy. Employment of local people is confined to digging these wells. All jobs, from drivers and above, are filled by labour imported from outside the area. Officers of the security personnel and most of their foot soldiers are carefully selected from one known ethnic category, so that not a single Dinar goes to those who do not deserve it.

DEFINING THE STATE AND ITS AUTHORITY

Scholars rarely agree on how to define the State. Nonetheless, a consensus occurs regarding its essence and constituents. Calsen refers to the State as "a constellation of the nation". Others like Degi stress the constituent elements of the state like territory, population and authority. Gamal Albanna, another scholar in this field identifies five requirements for an Islamic state:

1. Primary aim is to develop the land (*Allah said I am making a Khalifa on the land. Koran, Albaqra Sura, Chapter X, verse mm*)
2. An environment that guarantees freedom (no compulsion on faith)
3. Justice as the main axis of State operation (*be just for justice is the essence Almaida Sura* of piety; Prophet Mohamed said: I have declared injustice haram <strongly disallowed> for myself. I also made it haram for all of you so never be unjust)
4. Decision making rests on consultation (seek views of stakeholders first and when you act trust on Allah)
5. Rule based on Allah's diktat (Let the rule be based on Allah's words and let Allah be the sole God to be worshiped in the land)

In our modern understanding, a state must display the following:

a. Territory: A defined territory that is endorsed by relevant international authorities.
b. Population: People who live in the specified territory.
c. Ruling authority: The power that is legitimated to administer the territory and its people according to specified laws and institutions. The ruling authority must demonstrate its commitment to work for peace and for meeting basic needs of all within its domain.

Conditions for accepting the authority of the ruler/ governing power:

The authority must demonstrate its commitment to maintain sovereignty of land against foreign intruders; treat its citizens equally; afford them peace and protection; guarantee dignified life; spread freedom and dignity, and must enable its citizens to fully participate in conducting their public affairs. All that is to take place within an environment that is conducive for participation of all without religious, ethnic, skin colour and gender discrimination.

The State authority cannot only implement that without commitment to its national laws that regulate and divide powers among different State organs. Most important here is the separation between State powers, and in particular the political, the judicial and the legislative.

REFLECTION ON STATE AUTHORITIES

EXECUTIVE POWERS

These are vested in specified offices that are delegated to implement state policies regarding economy, politics, social needs, security and general State-citizen relationship. Executive state organs must be subordinate to and committed to State legislative authorities.

LEGISLATIVE AUTHORITIES

Duty of these bodies is to enact laws regarding state policies in the political, social, economic and ethical areas. Legislative authorities draw their laws from religious, traditional, natural and legal conventions. Legislative authorities should be committed to observe these laws that they make and ensure that State and the public will do like-wise.

JUDICIAL AUTHORITIES

Their main function is to implement the law, protect the State constitution and restore justice when disputes occur. These authorities can only function adequately if they maintain and respect their neutrality and independence. Independence of the judiciary should be maintained throughout its entire hierarchy ranging from its lowest level like the village court to its highest level, the Constitutional Court.

MEDIA

Media has only recently surfaced as an important player in modern State apparatus. It has since carved itself a space that has become indivisible from any democratic State. The media now plays an important role in guarding State laws and constitution, similar to the role traditionally played by legislative powers. Moreover, it has become the avenue for channelling complaints regarding abuse of power, infringement of law by the powerful, corruption and injustice at large. It has also become a voice for the powerless and a guardian for the dispossessed.

EXAMPLES OF IMBALANCE OF DIVISION OF POWERS

State authority is a source of power and a tool for achieving prosperity for all within the nation. Sudan state is no exception in this regard. At its independence, 1956, it declared itself a sovereign State and raised its flag together with other slogans promising full commitment to work for good of all within the new nation. Discrepancy between slogans and actions however appeared as early as the birth of the new state. Politics in Sudan was sectarian and dominated by the two religious houses, the house of the Mahdis and the house of the Mirghani. These two Houses corresponded (still do) to the two leading political parties: the Umma Party of the Mahdis and the Democratic Unionist Party of the Mirghanis. In some ways, these two Houses inherited colonial powers on golden plates. In order to monopolize power in the country, both of these parties pegged leadership of their parties to that of their respective religious sects. Hence party leader were also sect leaders. The trick was that sect leaders had to come from families of the founding fathers of these religious sects. Moreover, a second strategy was also devised for the same purpose that was of exporting electoral candidates. Important party members from the centre were encouraged to stand for elections in areas other than their own. The practice effectively made it impossible for the emergence of locally born political representatives. These practices ensured domination of the Northern Region over all other regions in the country and established a pattern for dealing with so-called marginalized areas. The pattern also meant that legislative powers remained under personnel who were primarily drawn from the Northern Region.

The pattern described above had (and still has) wide ramifications for political representation in the country. High representation of the Northern Region in the central government remained the same, irrespective of knowledge gains in other regions and changes in the political environment. Throughout its recent history, the Northern Region was represented by well over 50% at the central government. Its representation occasionally climbed over 70%. From independence to this day, not a single Prime Minister/ President came from any region other than the Northern Region. Like many Third World countries, Sudan was ruled by several governments which came to power through a coup. However, several attempts to overthrow governments failed simply because its leaders came from regions other than the Northern Region.

In the coming pages, we will examine the influence of the State on distributions of power in the country. Figures and statistics will be used to explain that, as follows:

MINISTERIAL REPRESENTATION

For the period 1954 to 1964, 73 ministerial positions were served in central government in Khartoum. The distribution of different regions is presented in Table 2.

TABLE 2: MINISTERIAL POSITIONS 1954 – 1964

No	REGION	POSITIONS	OVERALL %
1	Eastern Region	1	1.4%
2	Northern Region	58	79%
3	Central Region	2	2.8%
4	Southern Region	12	16%
5	Western Region	0	0%

To place Table 2 within perspective, we have to refer to Sudan's population some decades ago. The 1986 census is the mostly reliable for our purpose.

TABLE 3: SUDAN POPULATION DISTRIBUTION, 1986

No	REGION	POPULATION	%
1	Eastern Region	2,212,779	11.8%
2	Northern Region	1,016,406	5.4%
3	Central Region	4,958,038	26.5%
4	Southern Region	4,407,450	23.7%
5	Western	6,072,872	32.6%

Note that 5.4% of Sudan's population were represented at 79.5%, executive/ ministerial posts in the Khartoum, the seat of the central government. During that period, five different governments took office but the pattern remained the same.

TABLE 4: NATIONAL GOVERNMENTS 1954-1964

No	GOVERNMENT	YEARS	LEADER
1	1st National Government	Jan. 1954	Alazhari
2	2nd National Government	1955	Alazhari
3	3rd National Government	1956	Alazhari
4	Kkaleel Government	1958	Khaleel
5	1st Military Government	1958-1964	General Aboud

All of the above governments based their powers on the aforementioned religious sects. General Aboud was no exception.

Following a national uprising in October 1964, Aboud was removed from office, thus giving way for a democratic government 1964-1969. Let us now see what happened to executive representation under democratic Sudan.

TABLE 5: MINISTERIAL POSITIONS 1964-1969

REGION	POSITIONS	%
Eastern	2	2.05%
Northern	55	67.9%
Central	5	6.2%
Southern	14	17.3%
Western	5	6.2%

The total number of constitutional posts for this period was 81 positions. Strangely enough, Western and Southern Regions contributed a lot to bringing the interim Government under Presidency of Sir Alkatim who prepared the country for 1964's elections. Those who were selected as ministers from the Central Regions were of Northern Region origin.

THE REIGN OF NIMEIRI, 1969-1985

Nimeiri's military rule was characterised by internal instability leading to numerous cabinet reshuffles. In total, 115 ministers served in his different cabinets with the following regional distribution (see Table 6):

TABLE 6: MINISTERIAL POSITIONS, 1969-1985

REGION	POSITIONS	%
Eastern	4	2.5%
Northern	79	68.7%
Central	19	16.5%
Southern	9	7.8%
Western	4	3.5%

Despite tremendous differences between the politics of Nimeiri and what went before him, domination of the Northern Region seemed to have persevered. A continuous flow of new ministerial blood and the reputation of Nimeiri as a man for all Sudan did not dent the supremacy of the Northern Region. This situation increased the hegemony of the Northern Region and sabotaged all attempts to attract development projects for non-Northern Regions. A good example was the defunct Kafra road that was meant to connect Libya with Alfashir, the capital of Darfur in the Western Region. The desert highway road was to be financed wholly or partially by Libyan aid. Obstruction against construction of this road is well known to all and caused tremendous loss of faith in the central government in the Western Region.

Following the demise of Nimeiri, a transitional military government took over for a year to prepare the country for election. The new government operated under what came to be known as the Transitional Military Council, headed by Swar Aldahab. Table 7 shows the constitution of the Transitional Military Council.

Table 7: Transitional Military Council, 1985-1986

Region	Positions	%
Eastern Region	0	0%
Northern Region	21	70%
Central Region	3	10%
Southern Region	5	16.7%
Western Region	1	3.3%

Please note that the Sudanese Army has always been a national institution. That aspect of the army faired rather poor with the regional representation of the Council.

The Transitional Military Council was aided by senior members of the Transitional Government, but an imbalance remained as before.

SECOND DEMOCRACY 1986-1989

The Transitional Military Council kept its word. It organized democratic elections and handed down power to the new elected Prime Minister, Sadiq Almahdi, whose cabinet are presented in Table 8.

Table 8: Ministerial Positions of Almadhi's government 1986-1989

Region	Positions	%
Eastern Region	3	2.6%%
Northern Region	55	47.4%
Central Region	17	14.7%
Southern Region	15	12.9%
Western Region	26	22.4%

Almahdi was the only leader who came close to perfection in the sense of forming a government in which all Regions were reasonably represented, notwithstanding the evident over representation of the North. Although the North was also over represented and the cabinet did not reflect the regional distribution of Sudan's population, we would like to acknowledge that Almadhi deserves praise for having gone further than any other Sudanese leader. Almahdi was also the first head of State who allowed the important Ministry of Finance and Economy to be headed by someone from the Western and the Central Region. These were Ibrahim Mansour and Omer Bashir from the Western Region and Omer Nur Aldayim from the Central Region.

AL-BASHIR'S GOVERNMENT OF NATIONAL SALVATION, 1989 TO DATE

Almahdi was overthrown in a bloodless coupe, 1989 and a new government took office under the name "Revolution/Government of National Salvation". As the West has been instrumental in the formation of the ideology that inspired Al-bashir to take over, the Westerners were rewarded without challenging the domination of the North. This was reflected in the constitution of the Military Command Council that controlled Sudan for Al-bashir's early years (see Table 9):

TABLE 9: REVOLUTIONARY COMMAND COUNCIL, JUNE 1989

REGION	POSITIONS	%
Eastern	0	0%
Northern	10	66.7%
Central	0	0%
Southern	2	13.3%
Western	3	20%

When the power was settled in favour of the new government, the domination of the Northern Region was restored in line with previous political traditions. The new government operated under the slogans: Civilizational Project, Islamization of life, equality and justice and the principle of citizenship. Unfortunately, these slogans soon gave way to unchallenged hegemony of the Northern Region. The evidence for that can be seen in the cumulative high office positions that continued until the last cabinet reshuffle 1999. A total of 202 personnel are computed in Table 10.

TABLE 10: CONSTITUTIONAL/ MINISTERIAL POSITIONS, JULY 1989-DECEMBER 1999.

REGION	POSITIONS	%
Eastern	6	3%
Northern	120	59.4%
Central	18	8.9%
Southern	30	14.9%
Western	28	13.8%

As Table 10 shows, representation of the Northern Region reached 59.4% for a population that constituted 12.2% only. As such, the destiny of the remaining 87.8% of the population was subordinate to the will of the 12.2% who came from the Northern region. The Northern Region itself was not (and still is not) a homogeneous entity. In fact, the North contained many groups that were subject to the same level of injustice and marginalization, like the Manaseer and Mahas. The first claimed Arab descent while the latter were of Nubian origin. In fact the entire Northern Region was dominated by only three ethnic groups that also dominated the whole country. These were the Shaygia, the Jaalyeen and the Danagla.

Table 10 also indicates that the National Salvation government had come to wreck what it had formed before during its first Military Command Council. In so doing, the government demonstrated its inability to deviate from established patterns of injustice, despite the slogans that it raised during its inception. Even in situations when the government appointed some personnel from other regions, it opted for those migrants from the Northern Region. Appointing those of Northern origin resident in other region was a blatant attempt to deceive people and give the illusion of some air of regional representation.

In December 1999, following power struggle between Albashir and his ideologue Turabi, the government rushed in a number of Presidential Decrees. Changes contained in these Decrees showed little attempt to avoid tribalism and regionalism as promised in earlier slogans. This was (still is) evident from the choice of new recruits to high offices ranging from the Republican Palace to ministers and State governors. To dispel any accusation of bias in our analysis, we present below a list of their new appointees indicating their portfolios and regions. We will start with the Republican Palace (see Table 11)

TABLE 11: STAFF OF THE REPUBLICAN PALACE (DECEMBER 1999)

No.	Name	Position	Region
1	F. Marshall Omer A. Albashir	President	Northern
1	Ali Osman M. Taha	First Deputy President	Northern
3	George Kangoor Arop	Deputy President	Southern
4	Dr. Riak Mashar	Assistant President	Southern
5	Dr. Ibrahim Ahmed Omer	Assistant President	Northern
6	Lt General Bakri Hasan Salih	Minister for presidency of the Republic	Northern
7	Dr. Ahmed Ali Imam	Presidential Advisor	Northern
8	Dr. Nafayi Ali Nafayi	Peace Affairs	Northern
9	Dr. Altayib Mohamed Kheir	Security Affairs	Northern
10	Dr. Suaad Alfatih	Women and Children	Northern
11	Abdel Basit Sabdarat	Legal Politics	Northern
12	Salah Mohamed Salih	Water Resources	Northern

Following defection of Riak Mashar to SPLM, the Palace remained with 11 members one of them from South Renk (Southern Region) while the rest originated north of Aljaile (town north of Khartoum). Those 11 were left to rule a country that extended from Geneina to Port Sudan and from Nimuli to Halfa. One wonders how those people could have imagined the rest of the country and how many of them had seen a third of it, let alone its entirety.

Where was the justice promised by the government, in the field of division of power and where was the transparency often reiterated by official media? What was the role of this immense army of advisors? Had these appointments any purpose other than appeasing relatives and fellow members of ethnic groups? What are the jobs that they could do and which could not be accomplished by Ministers of the Federal Government (as distinct from State governments)?

Below are names of the Ministers of the Federal government for the post-Turabi period (12/1999 onwards; see Table 12)

TABLE 12: FEDERAL MINISTERS

NAME	REGION
F. Marshall Omer Ahmed Albashir	Northern
Ali Osman Taha	Northern
George Kangoor Arobe	Southern
Dr. Riak Mashar	Southern
Ibrahim Ahmed Omer	Northern
Dr. Mustafa Osman Ismael	Northern
Lt. general Abdel Rahman Siralkhatim	Northern
Dr. Mohamed Kheir Alzibair	Northern
Dr. Awad Ahmed Aljaz	Northern
Dr. Zibair Bashir Taha	Northern
Dr. Abdalla Hasan Ahmed	Northern
Dr. Qutbi Almahdi	Northern

Abdel Basit Sabdarat	Northern
Dr. Abdalla Mohamed Seed Ahmed	Northern
Ali Ganmar Osman Yasin	Northern
Kamal Ali Ahmed	Northern
Badria Sulaiman	Northern
Abdel Haleem Almuaafi	Central
Abul Gasim Mohamed Ibrahim	Central
Dr. Ghazi Salah Aldin Atabani	Central
Ahmed Ibrahim Altahir	Western
Lt. General Tigani Adam Tahir	Western
F. .Marshall Ibrahim Sulaiman	Western
Mekki Ali Bilal	Western
Dr. Alhaj Adam Yousif	Western
Mohamed Tahir Bilal	Eastern
Dr. Lam Akol	Southern
Alison Manafi Magaya	Southern
Joseph Malwal	Southern

Reading the Table above, the regional representation of the Federal Government is summarised below.

TABLE 13: REGIONAL REPRESENTATION OF THE FEDERAL GOVERNMENT, 1999.

REGION	NO OF POSITIONS	%
Eastern Region	1	3.3%
Northern Region	18	60.1%
Central Region	2	6.6%
Southern	4	13.3%
Western Region	5	16.7%

Chapter 4
Examples of Imbalance of
Division of Wealth

Division of wealth in any society is an important barometer of the legitimacy of its political system. A political system that thwarts its laws to preside over an unfair distribution of wealth is bound to witness rapid erosion of its legitimacy. Modern Sudan is a case in point here. We have carefully monitored the division of wealth in this country over a long time and have come to conclusions that are neither assuring, nor comfortable to confront. We have handed our leadership to those with whom we have fought together for our common national objectives. We have paid our allegiance and put our trust behind the appealing slogans which they raised and continued to do so until the present time. We have finally come to the conclusion that as we demand restoration of our rights, we are demanding the impossible. We are like a person who tries to straighten a shadow without thinking about the crookedness of the object that casts it in the first place.

During his reign 1958-1964, General Aboud extended the railway line to Nyala, opened two technical schools in Geneina and Nyala and two secondary schools in Alobeid and Port Sudan. Having done that, he then proceeded to redirect the rest of Sudan's wealth for the development of Central and Northern Sudan. Agricultural schemes of Khasm Algirba and New Halfa were given special attention, having been reserved for those who were displaced by the construction of the Oswan dam. The population of New Halfa were compensated for losing their original homeland and for the mistakes that were committed by previous rulers. However, had they not been indigenous to the Northern Region, they would not have been compensated.

249

Since independence, Sudan has known several development plans. Among them we mention the Ten Year Strategic Development Plan, the Five Year Development Plan and the Three Year Development Plan. Billions of dollars have been spent on these Plans, forming our present foreign debts and a burden on current and future generations. Most of these Plans have been located in the central and northern Sudan and we are yet to see a return that benefits all those who are responsible for its costs. Many of the schemes that emerged within these developmental plans have remained a drain on the national economy at the expense of all but the Central and the Northern Regions. A critical look at government budget allocations in recent years shows the perils of such development investment and the special place northern Sudan occupies in the hearts of Sudan's ruling elite. Not a single State in non-northern Sudan exceeded 36% of its already budgeted allocations. The Northern States were different. Actual disbursement shows that they never dropped below 60% of their planned budget allocations. Apparently, there is a story behind that. The Ministry of Economy and Finance has always been dominated by the Northern Region. Top positions like Minister, the Deputy Minister, Secretary Generals and chief administrators usually come from the North. Even the positions of drivers are also reserved for school drop outs from the North. The rest of the country has to contend with jobs in the Ministry as cleaners, tea makers, guards, etc. In such an environment, it is not surprising that non-northern States find it impossible to receive their allocated budgets while the Northern States have their facilitators at every venue inside the Ministry. This is very clear when you look at how universities and higher institutes have been performing. In particular, that is evident from the growth of Universities of Kasala and Kadugli (Eastern and Western Region respectively) with their peer Universities of Shandi and Atbara (Northern Region). The first category experienced difficulties while the last prospered even when the economy was facing major difficulties. Universities of the north benefited from substantial donations from public companies that were headed by officials from the Northern Region. Their donations were in fact borne by the same tax payers who come from the whole of the Sudan.

For our purpose here, we will focus on the major characteristics of the Three Year Programme that was ratified by the Government of National Salvation for the years 1999 to 2002.

4.1. THE AGRICULTURAL SECTOR

The irrigated sector, as distinct from the rain-fed sector of agriculture is an important component of the Sudanese economy. It has been developed with dual aims in mind. Firstly, to boost the export sector through an increase in cash products like cotton, peanuts, sesame seeds, etc. Secondly, to augment food production as a strategic sector, thus increasing production of millet, maize, rice, lentils, etc. This sector has been fortunate in attracting substantial funding, both from national resources as well as borrowed capital from abroad. Substantial expenditure in this sector also goes for infrastructure like dams, roads, bridges, etc. Despite substantial investment in this sector, its revenue to the nation is minuscule compared to rain-fed agriculture. The latter has remained a backbone of the export sector contributing peanuts, sesame, gum Arabic, hibiscus and animals. The high cost and low return aspect of the irrigated sector led to its continuous subsidization by the rain-fed sector. We note here that the irrigated sector dominates in Central and Northern Sudan while rain-fed agriculture features mainly in other parts the nation.

Lack of investment in areas of rain-fed agriculture has been a major cause of migration to cities, including the capital Khartoum. The North has however been protected against population depletion. Production of wheat has been moved from central Sudan to the north. Movement of wheat to the north has led to the emergence of new dams like Kajabar, Hamadab and Marawi and God knows what other dams follow. Palm trees that were displaced by these dams have been compensated for and many of them have been transported for transplantation in Khartoum. Compare this level of care with the impact of similar dams and irrigated schemes in the East like Algash, Tokar and Sitait. Displacement in these areas still remains unaided to this day. This is despite the fact that the east is among the least developed part of the country. Its population suffers disease, hunger, illiteracy and drought.

4.2. RAIN-FED AGRICULTURAL SECTOR

Two broad sub-sectors can be identified here; these are the traditional rain-fed sector and the mechanised rain-fed sector. This sector plays an important role in food production. Its programme of work is intended to include investment in agricultural services, pest control, provision of seeds and agricultural extension in general. A number of schemes were established within this sector with the aim of developing deprived areas and rehabilitating the drought stricken savannah belt. Rather than augment this sector, the government ordered liquidation of a number of them. These schemes are:

1. Nuba Mountain Agricultural Corporation
2. Blue Nile Agricultural Corporation
3. White Nile Agricultural Corporation
4. Agricultural Machinery Corporation
5. South Kordofan Agricultural Corporation

6. Mechanised Agriculture Corporation]
7. Jebel Mara Rural Development Scheme
8. Western Savannah Corporation

Note that none of these schemes were in the north and that these schemes were liquidated and not sold or privatised. We add that these schemes were developmental and their contribution was not confined to economic gains. As such we are bound to conclude that scrapping of these schemes indicates that development work is the preserve of north Sudan. Others have to contend without it. None of those in power who are calling for equality and development in the country have noticed the plain fact: that since Independence, Darfur has not secured a single developmental scheme which could finance a single Local Administrative Area for three months. Moreover, most agricultural schemes in central Sudan are headed by personnel from the north or otherwise those whose origin is in the north. Examples here include the Gezira Scheme, Rahad Scheme and the Blue Nile Scheme.

In addition to liquidation of public amenities, the government also resorted to aggressive privatisation that benefited certain circles. Below is a list of privatised public properties:

1. Abu Naama Jute Factory
2. Sata Company
3. Blue Nile Cardboard Factory
4. Port Sudan cotton Spinning Factory
5. Rabak Ginnery
6. Sudan Mining Corporation
7. Red Sea Hotel
8. Kosti Guest House
9. Sudan Cotton Company
10. White Nile Tannery

11. Ria Sweets Factory
12. Kirrikab Factory for Sweets
13. Khartoum Tannery
14. Kuku Company for Milk
15. Sudan Hotel
16. Atbara Gest House
17. Sudan Trade Bank

Some of these companies were sold to certain institutions and for logical reasons. For example, there was nothing wrong in selling Sudan Hotel to the National Fund for Social Insurance. Other sales were however of a dubious nature. Abu Naama Jute Factory was sold for Ls 800m, a sum that was well below its commercial value at the time, considering land, assets and machineries included in the sale. We were less surprised when we realised that the buyer was none other than Hashim Haju. Other sales also followed the same pattern. In sharp contrast to Hashim Haju, the Sudanese businessman Mohamed Jar Alnabi who is from the Western Region had to struggle exceptionally hard to survive with the regime. His effort to establish an oil refinery, a strategic acquisition at the time, did not endear him to the system. Had it not been for his resilience, he would have been driven into exile like the Ex-Governor of Darfur, Ibrahim Draig.

Sadly, the above shows how the country is run and how the public coffer is manipulated to serve certain individuals and certain areas. Barriers are also erected to prevent leaders from other parts of the Sudan to succeed. A good example is the endemic problem of drinking water in Alobeid city. It was the governor Ibrahim Alsanusi who decided to confront this problem and who tirelessly worked for a final solution. As an indigenous to the area, he was not allowed to reap the result of his work. At the last moment, he was replaced by one of those who deserve to succeed, a governor from the Northern Region.

We all remember the case of Alshafay Ahmed Mohamed who worked together with his predecessor Hasan Mohamedain to establish the National Council. Both of them are from the west and hence had to give way to a northerner to preside over the established Council.

Dr. Ali Alhaj is another example of the manner in which leaders are penalised for not originating in the north. He was the dynamic figure in the peace negotiations as well as establishment of the Federal Government System. In each of these successes, he was removed to allow other to crown his success. Despite continuous character assassination, Dr. Alhaj remained national in his work and did not give way to racist, regional or nepotistic temptations.

4.3. AGRICULTURAL SERVICES

Sudan has great agricultural potential that is yet to be adequately explored and properly exploited. So far, expenditure on agricultural and horticultural extension has been confined to the irrigated sector. For the farmers in the west, east and southern Sudan, agricultural extension is a riddle for which they do not qualify. Other agricultural services directed at small farmers have also been available only to farmers in northern Sudan. Using the Emergency Law that has been enacted recently, even the meagre resources available to the Western Region have been further eroded. Its only pest control plane has been removed on the account that pests did not pose a real threat to agriculture in Sudan. The definition of what constitute pests and grass-hoppers as provided by the Agricultural Pest Control Office in Darfur was not convincing enough for the bureaucrats in Khartoum. The result is that the Office lost the plane and its running cost and kept the grass-hoppers and other pests.

4.4. NATURAL RESOURCES

Environmental protection and reversal of desertification have been among the salient stated strategies of natural resource policies in the Sudan. Policies have been drafted with the aim of arresting desertification, protecting and promoting forests, locating new sources of cooking fuel and other similar measures. However, actions on the ground followed a different trend. Jebel Mara forests, rich savannah grass in western Darfur, Blue Nile natural endowment and the gum Arabic belt are all directed to serve the overseers of the Federal government and their affiliates in the north.

4.5. ANIMAL RESOURCES

As a desert plain, the Northern Region has no significance in the field of animal export. Nonetheless, amid international concern about animal disease, the north was declared – internationally- by the government as an area free of animal diseases. Soon after that, centres of animal exports in the west were moved to the north together with appropriate infrastructural rehabilitation to facilitate that. Officials who contested this, were either subjected to threats or enticement to buy into the new policy of the day. Customs tax centres were also moved to the north. Despite difficulties, truck drivers involved in animal export had no choice but to clear their departing products in Dongula in the north. Financial services also had to follow suit. The Branch of Sudan Bank in Alfashir in the west had to give way to a Bank Branch in Dongula despite the fact that Alfashir is a capital animal producing region, while Dongula is a capital with no land to support animal wealth and a population that is half of that of Alfashir.

4.6. INDUSTRIAL SECTOR

Rural industry and industrial villages have been among the fundamentals of development in India and China. The pattern of development is different in the Sudan. Rural areas are emptied of their labour force in favour of bloated cities where the meagre industrial development is concentrated. In these industrial centres, power is firmly placed under the grip of a northern elite who in turn continue depleting other regions of their wealth. This is despite the fact that substantial natural wealth like iron, petrol, gas, gold, etc. is found in these non-Northern Regions. As long as we continue along this road, it will be a long time before we can see a single industrial scheme outside Central and Northern Sudan. It is in these Regions that we find military industry, currency coinage, Bank Notes Printing Houses, electricity, sugar industries, etc.

4.7. WATER AND ENERGY

It is hard to write about expansion in oil drilling and development in the Sudan without a deep feeling of embarrassment. The Ministry of Energy is now, more or less, a homestead of extended families belonging to one ethnic group from the north. This group and its commercial companies have monopolized all the high paying posts in the venture, down to that of drivers. The local people who supposedly own the oil land are to be content with digging trenches and laying the oil pipelines.

Water development is currently reserved for the eve-expanding capital Khartoum. The rest of the country is left out, dying of thirst as well as of diseases like malaria, **kalazar, bilharsiasis,** and other water borne diseases.

4.8. TRANSPORT AND COMMUNICATION

Current State strategies in the field of transport and communication state the following objectives:

a. Integration and improvement of transport and communication services through continuous maintenance of existing national roads and constructions of new national networks that are geared towards economic development.
b. Orientation of new investment towards schemes and projects that have clear objectives, leading to increased production.
c. Encouragement of the private sector to invest in transport and communication through sales of public amenities or joint ownership with the State.
d. Making full use of available opportunities, resources and potentials to that effect.

Despite the obvious importance of transport and communication and their centrality to any developmental plans, they have been relegated to marginal ministries that have no power in the allocation of national budgets. As such, the Department of Transport and Communication has remained subordinate to other ministries like Economics and Finance that operate under different and often contradictory agenda.

While the principle of integrated transport network is agreeable, the term itself has remained either ill defined or simply meaningless. It is not at all clear whether the policy of integration is meant to feature at the level of the nation, the State or a combination of both.

The strategy refers "correctly" to projects and schemes that have clear objectives without being specific as to the delineation of these objectives. Lack of clarity in these issues leaves options open for individual ministers to tune national budgets to their regional and ethnic interests. For example, the Saudi Islamic Bank earmarked funding for the Western Road (Alobeid-Alfashir). That fund was later redirected by the Ex-Minster of Finance Dr. Abdel Wahab Osman to the Wheat Project in the north. This project came as a policy of indigenising production of wheat in northern Sudan, a project poorly competing with the national economic gains of the Western Road. This is despite the fact that previous economic feasibility studies had been in favour of the Alobeid – Alfashir Road and equally the Southern Kordofan Nuba Circular Road.

4.9. EDUCATION AND OTHER DEVELOPMENTAL SERVICES

Tremendous disparities obtain with regard to educational services. While certain areas have seen a progressive increase in the number of children who have progressed to secondary schools, pupils in the marginalized areas have been grounded at the primary level. In the State of Western Darfur, primary schools remained closed for two years for lack of books and staff salaries. In fact, books rotted in their stores due to lack of funds. There were more than one and a half million people in the State of Western Darfur. Only 4,211 children were able to sit for the final Primary School Examination. This number is less than the number of primary school leavers in a single Local Administrative Area in the Northern Region. The comparison becomes somewhat bizarre when we realise one Local Administrative Area in Darfur has a population that is equal to that of the entire Northern Region.

At a different level, marginalized regions also suffer at the hands of the State Support Fund. This is a national fund expected to fund State developmental projects. As decreed, no State is to access the fund without sound feasibility studies. While this principle makes sense, it is here that northern control reigns supreme. Poorer states are deprived of the cost of feasibility studies and hence credible competition for funding. The result is obvious. The National State Support Fund channels its entire budget to funding projects other than those in the Western, Southern and Eastern Regions.

NATIONAL FINANCIAL INSTITUTIONS

Stat financial sector is one of those sectors that have remained off limits for Regions other than the Northern Region. For example since the establishment of the Bank of Sudan in 1956 and to this day, not a single manager of this Bank came from the Eastern, Western or Southern Region. Those managers who came from the Central Region were in fact members of ethnic groups that originated in the Northern Region. The case of the management of the Bank of Sudan can equally be applied to other major Sudanese banks like Khartoum Bank, Sudan Agricultural Bank and the Industrial Development Bank. The appointment of managers to newly created banks and other recent public financial institutions in the country also followed the same patterns.

A. CHAMBER OF ZAKAT (ISLAMIC TAX)

Although this institution is essentially religious, it too could not escape the process of northern ethnification, i.e. bringing it under the control of the Shaygia, the Jaalyeen and the Danagla. Recent power struggles between the Secretary General and the Manager General of the Chamber of Zakat can be seen within the same process.

B. Sudan Development Corporation

No Manager General of this institution ever came out of the three ethnic groups (Shaygia, Jaaliyeen and Danagla).

C. Islamic Trust

Throughout the life of Al-bashir's government, this institution has never been led by any manager from outside the Northern Region.

D. Integration Fund.

This fund was originally established for noble reasons. However, when it was placed under directorship of someone from a region other than the favourite one, all hell broke loose. All obstacles were placed in front of the non-northern director in order to ensure his failure. This went on despite the impressive profile of the Director who succeeded in attracting Libyan firms for Red Sea fishing, provided badly needed school uniforms, and created employment for a substantial number of people. Despite the appeals of many prominent people, the Fund was liquidated and replaced by Sineen Corporation under the same directorship. When Sineen proved its success like its predecessor under the same previous manager of Integration Fund, opposition was revived. A new manager from the right region was put in charge. His school drop-out relative now works there and is paid in Dollars, not in Sudanese Dinars, in a UN sponsored project.

Control of the Northern Region over public finance also features in other institutions including the following:
+ Application of Sharia (Islamic Law) Fund
+ Philanthropic Corporation for Support of Armed Forces

+ Martyr's Organisation
+ Call for Jihad
+ Bir (Charity) International
+ Martyr Zibair Charity Organisation
+ Marine Lines
+ Philanthropic Insurance Fund

NATIONAL INSURANCE FUND

This Fund was originally headed by Major General Mahir Sulaiman who is not from the Northern Region. His success attracted the attention of his relevant Federal State Minister who was not pleased by what he saw. Confrontation followed and the Fund was subsequently restored to the control of the Northern Region.

When we raise issues of injustice, corruption and mismanagement, we get accused of racism. Others are free to abuse their position and enrich themselves at the expense of the tax payers in the open. Let us give one example known to many in the country. A General Director of a well known public company was moved to head another public company. He requested payment of $17,000 as travel expenses for himself and his family against his new company. He also demanded payment of the same expenses from the previous company insisting payment be made outside the state. He also applied for two years house rent in cash, 7 million Sudanese pounds for furniture, in addition to his salary of 10 million pounds a month. All was paid to him to the last penny. Now, this explains why higher jobs have to be reserved only for those from the Northern Region and that there is little or nothing left for other regions.

COMMITTEE FOR DIVISION OF RESOURCES

The discovery of petrol and resumption of its export introduced a new type of wealth into the nation. This new wealth was territory bound and could not be simply relocated to the Northern Region. Something had to be done to ensure the flow of wealth to the North and there was no dearth of genius thinking in our leadership. It was easy. A Presidential Decree was to take care of it. Here is the Decree in full:

"Decree No 334, Year 1999: Creation of a National Committee, for drafting proposal for division of national wealth between Federal Government and State governments.

Following examination of the recommendations of the Minister for Federal Relations and the decision of the Council of Ministers No. 839, Year 1998 regarding the constitution of a National Committee for division of national resources between the Federal Government and state governments, and in accordance with Constitutional Articles 113, 114, and 115, The President decrees the following: Establishment of a National Committee for the purpose of drafting proposals for division of national wealth between the Federal and State Governments. The committee consists of the following:

TABLE 14:

NATIONAL COMMITTEE FOR DIVISION OF NATIONAL WEALTH

No	Name	Position	Region*
1	Abdel RahimMohamed Hamdi	Chair	Northern
2	Dr. Taj Alsir Mahjoub	Secretary and Member	Northern
3	Dr.Taj Alsir Mustafa	Member	Northern
4	M. General Abul Qasim M. Ibrahim	Member	Northern
5	Dr. Khalid Sir Alkhitim	Member	Northern
6	Farah Hasan	Member	Northern

7	Dr. Ahmed Majzoub Ahmed	Member	Northern
8	Abdel Wahab Ahmed Hamza	Member	Northern
9	Dr. Jumaa Kindi Komi	Member	Western
10	Dr. Swar Aldahab Ahmed Iesa	Member	Northern
11	Jamie Leemy	Member	Southern
12	Dr. Ali Abdalla Ali	Member	Northern
13	Dr. Awad Alseed Alkarsabi	Member	Northern
14	Moses Mashar	Member	Southern
15	Ahmed Ibrahim Turuk	Member	Eastern
16	Dr. Izzaldin Ibrahim Altigani	Member	Northern
17	Dr. Mohamed Kheir Alzibair	Member	Northern
18	Gindeel Ibrahim	Member	Northern
19	Fareed Omer Medani	Member	Northern
20	Badr Aldin Taha	Member	Central
21	Sheikh Beesh Kore	Member	Southern
22	Omer Taha Abu Samra	Member	Northern
23	Dr. Bidoor Abu Affan	Member	Northern
24	Tariq Mubarak	Member	Northern
25	Hasan Jiha Ali	Member	Northern

* added by authors

TABLE 15: SUMMARY OF TABLE 14, DIVISION OF NATIONAL WEALTH

REGION	SEATS	%
Eastern	1	4%
Northern	19	76%
Central	1	4%
Southern	3	12%
Western	1	4%

The hegemony of the Northern Region over all other Regions is obvious (Table 15). Such a powerful position enables the committee to become yet another tool for furthering interests of the Northern Region.

FUTURE VISIONS

The injustice and mal-division of power and wealth in the Sudan have eroded the sense of belonging to a unified society where all could aspire to share benefits as well as duties and responsibilities. The situation in which citizens compromise their personal interests in return for peaceful co-existence with others in their society is what early philosophers called "the social contract". The inability of our leaders to respect this simple fact has undermined the very fabric of our Sudanese society. Ensuing problems include the following:

Internal Immigration

Emigration is not natural and is rarely built into the culture of most Sudanese societies. Most rural Sudanese prefer to remain in their homes surrounded by their familial human and non-human surroundings. However, rural people are also thinking individuals who have to evaluate their options and ensure reasonable future prospects for themselves and their future generations. The current pattern of development in the country consists of a continuous transfer of surplus from rural areas to cities and from marginalized regions to the Northern Region. Not surprisingly, rural villages, particularly in marginalized regions are emptied of their human resources. Young people in particular vacate these rural centres in their desperate attempt to flee poverty, illiteracy and ill health. At the same time, shanty towns continue to grow, forming belts of poverty around every city in the country. This has serious implications at both ends.

Rural areas have been depleted of their human resources, particularly the young, energetic and creative. Cities in turn cannot cope as their resources, employment opportunities and services collapse under pressure of ever growing populations.

EDUCATION LOSS

Educational services have so far been concentrated in Khartoum, the Northern Region and certain parts of the Central Region. Within these locales, the cost of education has been beyond the riches of the average citizen. In fact, education has become more and more confined to the wealthy, including families of high government employees. Much more recently, education has devolved and been placed under State authorities. Many States rose to the challenge and used the then rationed sugar to finance their own State education. That policy did not last for long. The government moved to remove sugar from the list of rationed items and left it to the open market. Obviously, that deprived States of the revenue raised by tax on sugar, thus resulting in the collapse of the educational system in all marginalized States. To this day, not a single leader called for an examination of this costly problem with a view to overcoming it. We are bewildered about previous slogans of compulsory education and free education that preceded it and equally free medicine. It is our contention that the Northern Region is deliberate in inflicting illiteracy and ignorance on others as part of its project of hegemony over the Sudan.

SPREAD OF DISEASES

The Eastern Region gives a good example of the collapse of the health system in the Sudan and the impotence of those who are in charge in Khartoum. Kasala and Gadharif cities offer health services to patients that are four times their capacity – by national standards. They both depend on internally generated and charity funds in offering their services. National health system and national disease prevention have receded to feature only on National TV programmes. Instead, the government introduced the so-called national health insurance for those who can pay for it. The policy led to a mushrooming of health hotels, some rated at five stars and above, for the haves, leaving the have-nots forgotten.

The entire State of Western Darfur has two medical specialists in the field of obstetrics and gynaecology, one in Geneina and the other in Zalengay. They are to serve a population of 1,650,000 aided by few medical students who visit the area for training and for escaping mandatory Military Service.

Let us give one example to highlight the dearth of heath services in Darfur. The city of Geneina got its first x-ray machine in 1978. It lasted for seven or so years. Since the 1980s, patients requiring x-rays had to leave for Nyala or Khartoum for an x-ray, a trip of two to six days for those who could not afford air tickets.

Erosion of Peace and Harmony

Continuous feelings of injustice, favouritism in job allocations, removal of employees from their jobs to leave room for designated individuals, etc, have all created a sense of exclusion and lack of belonging. This has led marginalized people either to opt out of the society or to turn to violence to redress their perceived maltreatment. Loss of faith in authority and leadership is eating quickly into the very fabric of Sudanese society.

Regional Associations

Continuous marginalisation of certain groups and loss of faith in all those in power have resulted in new ways of campaigning for basic rights. Among others, this has led to a mushrooming of ethnic and regional groups acting in desperate attempts to remind leaders of their role regarding distribution of power and wealth in the country, albeit in a peaceful manner.

Thus we have the Bija Association, the Nuba Mountain Associations, Darfur Associations, in addition to lobby groups from within the National Parliament.

ARMED MOVEMENTS

Over the years, various regional armed movements appeared in the Sudan in response to injustice perpetrated by successive Khartoum governments. These movements include Anyana I and II, Sudan Liberation Movement, Sudan People's Liberation Force, Ingessana Coalition and the Nuba Mountain Freedom Movement. For all of these groups, independence of the country was no more than a replacement of one master by another.

LOSS OF CREDIBILITY

Loss of credibility is certainly the worst outcome of the imbalance of power and wealth in the Sudan. Lack of faith in Khartoum government has been a phenomenon felt in all Regions, with the North being the only exception. Since Independence, the last of Government of Sadiq Almadhi was perhaps the only exception whereby some efforts had been shown in its mild attempt to be somewhat inclusive. Other governments have simply pursued policies of entrenching domination of the north and a few areas in the centre over all other Regions. The last government (Al-bashir's National Salvation) is certainly the worse of them all. It combined politics with ethnicity and Islam to concentrate power and wealth in the North. In this project, regionalism goes hand in hand with racism, and often disguised under an Islamic flag to realise government goals. Not only is Sudan further dissected into clearly power demarcated Regions, cities too are falling under the same onslaught. They are to be ruled by their inhabitants who originate in the North.

ISLAMIC RULE

Since its accession to power, this government has been selling itself as a champion of Islam. Its major slogan has been to construct a State built on "Knowledge/Science and Submission to Islam". Such a State is expected to be a model of justice, equality and faith. We hereby offer our understanding of the five major criteria for an Islamic State:

I. Land Development (I'mar Alarad)

As stated in the Koran, man is the successor of God on earth and is entrusted with its development (I'mar). The State or the government is the body that is in charge of this, and is thus obliged to devise and implement and monitor all relevant policies. In so doing, the state is to guarantee equality of all in front of the laws in the designated land. In accordance with God's Decrees, the State should ensure prevalence of justice, protection of the weak and eradication of oppression and excesses of the powerful. The State is obliged to fight nepotism, favouritism and unfair enrichment of the few at the expense of the many. Only through this can the State claim to be an adequate representative and a true successor to God.

II. Freedom

The second criterion of an Islamic state is freedom as enshrined in the Koran ("Let there be no compulsion in religion: Truth stands out Clear from Error" The Cow, Verse 256). The divine order presupposes freedom, treating the individual as a thinking citizen capable of making his/her own choice. It is only through enabling people to make their choice that we can guarantee true debate and exchange of different views that can lead to effective use of resources and continuous development. Islam teaches us to exchange views in a free environment that is cleared of autocracy and the arrogance of rulers; an environment in which the ruler is subordinate to the consensus based on the views of ordinary citizens. This was the method used by the Prophet and his immediate Successors. Abu Bakr, the first successor of the Prophet once said: "Support me if I do well and correct me when I make mistakes". His successor Omer also followed the same philosophy. As narrated, a woman opposed one of his decisions and quoted the Koran to support her argument. Omer listened and obliged saying "Omer erred while a woman delivered the right view. All of you are more knowledgeable than Omer". This is why early Islamic States prospered and extended their borders from the Indian to the Atlantic oceans.

Arrogant leaders who refuse to listen to their subjects are ultimately bound to depend on oppressive institutions if they are to preserve their power. In their pursuit of remaining in power, these leaders, hypocritically, preach the word of God and His Prophet amid corruption, injustice and tyranny. They however never recall the words of the Prophet, "If Fatima, the daughter of Mohamed is to steal, I will certainly amputate her hands as we do to other thieves". Such a level of justice requires an environment of freedom, in which citizens guide their leaders in the fight against corruption, nepotism and injustice.

III. JUSTICE

The third criterion of an Islamic state is working for justice. Justice is the essence of good leadership. With its presence, a non-Muslim king can guarantee his success in a Muslim community. In its absence, even the most Muslim king is bound to fail. The high place accorded to justice is indicated by its use as one of the Most Beautiful Names of Allah.

Justice that we require in the Sudan is that which includes division of resources in accordance with equality of all citizens as members of the same country. Resources are to be divided according to clearly laid down priorities that are transparent and evident to all. Such an approach ensures consensus and evades a feeling of deceit. Control over public wealth should be open to all, according to their experience, qualifications and commitment to national interests. It should not be a preserve of a select minority whose members collaborate to protect the corrupt and shield the incompetent. While stories of corruption in many public financial institutions are rampant in the state, the response of the government seems to have focused on a limited number of Banks. So far all of these Banks and financial institutions seem to have links to regions other than the Northern Region.

Justice presupposes opening high office to all qualified citizens. This is not the case in the Sudan. The presidency of the State, for example, has always been monopolized by certain ethnic groups. This has been the case throughout the independent history of the Sudan. The position of the head of the Judicial System has also fallen under the same menace of ethnic domination.

IV. Shura (Consultation)

We introduce shura or consultation as the fourth criteria of Islamic rule. Islam stipulates the use of consultation for all public decision, small and big alike. The shura is a right of all citizens in an Islamic state, and the ruler is clearly instructed to avoid monopoly over decision-making. The following are clearly stated in Islamic jurisprudence:

a. The ruler is obliged to consult widely prior to taking any major decision. Consultation allows the ruler to examine various views that are not available to a single individual, no matter how wise he or she is. Consultation also allows the ruler to avoid pitfalls of emotional and personal inclinations.

b.   Absence of consultation leads to abuse of power and breeds arrogance. Major decisions are public matters and should not be left to a single individual. The duty of all citizens to contribute to such consultation is so crucial in Islam that it is elevated to the level of Jihad: "The best of Jihad is a word of truth to an unjust ruler". In a modern state, civic societies, organisations, media, etc are all obligated to speak out and contribute to the decision making process.

V. Adoption of Divine Governance

Our fifth criteria of an Islamic rule is its conformity with divine laws as enshrined in the Koran, the prophetic traditions and other good sources of Islamic jurisprudence. In this system, submission must be made to God alone and this applies to the ruler and ruled alike. The rule here is nothing but a means towards entrenchment of the rule of God. Islam grants the ruler rights but equally that comes with corresponding responsibilities. So heavy are these responsibilities and that is what led Omer, the second successor of Prophet Mohamed to lament: "I wish the mother of Omer had never given birth to me", or elsewhere: "You are all shepherds and every one of you is responsible for his flock, (i.e. subjects) in front of Allah".

The ruler must constantly remember that he has to defend himself on the Day of Judgement. Those who are related to the ruler should not abuse that relationship. Early Islamic rulers had always seen such a relationship as a liability and never an asset. A relative of a ruler is the first to be called to action and first to be scrutinized for mistakes. Such was the case with Abdullah, the son of Successor Omer who was the first to be investigated and the last to receive his legitimate share in his community.

HARVEST OF DESTRUCTION

We would like to step back and contemplate our rulers and assess the reasons behind their incessant control over power and their use of every possible means to retain it. Here are our conclusions:

I.

Those who are in charge seem to have succumbed to their inner instinct for power and domination over others. Their thirst for power has gone out of control as they have lost the most important bridle and that is fear of God and the After Death punishment.

Success in monopolising power for so long gave members of this group an illusion that their rise to power is natural and is a direct result of their superior capabilities, tribes and regional origin. Nothing better illustrates this more than their popular saying that they will never hand in the Sudan to anybody except to Jesus and the Messiah at the end of the current world (Biblical story about end the world). Despite their deceptive talk about Islam, those people have never learnt the simple Islamic teaching that it is God that gives power to some and takes it from others; that it is God's kingdom that lasts, not that of His creatures.

II.

In the last ten years or so, corruption has become so widespread that it has acquired semi legal status. Corrupt government officials are often described as being involved in establishing themselves or forming personal wealth. Public office has become a means of acquiring villas, expensive cars or extra wives. Corruption has become indivisible from the state that the judicial powers have to be tuned to protect the inner circle of the favoured ruling elite. Thus sharia (Islamic) laws are interpreted to strike those who encroach on private property and spare those who steal from the public coffer. The result is obvious. Amputation, flogging and extended prison sentences became the punishment of the destitute and dispossessed who are likely to steal a transistor radio, a watch or a camel. The same laws and hence punishment do not apply to those who steal public money no matter how huge are their unlawful gains. The latter group of thieves consists of government officials, mostly among the favoured few. Not surprisingly, poverty of the many grew in tandem with growth of wealth as illustrated by the substantial increase in new villas, expensive cars and luxurious life styles. This trend is very much facilitated by the unwritten code which enabled a small minority to control almost all key financial positions in the country and at the same time preside over the judicial system.

III.

While enriching themselves, our ruling elite also devised a system where nobody else succeeded in the economic sphere. The rule is simple: "starve your dog and he will follow you", forgetting that it is God who provides sustenance and that He can change fortunes overnight. Moreover, the ruling elite also made sure that success in any public office can only be achieved if the occupant is a Northerner. Otherwise all obstacles are erected to guarantee failure of the government official. This pattern has been clear in the following cases:

1. The old colonial dictum: "divide and rule" has been refashioned by our leaders and used in various ways to achieve their objectives. It is combined with other tactics including rewards and punishment, character assassination and embellishment of puppets. Turning ethnic groups against each other has been a dominant feature of this current regime. Examples here are the Hadandwa against the Beni Amir , the Ara'ar against the Bashshareen and the Halanga against the Rashida in the Eastern Region. The Southern Region has also been placed under the same destructive policy. Thus you witness the Dinka against the Nuer, the Nuer against the Shiluk, the Manari against the Zande and so forth. The Western Region also has its share of this divisive policy culminating in conflicts between the Nuba and the Misairiya, the Slamat and the Silaihat, the Zaghawa and the Rizaigat and so forth. Much more recently, a broader gulf has been created in Darfur between the so-called Arab alliance on one hand, and the Zurga (black) on the other. The national security offices and media have also been employed to stimulate such conflicts. This has often appeared in the form of false statements attributed to certain groups threatening their neighbours.

2. Character assassination of leaders who raise their voices against injustice has also been a favoured tactic for this government. The case of Colonel Malwal, the southern leader, is known to all in the Sudan. He was removed from the Command Council of the government following false accusations staged-managed by the certain circles within the regime.

    When this government came to power, General Bakri Almak rose to become the Governor of the

Eastern Region. False accusations similar to those Colonel Malwal received were devised to remove him from office. The only reason we can come up with is that he comes from the wrong Region (Central).

Khartoum State also saw similar dirty plays. Khartoum has always been seen as an extension of the Northern Region. That became clear when Badr Aldin Yhia who is Khartoumese became State Governor of Khartoum. He was subjected to vicious attack using the might of the government controlled media. Attacks continued until he was finally driven out of office. He was replaced by Dr. Majzoub Alkhalifa who is a Northerner, and even better, famous for his chauvinistic inclination to the Jaalyeen ethnic group.

CONCLUSION

This document, which is factual in its data and clear in its representation, is compiled under the slogan: "Justice". Our choice is inspired by the fact that "Justice" is derivative of one of the 99 Names of Allah. Justice and equality are our demand. Remaining within Islamic slogans which this government claims to raise, we indicate that Justice and equality are essential to full realisation of Islamic rule. That can only be realised if we are prepared to speak out for justice. Prophet Mohamed once said: "Support your brother whether he is just or otherwise". In so saying, he does not mean standing with injustice. Rather, what he meant is that you take your unjust brother by the hand, and direct him to where justice lies. This is our approach to our brothers in the Northern Region.

Sudan was not ideal at its Independence in 1956. Resources were poorly divided among different provinces at the time. By the 1970s some progress was made and gaps between provinces started narrowing. The last two decades have been different. Resources were moved to concentrate in the Northern and Central Regions leading to impoverishment of other regions. As a result, marginalized regions became zones of out migration. People had to move in search of food, work and services, all of which concentrated in the Central and Northern Regions.

Destruction of marginalized regions has become a feature of Sudan, particularly during the reign of the current regime. Much worse are the marginalized regions that are governed by Governors who do not come from the Northern Regions. The State of Western Darfur and the State of Southern Kordofan provide a good example in this regard. They were both brought to their knees simply because their governors happen to be from within these States. When they were replaced by Governors of the "right northern ethnic groups", funds were released and the States became somewhat functional. So acute was this problem that a pillar of the government in Khartoum declared Federal funding for western states could only be released following his personal approval, verbal or written. Such policies are bound to lead to alienation and subsequent loss of faith in Sudan as a united country. We hereby appeal to those who are in charge to think hard. We understand that justification has always been made to behave in a specific way but the road to move forward is clear. Our northern brothers must be ready to compromise and be fair in dealing with national issues. They must open up government positions to all, according to their qualifications, competence and experience. They must stop abusing their positions and halt directing illegitimate resources to their own home areas. Finally, they must follow the justice slogans that they raise in their public speeches.

This regime took over (1989) to augment the project of Sudan as a model of an Islamic state. Muslim countries everywhere are looking at our experience. Its failure is a failure of

Islam as much as it is a failure of Sudan as a nation. It is time to set things right. We appeal to those who are in charge to unite and commit themselves to justice, the protection of individual rights and the promotion of the national interest.

Lastly, we would like to promise our readers more detailed information in Part II of this work.

REFERENCES

1. Directory of Federal Rule, Sudan.
2. People Councils Publications.
3. Presidential/Republican Decrees
4. Public Administration Regulations
5. Sudan National Census, 1993.
6. Mekki Othman, 1997. Finance Ministers Whom I knew. (No Publishing House).
7. IMF Publications.
8. Institute for Arab Planning. Kuwait. March 1997.
9. National Fund for Social Insurance, Sudan.
10. Sudan Sea Lines Publications.
11. Newspaper articles
12. Diplomatic Publications, Jordan.
13. Bank of SudanPublications
14. World Bank Publication.

Part 2
(FIRST APPEARED AUGUST 2002)

INTRODUCTION

As it has appeared in the communiqué of the Justice and Equality Movement (JEM), Sudan's unity is now under serious threat. This is a result of injustice perpetrated by a small group of autocratic rulers. There is however a glimpse of hope to avert this imminent crisis and move towards a comprehensive solution of Sudan's impasse. As envisaged, this can take place through a comprehensive congress that encourages free and honest debate, under the slogan "Be just: That is Next to Piety" (Koran, Almaaida, Verse 8).

Using statistical evidence, we will proceed to expose injustice in the Sudan, particularly during the current reign of "the Government of National Salvation". We will show how different regions of the country have been made to endure mal-distribution of power, wealth, services and development opportunities.

Information contained in our statistics is drawn from various sources including government official and strategic reports, presidential Decrees and Chambers of Sudan Civil Service.

And now to the talk of figures:

TABLE 16: SUDAN POPULATION, THE YEAR 2000

No	State	Estimated Population	Annual Rate of Growth
1	Northern	582,000	1.75%
2	River Nile	900,000	1.96%
3	Red Sea	721,000	0.52%
4	Kasala	152,000	2.51%
5	Gadharif	1409,000	3.337%
6	Khartoum	4740,000	4.04%
7	Gezira	3374,000	3%
8	Sinnar	1173,000	2.59%
9	White Nile	1476,000	2.59%
10	Blue Nile	636,000	3.01%
11	North Kordofan	1483,000	1.55%
12	West kordofan	1124,000	1.7%
13	South Kordofan	1111,000	1.38%
14	North Darfur	1455,000	2.23%
15	West Darfur	1777,000	2.38%
16	South Darfur	2760,000	3.48%
17	Upper Nile	1453,000	0.93%
18	Bahr Alghazal	2321,000	2.36%
19	Equatorial	1261,000	1.01%
Total		31,181,000	

For simplicity of information presentation, we have opted to revert to older division of Sudan into Regions. The following terms are hence used:

1. Central Region: Gezira, Blue Nile, Sinnar and White Nile States,
2. Darfur Region: North and South Darfur States,
3. Southern Region:
   a. Old-Equatorial Region: Bahr Aljabal, East and West Equatorial States,

b. Ex-Bahr Alghazal Region: Buhairat, Warab, East and West Bahr Alghazal and

c. Upper Nile Region: Jungole, Unity and Upper Nile States.

4. Khartoum Region: National Capital Khartoum,

5. Kordofan Region: North and South Kordofan States,

6. Easter Region: Consists of Red Sea State, Gadharif and Kasala States,

7. Northern Region: The River Nile State and the Northern State.

TABLE 17: REGIONAL POPULATION COMPOSITION

No	Region	Population	% of Population
1	Central Region	6,559,000	20%
2	Darfur Region	5,992,000	20%
3	Southern Region	5,035,000	16%
4	Khartoum Region	4,740,000	15%
5	Kordofan Region	3718,000	12%
6	Easter Region	3,655,000	11%
7	Northern Region	1482,000	5%
Total		31,181,000	100%

TABLE 18: REVOLUTIONARY COMMAND COUNCIL

No	Name/Region	Khartoum	Eastern	Kordofan	Northern	Darfur	Central	Southern
1	Brigadier O. H AlBashir	-	-	-	*	-	-	-
2	Brigadier Zebair M Salih	-	-	-	*	-	-	-
3	Brigadier Faisal A Abu Salih	-	-	-	*	-	-	-
4	Brigadier Tigani A Al-Tahir	-	-	-	-	*	-	-
5	Brigadier Osman H. Ahmed	-	-	-	*	-	-	-
6	Colonel Bio Yo Kwan	-	-	-	-	-	-	*
7	Colonel Ibrahim N Iydam	-	-	*	-	-	-	-
8	Colonel Dominic Kasiano	-	-	-	-	-	-	*
9	Colonel M Malwal Arob	-	-	-	-	-	-	*
10	Colonel Sulaiman M Sulaiman	-	-	-	*	-	-	-
11	Colonel Faisal M Mukhtar	-	-	-	-	-	*	-
12	Coleonel Salah M Karrar	-	-	-	*	-	-	-
13	Lt. Colonel Mohamed A Khalifa	-	-	-	-	*	-	-
14	Lt. Colonel Bakri H Salih	-	-	-	*	-	-	-
15	Major Ibrahim S. Al-Din	-	-	-	*	-	-	-
	Total	0	0	1	8	2	1	3

When the Council was dissolved, all of its members were retired except four who happened to be from the Northern Region.

TABLE 19: SUMMARY OF TABLE 18

Total / Regions	Ktm	East	Krdfn	Nrth	Dfr	Cent	Sth
15	0	0	1	8	2	1	3
%	0%	0%	7%	53%	13%	7%	20%

282

TABLE 20: PRESIDENT – OF THE REPUBLIC–, DEPUTIES AND ASSISTANTS OF THE PRESIDENT

-	NAME	POSITION HELD	DURATION
1	F. Marshal O. H Albashir	President	19/7/89 to date *
2	F. Marshal Zibair M Salih	Vice President	9/7/89- 12/2/98
3	M. General George K Arob	Vice President	14/2/94 – 14/10/00
4	Ali Osman Taha	First Vice President	17/2/98 to date
5	Prof Moses Machar	Vice President	12/2/01 to date
6	Dr. Riak Mashar	Assistant President	6/8/97 – 24/7/01
7	Prof. Ibrahim A. Omer	Assistant	25/1/20 – 8/7/00
8	Angelo Beeda	Council Coordinator	24/7/00 – 12/2/01
9	General Malwal Deng	Council Coordinator	12/2/01 to date
10	Mubarak Alfadhil	Assistant President	20/8/02 to date
11	Dr. Riak Gaye	Council Coordinator	Not supplied- to date

* To date of compilation of original manuscript.

TABLE 21: SUMMARY OF TABLE 20

TOTAL / REGIONS	KTM	EAST	KRDFN	NRTH	DFR	CENT	STH
11	2	0	0	3	0	0	6
%	18%	0%	0%	27%	0%	0%	55%

TABLE 22 : PRESIDENTIAL ADVISORS

NAME	AUTHORITY POSITION	FROM	TO	REGION
Ahmed Ibrahim Al Tahir	Legal Advisor	14/2/94	8/3/98	Kordofan
Brig. Bakri Hasan Salih	Security Advisor	17/4/96	8/3/98	Northern
Lt. Colonel Ibrahim Shams Al Din	Defence Advisor	17/4/96	12/12/97	Northern
Prof Ibrahim Ahmed Omer	Advisor for Islamization*	24/4/96	2/12/96	Northern
Dr. Ahmed Ali Imam	Advisor for Islamization	8/3/98	To date	Northern
Adam Tahir Hamdoun	Peace Advisor	8/3/98	6/3/99	Darfur
Dr. Isam Siddeeq	Economic Advisor	8/3/98	24/1/00	Northern
Dr. Nafiy Ali Nafiiy	Peace Advisor	6/3/98	8/7/00	Northern
Abdel Basit Sabadrat	Political and legal Advisor	24/1/00	22/2/01	Northern
Lt.General Altayib M. Kheir	Security Advisor	24/1/00	19/5/03	Northern

Name	Authority position	From	To	Region
Ahmed Ibrahhim Al Tahir	Peace Advisor	10/7/00	20/2/01	Kordofan
Badria Sulaiman	Legal Advisor	22/2/01	To date	Khartoum
Mekki Ali Bilal	Peace Advisor	22/2/01	10/5/01	Kordofan
Mahdi Ibrahim	Political Advisor	22/2/01	13/6/01	Central
Dr. Ghazi Salah Al Din	Peace Advisor	13/6/01	To date	Khartoum
Lt. General Abdel Rahim M. Hesain	Advisor of President	10/7/00	22/2/01	Northern
Prof. Suaad Al Fatih	Advisor for women and children	18/2/00	22/2/01	Northern
Dr. Qutbi Al Mahdi	Political Advisor	13/6/01	To date	Northern
Badr Al Din Sulaiman	Economic Advisor	8/7/01	To date	Northern
Ali Hasan Taj Al Din	Advisor for Africa	No date	To date	Darfur

* Islamization is a translation of the Arabic Term "tasseel"

TABLE 23: SUMMARY OF TABLE 22

Total / Regions	Ktm	East	Krdfn	Nrth	Dfr	Cent	Sth
20	4	0	3	10	2	1	0
%	20%	0%	15%	50%	10%	5%	0

TABLE 24: PRESIDENTIAL MINISTERS

Name	From	To	Region
Colonel Abdel Aal Mahmoud	30/6/89	?	Northern
Brigadier Abdel Rahim M Hesain	13/7/1994	8/3/1998	Northern
M. General Bakri H. Salih	8/3/1998	24/1/2000	Northern
M. General Bakri H Salih	24/1/2000	10/7/2000	Northern
L. General Salih M. Salih	22/2/2001	To date	Northern
Altayib M. Kheir	19/5/2003	To date	Northern

TABLE 25: SUMMARY OF TABLE 24

Total / Regions	Ktm	East	Krdfn	Nrth	Dfr	Cent	Sth
6	0	0	0	6	0	0	0
%	0%	0%	0%	100%	0%	0%	0%

TABLE 26: MINISTRY OF INTERNAL AFFAIRS

NAME	FROM	TO	REGION
Brigadier Faisal Abu Salih	9/7/1989	13/4/1991	Northern
Lt. General Zubair M Salih	13/4/1991	18/1/1993	Northern
General Abdel Rahim M. Hesain	18/1/1993	13/7/1994	Northern
General Altayib M. Kheir	13/7/1994	16/8/1995	Northern
General Bakri H. Salih	20/4/1996	8/3/1998	Northern
General Abdel Rahim M Hesain	8/3/1998	10/7/2000	Northern
Lt. General Alhadi A. Mohamed	10/7/2000	22/2/2001	Northern
General Abdel Rahim M Hesain	22/2/2001	To date	Nortehrn

TABLE 27: SUMMARY OF TABLE 26

TOTAL / REGIONS	KTM	EAST	KRDFN	NRTH	DFR	CENT	STH
8	0	0	0	8	0	0	0
%	0%	0%	0%	100%	0%	0%	0%

TABLE 28: PRESIDENTIAL COUNCIL MINISTERS

NAME	FROM	TO	REGION
Lt. Colonel Al-Tyaib Ibrahim M Kheir	9/7/89	30/8/91	Northern
Dr. Awad Al Jaz	30/8/91	18/8/95	Northern
General M A Salah Karrar	20/4/96	8/3/98	Northern
Colonel Mohamed Alamin Khalifa	8/3/98	15/12/99	Darfur
Abdalla Hasan Ahmed	24/1/00	8/7/00	Northern
F. Marshal Abdel Rahim Sir Alkhetim	10/7/00	22/2/01	Northern
Lt. General Alhadi A. Mohamed	22/2/01	To date	Northern
Badria Sulaiman	25/1/00	22/2/01	Khartoum
Martin Malwal Arob	22/2/01	To date	Southern
Abdalla Safi Alnour	?	To date	Darfur

TABLE 29: SUMMARY OF TABLE 28

TOTAL / REGIONS	KTM	EAST	KRDFN	NRTH	DFR	CENT	STH
10	1	0	0	6	2	0	1
%	10%	0%	0%	60%	20%	0%	10%

TABLE 30: MINISTRY OF DEFENCE

NAME	FROM	TO	REGION
F. Marshal Omer H A Albshir	9/7/89	19/10/93	Northern
F. Marshal Hassan Abdel Rahman	19/10/93	8/3/98	Khartoum
F. Marshal Ibrahim Sulaiman	8/3/98	6/3/99	Darfur
F. Marshal Abdel Rahim Sir Alkhetim	6/3/99	10/7/00	Northern
Lt. General Bakri Hasan Salih	10/7/00	To date	Northern

TABLE 31: SUMMARY OF TABLE 30

TOTAL / REGIONS	KTM	EAST	KRDFN	NRTH	DFR	CENT	STH
5	1	0	0	3	1	0	0
%	20%	0%	0%	60%	20%	0%	0%

TABLE 32: MINISTRY OF AVIATION AND NATIONAL SURVEY

NAME	FROM	TO	REGION
Retired Lt. General Tigani Adam Tahir	9/2/95	20/4/96	Darfur
Retired Lt. General Tigani Adam Tahir	20/4/96	8/3/98	Darfur
Hamid M. Ali Torain	8/3/98	6/3/99	Darfur
Mekki Ali Bilal	6/3/99	24/1/00	Kordofan
F. Marshal Ibrahim Sulaiman	24/1/00	10/7/00	Darfur
Dr. Shamboul Adlan	10/7/00	22/2/01	Central
Joseph Malwal	22/2/01	To date	Southern

TABLE 33: SUMMARY OF TABLE 32

TOTAL / REGIONS	KTM	EAST	KRDFN	NRTH	DFR	CENT	STH
7	0	0	0	0	5	1	1
%	0%	0%	0%	0%	72%	14%	14%

TABLE 34: MINISTRY OF TRADE FOREIGN AFFAIRS POLICY

NAME	FROM	TO	REGION
Dr. Farouq Albushra	9/7/1989	11/1990	Northern
Dr. Awad Aljaz	11/8/1990	30/8/1991	Northern
Dr. Ibrahim Ibaidalla	30/8/1991	8/7/1993	Northern

Name	From	To	Region
Dr. Taj Alsir Mustafa	8/7/1993	9/2/1995	Northern
Dr. Taj Alsir Mustafa	9/2/1995	20/4/1994	Northern
Osman Alhadi Ibrahim	20/4/1996	6/3/1999	Northern
Adam Tahir Hamdoun	6/3/1999	24/1/2000	Darfur
Mekki Ali Bilal	24/1/2000	22/2/2001	Kordofan
Abdel Hamid Musa Kasha	22/2/2001	To date	Darfur

TABLE 35: SUMMARY OF TABLE 34

Total / Regions	Ktm	East	Krdfn	Nrth	Dfr	Cent	Sth
9	0	0	1	6	2	0	0
%	0%	0%	11%	67%	22%	0%	0%

TABLE 36: MINISTRY OF AGRICULTURE AND FORESTRY

Name	From	To	Region
Prof. Ahmed Ali Jenaif	9/7/1989	20/4/1996	Northern
Dr. Nafey Ali Nafey	20/4/1996	6/3/1999	Northern
Osman Alhadi Ibrahim	6/3/1999	24/1/2000	Northern
Dr. Alhaj Adam Yousif	24/1/2000	8/7/2000	Darfur
Abdel Hamid Musa Kasha	10/7/2000	22/2/2001	Darfur
Dr. Majzoub Alkhalifa	22/2/2001	To date	Northern

TABLE 37: SUMMARY OF TABLE 36

Total / Regions	Ktm	East	Krdfn	Nrth	Dfr	Cent	Sth
6	0	0	0	4	2	0	0
%	0%	0%	0%	67%	33%	0%	0%

TABLE 38: MINISTRY OF IRRIGATION AND WATER RESOURCES

Name	From	To	Region
Dr. Yaqoub Musa Abu Shora	9/7/1989	19/8/1997	Central
Dr. M Shareef Altuhami	8/3/1998	20/10/1999	Central
Kamal Ali Mohamed	6/3/1999	To date	Northern

TABLE 39: SUMMARY OF TABLE 38

TOTAL / REGIONS	KTM	EAST	KRDFN	NRTH	DFR	CENT	STH
3	0	0	0	1	0	2	0
%	0%	0%	0%	33%	0%	67%	0%

TABLE 40: MINISTRY OF ENERGY AND MINING

NAME	FROM	TO	REGION
Abdel Munim Khogali Osman	9/7/1989	30/8/1991	Khartoum
Dr. Osman Albdelwahab	30/8/1991	18/1/1993	Central
General Salah Karrar	18/1/1993	18/8/1995	Northern
Awad. A. Alzaz	20/4/1996	18/8/1995	Northern

TABLE 41: SUMMARY OF TABLE 40

TOTAL / REGIONS	KTM	EAST	KRDFN	NRTH	DFR	CENT	STH
4	1	0	0	2	0	1	0
%	25%	0%	0%	50%	0%	25%	0%

TABLE 42: MINISTRY OF INDUSTRY

NAME	FROM	TO	REGION
Dr. Mohamed Omer Abdalla	9/7/1989	20/1/91	Kordofan
Dr. Taj Alsir M. Abdel Salam	20/1/1991	9/2/1995	Northern
Badr Eldin Sulaiman	9/2/1995	6/3/1999	Northern
Dr. Abdel Halim I Almutaafi	24/1/2000	22/2/2001	Central
Dr. Jalal Yousif Aldigair	22/2/2001	To date	Khartoum

TABLE 43: SUMMARY OF TABLE 42

TOTAL / REGIONS	KTM	EAST	KRDFN	NRTH	DFR	CENT	STH
5	1	0	1	2	0	1	0
%	20%	0%	20%	40%	0%	20%	0%

TABLE 44: MINISTRY OF HOUSING, WORKS AND PUBLIC SERVICES

NAME	FROM	TO	REGION
Retired Lt. General, Mohamed Mamoun Almardi	9/7/1989	10/4/1990	Northern
Dr. Hesain Sulaiman Abu Salih	10/4/1990	20/1/1991	Northern
Osman Abdel Gadir Abdel Lateef	20/1/1991	18/1/1993	Central

TABLE 45: SUMMARY OF TABLE 44

TOTAL / REGIONS	KTM	EAST	KRDFN	NRTH	DFR	CENT	STH
3	0	0	0	2	0	1	0
%	0%	0%	0%	67%	0%	33%	0%

TABLE 46: MINISTRY OF ROADS AND COMMUNICATION

NAME	FROM	TO	REGION
Osman Abdel Gadir Abdel Lateef	29/2/1995	20/4/1996	Central
Retired Lt. General Alhadi Bushra	20/4/1996	6/3/1999	Northern
Mohamed Tahir Bilal	24/1/2000	To date	Eastern

TABLE 47: SUMMARY OF TABLE 46

TOTAL / REGIONS	KTM	EAST	KRDFN	NRTH	DFR	CENT	STH
3	0	1	0	1	0	1	0
%	0%	33%	0%	33%	0%	33%	0%

TABLE 48: MINISTRY OF NATIONAL ASSEMBLY RELATIONS (AFFAIRS)

NAME	FROM	TO	REGION
Retired Major Abu Qasim M Ibrahim	20/4/96	24/1/00	Khartoum
Abdel Basit Sabdarat	22/2/01	To date	Northern

TABLE 49: SUMMARY OF TABLE 48

TOTAL / REGIONS	KTM	EAST	KRDFN	NRTH	DFR	CENT	STH
3	0	1	0	1	0	1	0
%	0%	33%	0%	33%	0%	33%	0%

TABLE 50: MINISTRY OF INVESTMENT AND INTERNATIONAL COOPERATION

Name	From	To	Region
Dr. Ali Alhaj Mohamed	18/1/1993	8/7/1993	Darfur
Dr. Ibrahim Ibaidallah	8/7/1993	9/2/1995	Northern
Abdalla Hasan Ahmed	8/3/1998	24/1/2000	Northern
Dr. Karm Aldin Abdel Moula	22/2/2001	To date	Darfur
Shareef Omer Badr	?	To date	Central

TABLE 51: SUMMARY OF TABLE 50

Total / Regions	Ktm	East	Krdfn	Nrth	Dfr	Cent	Sth
5	0	0	0	2	2	1	0
%	0%	0%	0%	40%	40%	20%	0%

TABLE 52:
MINISTRY OF CULTURE, HERITAGE, ECOLOGY AND TOURISM

Name	From	To	Region
Mohamed Tahir Iela	9/2/1995	24/1/2000	Eastern
Retired Lt. General Tigni Adam Tahir	24/1/2000	22/2/2001	Darfur
Abdel Basit Abdel Majid	22/2/2001	To date	Northern
Abdel Basit Abdel Majid	-	-	Northern
Abdel Jalil Basha	-	To date	Kordofan

TABLE 53: SUMMARY OF TABLE 52

Total / Regions	Ktm	East	Krdfn	Nrth	Dfr	Cent	Sth
5	0	1	1	2	1	0	0
%	0%	20%	20%	40%	20%	0%	0%

TABLE 54: MINISTRY OF SURVEY AND CONSTRUCTIONAL DEVELOPMENT

Name	From	To	Region
General GalwaK Deng	20/4/1996	6/3/1999	Southern
Joseph MalwaK Deng	24/1/2000	22/2/2001	Southern

Table 55: Summary of Table 54

Total / Regions	Ktm	East	Krdfn	Nrth	Dfr	Cent	Sth
2	0	0	0	0	0	0	2
%	0%	0%	0%	0%	0%	0%	100%

Table 56: Ministry of Guidance and Orientation

Name	From	To	Region
Abdalla deng Nial	9/7/1989	8/7/1993	Southern
Dr. Isam Ahmed Albashir	22/1/2001	To date	Northern

Table 57: Summary of Table 56

Total / Regions	Ktm	East	Krdfn	Nrth	Dfr	Cent	Sth
2	0	0	0	1	0	0	1
%	0%	0%	0%	50%	0%	0%	50%

Table 58: Ministry of Animal resources

Name	From	To	Region
Musa Almak Kor	20/4/1996	8/3/1998	Southern
Joseph Malwal Deng	8/3/1998	24/1/2000	Southern
Dr. Abdalla M. Seed Ahmed	24/1/2000	22/2/2001	Northern
Dr. Riak Gaay	22/2/2001	-	Southern
Galwak Deng	-	To date	Southern

Table 59: Summary of Table 58

Total / Regions	Ktm	East	Krdfn	Nrth	Dfr	Cent	Sth
5	0	0	0	1	0	0	4
%	0%	0%	0%	20%	0%	0%	80%

Table 60: Ministry of Youth and Sport

Name	From	To	Region
Lt. General Ibrahim Nayil Idam	11/11/1989	8/7/1993	Kordofan
General Yousif Abdel Fattah	8/3/1998	22/2/2001	Khartoum
Hasan Osman Rizig	22/2/2001	To date	Northern

TABLE 61: SUMMARY OF TABLE 60

TOTAL / REGIONS	KTM	EAST	KRDFN	NRTH	DFR	CENT	STH
3	1	0	1	1	0	0	0
%	33%	0%	33%	33%	0%	0%	0%

TABLE 62: MINISTRY OF COMMUNICATION AND TOURISM

NAME	FROM	TO	REGION
Retired Lt. General Ibrahim Nayil Idam	8/7/93	13/7/94	Kordofan
Dr. Kabshore Komo Gimbeel	13/7/94	20/4/96	Kordofan

TABLE 63: SUMMARY OF TABLE 62

TOTAL / REGIONS	KTM	EAST	KRDFN	NRTH	DFR	CENT	STH
2	0	0	2	0	0	0	0
%	0%	0%	100%	0%	0%	0%	0%

TABLE 64: MINISTRY OF HUMANITARIAN RELIEF AND REFUGEE AFFAIRS

NAME	FROM	TO	REGION
Peter Ourath Ador	9/7/1989	20/1/1991	Southern
Ibrahim Mahmoud	22/2/2001	To date	Eastern

TABLE 65: SUMMARY OF TABLE 64

TOTAL / REGIONS	KTM	EAST	KRDFN	NRTH	DFR	CENT	STH
2	0	1	0	0	0	0	1
%	0%	50%	0%	0%	0%	0%	50%

TABLE 66: MINISTRY OF STATE RELATIONS

NAME	FROM	TO	REGION
Natalie Bankar Casio	9/7/1998	30/7/1992	Southern
Lt. Colonel Galwal Deng	20/7/1992	18/1/1993	Southern
Dr. Ali Alhaj	8/7/1993	8/3/1998	Darfur
Ahmed Ibrahim Altahir	8/3/1998	10/7/2001	Kordofan
F. Marshal Ibrahim Sulaiman	10/7/2000	22/2/2001	Darfur
Dr. Nafye Ali Nafye	22/2/2001	To date	Northern

TABLE 67: SUMMARY OF TABLE 66

Total / Regions	Ktm	East	Krdfn	Nrth	Dfr	Cent	Sth
6	0	0	1	1	2	0	2
%	0%	0%	17%	17%	34%	0%	34%

TABLE 68: MINISTRY OF EDUCATION

Name	From	To	Region
Mahjoub Albadawi Mohamed	9/7/1989	10/4/1990	Northern
Abdalla Mohamed Ahmed	10/4/1990	20/1/1991	Central
Abdel Basit Sabdarat	20/1/1991	30/10/1993	Northern
Dr. Kabshore Komo Gimbeel	9/2/1995	6/3/1999	Kordofan
Hamid Mohamed Torain	6/3/1999	24/1/2000	Darfur
Abdel Basit Sabdarat	24/1/2000	22/2/2001	Northern
Ali Tameem Fartak	22/2/2001	-	Southern
Ahmed Babikir Nahar	-	To date	Darfur

TABLE 69: SUMMARY OF TABLE 68

Total / Regions	Ktm	East	Krdfn	Nrth	Dfr	Cent	Sth
6	0	0	1	3	2	1	1
%	0%	0%	12%	39%	25%	12%	12%

TABLE 70: MINISTRY OF HIGHER EDUCATION AND SCIENTIFIC RESEARCH/ -SCIENCE AND TECHNOLOGY

Name	From	To	Region
Dr. Ibrahim Ahmed Omer	20/1/1991	20/4/1996	Northern
Dr. Abdel Wahab Bob	20/4/1996	2/12/1996	Northern
Dr. Ibrahim Ahmed Omer	2/12/1996	24/1/2000	Northern
Prof. Zibair Bashir Taha	22/2/2001	22/2/2001	Northern
Prof. Mubarak Almajzoub	22/2/2001	To date	Central
Prof. Zibair Bashir Taha	29/2/2001	To date	Central

TABLE 71: SUMMARY OF TABLE 70

TOTAL / REGIONS	KTM	EAST	KRDFN	NRTH	DFR	CENT	STH
6	0	0	0	4	0	2	0
%	0%	0%	0%	67%	0%	33%	0%

TABLE 72: MINISTRY OF HEALTH

NAME	FROM	TO	REGION
Dr. Mohamed Shakir Alsarraj	9/7/1989	12/2/1992	Khartoum
General Faisal Ali Medani	12/2/1992	18/1/1993	Northern
Colonel Galwal Deng	18/1/1993	20/4/1996	Southern
Ihsan Alghabshawi	20/4/1996	8/3/1998	Northern
F. Marshal Babo Nimir	8/3/1998	24/1/2000	Kordofan
Major Abu Algasim M. Ibrahim	24/1/2000	22/2/2001	Northern
Dr. Ahmed Bilal Osman	22/2/2001	To date	Central

TABLE 73: SUMMARY OF TABLE 72

TOTAL / REGIONS	KTM	EAST	KRDFN	NRTH	DFR	CENT	STH
7	1	0	1	3	0	1	1
%	14%	0%	14%	43%	0%	14%	14%

TABLE 74: MINISTRY OF TRANSPORT

NAME	FROM	TO	REGION
Ali Ahmed Abdel Haleem	9/7/1989	20/1/1991	Northern
Colonel Salah Karrar	20/1/1991	18/1/1993	Northern
Osman Abdel Gadir Abdelateef	18/1/1993	9/2/1995	Central
Dr. Alfatih Mohamed Ali	9/2/1995	20/4/1996	Northern
Lt. General Albino Akol	20/4/1996	8/3/1998	Southern
Dr. Lam Akol	8/3/1998	-	Southern
Alwaseela Alsheikh Alsammani	-	To date	Central

TABLE 75: SUMMARY OF TABLE 74

TOTAL / REGIONS	KTM	EAST	KRDFN	NRTH	DFR	CENT	STH
7	0	0	0	3	0	2	2
%	0%	0%	0%	42%	0%	29%	29%

TABLE 76: MINISTRY OF SOCIAL PLANNING / WELFARE AND SOCIAL DEVELOPMENT

NAME	FROM	TO	REGION
Dr. Hesain. S. Abu Salih	20/1/1991	18/1/1993	Northern
Ali Osman M. Taha	18/1/1993	9/2/1995	Northern
Mohamed Osman Khalifa	9/2/1995	8/3/1998	Northern
General Altayib Ibrahim M Kheir	8/3/1998	24/1/2000	Northern
Dr. Qutbi Almahdi	24/1/2000	22/2/2001	Northern
Samia Ahmed Mohamed	22/2/2001	To date	Northern

TABLE 77: SUMMARY OF TABLE 76

TOTAL / REGIONS	KTM	EAST	KRDFN	NRTH	DFR	CENT	STH
6	0	0	0	6	0	0	0
%	0%	0%	0%	100%	0%	0%	0%

TABLE 78: MINISTRY OF FINANCE AND NATIONAL ECONOMY

NAME	FROM	TO	REGION
Dr. Sayed Ali Zeki	9/7/1989	10/1/1990	Kordofan
Abdel Rahim Hamdi	10/4/1990	30/10/1993	Northern
Abdalla Hasan Ahmed	30/10/1993	20/4/1996	Northern
Dr. Abdel Wahab Osman	20/4/1996	24/1/2000	Northern
Dr. Mohamed Kheir Alzibair	24/1/2000	22/2/2001	Northern
Abdel Rahim Hamdi	22/2/2001	-	Northern
Zibair Mohamed Alhasan	-	To date	Northern

TABLE 79: SUMMARY OF TABLE 78

TOTAL / REGIONS	KTM	EAST	KRDFN	NRTH	DFR	CENT	STH
7	0	0	1	6	0	0	0
%	0%	0%	15%	85%	0%	0%	0%

TABLE 80: MINISTRY OF JUSTICE

NAME	FROM	To	REGION
Hasan Ismael Albeeli	9/7/1989	11/8/1990	Northern
General Ahmed Mahoud Hasan	11/8/1990	12/2/1992	Northern
Dr. Abdel Samee Omer Ahmed	11/2/1992	30/10/1993	Northern
Dr. Abdalla Idris Mohamed	30/10/1993	18/1/1994	Northern
Abdel Aziz Shiddu	18/1/1994	20/4/1996	Central
Abdel Basit Sabdarat	20/4/1996	8/3/1998	Northern
Ali Mohamed Osman Yaseen	8/3/1998	To date	Kordofan

TABLE 81: SUMMARY OF TABLE 80

TOTAL / REGIONS	KTM	EAST	KRDFN	NRTH	DFR	CENT	STH
7	0	0	1	5	0	1	0
%	0%	0%	15%	70%	0%	15%	0%

TABLE 82: MINISTRY OF CULTURE AND INFORMATION

NAME	FROM	To	REGION
Ali Mohamed Shummu	9/7/1989	10/4/1990	Central
Mohamed Khogali Salheen	10/4/1990	20/1/1991	Khartoum
Abdalla Mohamed Ahmed	20/1/1991	6/11/1991	Central
Colonel Sulaiman M. Sulaiman	21/5/1992	30/10/1996	Northern
Abdel Basit Sabdarat	30/10/1993	20/4/1996	Northern
General Altayib Ibrahim M. Kheir	20/4/1996	8/3/1998	Northern
Dr. ghazi Salah Aldeen Atabani	8/3/1998	13/6/2001	Khartoum
Mahdi Ibrahim	13/6/2001	-	Central
Zahawi Ibrahim Malik	-	To date	Khartoum

TABLE 83: SUMMARY OF TABLE 82

TOTAL / REGIONS	KTM	EAST	KRDFN	NRTH	DFR	CENT	STH
9	3	0	0	3	0	3	0
%	33%	0%	0%	33%	0%	33%	0%

TABLE 84: MINISTRY OF FOREIGN AFFAIRS

NAME	FROM	TO	REGION
Ahmed Ali Sahloul	9/7/1989	13/2/1993	Northern
Dr. Sulaiman Abu Salih	13/2/1993	9/2/1995	Northern
Ali Osman Taha	9/2/1995	17/2/1998	Northern
Dr. Mustafa Osman Ismael	17/2/1998	To date	Northern

TABLE 85: SUMMARY OF TABLE 84

TOTAL / REGIONS	KTM	EAST	KRDFN	NRTH	DFR	CENT	STH
4	0	0	0	4	0	0	0
%	0%	0%	0%	100%	0%	0%	0%

TABLE 86: MINISTRY OF ELECTRICITY

NAME	FROM	TO	REGION
Ali Tameem Fartak	-	To date	Southern

TABLE 87: SUMMARY OF TABLE 86

TOTAL / REGIONS	KTM	EAST	KRDFN	NRTH	DFR	CENT	STH
1	0	0	0	0	0	0	1
%	0%	0%	0%	0%	0%	0%	100%

TABLE 88: SUMMARY OF ALL NATIONAL MINISTERIAL POSITIONS TABLE 23 TO TABLE 87

TOTAL / REGIONS	KTM	EAST	KRDFN	NRTH	DFR	CENT	STH
171	10	2	11	89	19	18	22
%	6%	1%	6%	52%	11%	11%	13%

GOVERNORS OF NORTHERN STATES (MAINLY MUSLIM PART OF THE COUNTRY)

TABLE 89: GOVERNORS OF KHARTOUM STATE

GOVERNOR	FROM	To	REGION
General Mohamed Osman Saeed	9/7/1989	14/2/1994	Northern
Badr Aldin Taha	14/2/1994	26/9/1996	Khartoum
Majzoub Alkhalifa	29/9/1996	22/2/2001	Northern
Dr. Abdel Halim Almutaafi	22/2/2001	To date	Central

TABLE 90: SUMMARY OF TABLE 89

TOTAL / REGIONS	KTM	EAST	KRDFN	NRTH	DFR	CENT	STH
4	1	0	0	2	0	1	0
%	25%	0%	0%	50%	0%	25%	0%

TABLE 91: GOVERNORS OF THE GEZIRA STATE

GOVERNOR	FROM	To	REGION OF STATE	REGION OF GOVERNOR
Lt. General Abdel Wahab Abdel Raouf	9/7/89	8/2/91	Central Region	Northern
Colonel Sulaiman M. Sulaiman	8/2/91	21/5/92	Central Region	Northern
Colonel Alawad Mohamed	21/2/94	14/2/94	Central Region	Northern
Dr. Ibrahim Ibaidalla	14/8/97	9/8/97	Gezira	Northern
Shareef Ahmed Omer	19/8/97	-	Gezira	Central
Abdel Rahman Sir Alkhatim	-	To date	-	Northern

TABLE 92: SUMMARY OF TABLE 91

TOTAL / REGIONS	KTM	EAST	KRDFN	NRTH	DFR	CENT	STH
6	0	0	0	5	0	1	0
%	0%	0%	0%	83%	0%	17%	0%

TABLE 93: GOVERNORS OF WHITE NILE STATE

GOVERNOR	FROM	TO	REGION
Abdalla Deng Nial	14/2/1994	27/5/1995	Southern
Dr. Abdalla M Seed Ahmed	27/5/1995	9/8/1997	Northern
Dr. Abdel Halim Almutaafi	19/8/1997	24/1/2000	Central
Badawi Alkheir Idris	24/1/2000	22/2/2001	Northern
Abdel Rahman Nur Aldin	22/2/2001	-	Northern
Majzoub Yousif Babikir	-	To date	Khartoum

TABLE 94: SUMMARY OF TABLE 93

TOTAL / REGIONS	KTM	EAST	KRDFN	NRTH	DFR	CENT	STH
6	1	0	0	3	0	1	1
%	16%	0%	0%	50%	0%	16%	16%

TABLE 95: GOVERNORS OF SINNAR STATE

GOVERNOR	FROM	TO	REGION
Lt. General Mohamed Osman Saeed	14/2/1994	18/6/1994	Northern
Ahmed Osman Alhaj	18/6/1994	-	Northern
Dr. Abdalla Mohamed Sid Ahmed	18/6/1994	27/5/1995	Northern
Colonel Algaili Ahmed Shareef	27/5/1995	9/8/1997	Central
Dr. Yagoub Abu Shora	19/8/1997	24/1/2001	Central
Dr, Younis Alshareef Alhasan	24/1/2000	10/6/2001	Kordofan
Mohamed Hamid Albala	24/7/2001	To date	Central

TABLE 96: SUMMARY OF TABLE 97

TOTAL / REGIONS	KTM	EAST	KRDFN	NRTH	DFR	CENT	STH
7	0	0	1	3	0	3	0
%	0%	0%	14%	43%	0%	43%	0%

TABLE 97: GOVERNORS OF THE BLUE NILE STATE

GOVERNOR	FROM	TO	REGION
Abdalla Abu Fatima	24/2/1994	14/12/1995	Eastern
Colonel Babikir J. Kabalo	14/12/1995	9/8/1997	Khartoum

Governor	From	To	Region
Abdel Raham Abu Median	19/8/1997	24/1/2000	Central
Lt. General Hasan Hamdain	24/1/2000	22/2/2001	Central
Lt. General Alhadi Albushra	22/2/2001	-	Northern
Abdalla Osman Alhaj	-	To date	Northern

TABLE 98: SUMMARY OF TABLE 97

Total / Regions	Ktm	East	Krdfn	Nrth	Dfr	Cent	Sth
6	1	1	0	2	0	2	0
%	17%	17%	0%	33%	0%	33%	0%

TABLE 99: GOVERNORS OF NORTHERN KORDOFAN STATE

Governor	From	To	Region
Lt. General Awadalla M. Alfatih	9/8/1989	8/2/1991	Northern
Colonel Faisal Medani Mukhtar	8/2/1991	12/2/1992	Northern
Lt. General Sayed Alhesaini	18/3/1992	14/2/1994	Khartoum
Mohamed Alhasan Alamin	14/2/1994	9/8/1997	Khartoum
Ibrahim Alsanousi	19/8/1997	24/1/2000	Kordofan
Osman Alhadi Ibrahim	24/1/2000	22/2/2001	Northern
General Alwad Mohamed Alhasan	22/2/2001	-	Northern
Ghulam Aldin Omsan Ahmed	-	To date	Northern

TABLE 100: SUMMARY OF TABLE 99

Total / Regions	Ktm	East	Krdfn	Nrth	Dfr	Cent	Sth
8	2	0	1	5	0	0	0
%	25%	0%	13%	62%	0%	0%	0%

TABLE 101: GOVERNORS OF SOUTHERN KORDOFAN STATE

Governor	From	To	Region
Habeeballa Ahmed Makhtoum	14/2/1994	9/8/1997	Darfur
Lt. General Baballa Biraima	19/8/1997	24/1/2000	Kordofan
Majzoub Yousif Babikir	24/1/2000		Khartoum
Soumi Zaidan Attiya	-	To date	Kordofan

TABLE 102: SUMMARY OF TABLE 101

TOTAL / REGIONS	KTM	EAST	KRDFN	NRTH	DFR	CENT	STH
4	1	0	2	0	1	0	0
%	25%	0%	50%	0%	25%	0%	0%

TABLE 103: GOVERNORS OF NORTHERN DARFUR STATE

GOVERNOR	FROM	To	REGION
Lt. General Abu Gasim Ibrahim	9/8/1989	6/8/1991	Northern
Colonel Altayib Ibrahim M Kheir	6/8/1991	14/2/1994	Northern
Prof Tigani Alamin	14/2/1994	14/12/1995	Kordofan
Dr. Younis Shareef Alhasan	14/12/1995	9/8/1997	Kordofan
General Abdalla Ali Safi Alnur	9/8/1997	22/2/2001	Darfur
F. Marshall Ibrahim Sulaiman	22/2/2001	-	Darfur
Osman M. Yousif Kibir	-	To date	Darfur

TABLE 104: SUMMARY OF TABLE 103

TOTAL / REGIONS	KTM	EAST	KRDFN	NRTH	DFR	CENT	STH
7	0	0	2	2	3	0	0
%	0%	0%	29%	29%	42%	0%	0%

TABLE 105: GOVERNORS OF SOUTHERN DARFUR STATE

GOVERNOR	FROM	To	REGION
Colonel Babikir Jabir Kaballo	14/12/1994	14/12/1995	Khartoum
Dr. Ismael Abel Haleem Alutaafi	14/2/1995	9/8/1997	Central
Dr. Alhaj Adam Yousif	19/8/1997	24/1/2001	Darfur
Alhiraika Izza Din	24/1/2000	22/2/2001	Kordofan
Lt. General Salah Ali Alghali	22/2/2001	-	Darfur
F. Marshall Adam Hamid	-	To date	Darfur

TABLE 106: SUMMARY OF TABLE 105

TOTAL / REGIONS	KTM	EAST	KRDFN	NRTH	DFR	CENT	STH
6	1	0	1	0	3	1	0
%	16%	0%	16%	0%	50%	16%	0%

TABLE 107: GOVERNORS OF WESTERN DARFUR STATE

Governor	From	To	Region
Mohamed Ahmed Alfadul	14/2/1994	27/5/1995	Central
General Hasan Hamadain	27/5/1995	9/8/1997	Central
Ibrahim Yahia Abdel Rahman	19/8/1997	24/1/2000	Darfur
Omer Haroun Abdalla	24/1/2000	-	Darfur
Lt. General Sulaiman Adam Abdalla	-	To date	Darfur

TABLE 108: SUMMARY OF TABLE 107

Total / Regions	Ktm	East	Krdfn	Nrth	Dfr	Cent	Sth
5	0	0	0	0	3	2	0
%	0%	0%	0%	0%	60%	40%	0%

TABLE 109: GOVERNORS OF THE RED SEA STATE

Governor	From	To	Region
Badawi Alkheir Idris	14/2/1994	9/8/1997	Northern
Abu Ali Majzooub	19/8/1997	22/2/2001	Eastern
Lt. General Hatim Alwaseela Sammani	22/2/2001	To date	Central

TABLE 110: SUMMARY OF TABLE 109

Total / Regions	Ktm	East	Krdfn	Nrth	Dfr	Cent	Sth
3	0	1	0	1	0	1	0
%	0%	33%	0%	33%	0%	33%	0%

TABLE 111: GOVERNORS OF KASALA STATE

Governor	From	To	Region
Lt. General Yousif B Sarraj	9/7/1989	8/2/1991	Northern
Colonel Alawad Mohamed Alhasan	8/2/1991	21/5/1992	Northern
Colonel Aljaili Ahmed Alshareef	21/5/1992	14/2/1994	Central
Lt. General Abul Gasim M. Ibrhim	14/2/1994	9/8/1997	Northern
Ibrahim Mahmoud Hamid	19/8/1997	22/2/2001	Eastern
F. Marshall Adam Hamid Musa	22/2/2001	-	Darfur
Farouq Mohamed nur	-	To date	Khartoum

TABLE 112: SUMMARY OF TABLE 111

TOTAL / REGIONS	KTM	EAST	KRDFN	NRTH	DFR	CENT	STH
7	1	1	0	3	1	1	0
%	14%	14%	0%	43%	14%	14%	0%

TABLE 113: GOVERNORS OF GADHARIF STATE

GOVERNOR	FROM	TO	REGION
Shareef Ahmed Badr	14/2/1994	9/8/1997	Central
Dr. Ibrahim Ibaidalla Hasan*	19/8/1997	24/1/2000	Northern
Prof. Alamin Daffala	24/1/2000	-	Northern
Dr. Abdel Rahman Alkhidir	-	To date	Northern

* Voted in by Executive Council

TABLE 114: SUMMARY OF TABLE 113

TOTAL / REGIONS	KTM	EAST	KRDFN	NRTH	DFR	CENT	STH
4	0	0	0	3	0	1	0
%	0%	0%	0%	75%	0%	25%	0%

TABLE 115: GOVERNORS OF THE NORTHERN STATE

GOVERNOR	FROM	TO	REGION
Lt. General Altahir M Yasin	9/7/1989	8/2/1991	Kordofan
Lt. General Musaaid Alniwairi	8/2/1991	16/9/1993	Central
Shareef Ahmed Omer Badr	16/9/1993	14/2/1994	Central
General Alawad Mohamed Hasan	14/2/1994	27/5/1995	Northern
Alhaj Adam Yousif	27/5/1995	9/8/1997	Darfur
Badwai Alkheir Idris	19/8/1997	24/1/2000	Northern
Dr. Mutasam Abdel Raheem	24/1/2000	-	Northern
Alhadi Bushra	-	To date	Northern

TABLE 116: SUMMARY OF TABLE 115

TOTAL / REGIONS	KTM	EAST	KRDFN	NRTH	DFR	CENT	STH
8	0	0	1	4	1	2	0
%	0%	0%	12%	50%	12%	25%	0%

TABLE 117: GOVERNORS OF THE RIVER NILE STATE

GOVERNOR	FROM	TO	REGION
Colonel Aljaili Ahmed Alshareef	14/2/1994	27/5/1995	Central
General Abdel Rahman Sir Alkhatim	27/5/1995	9/8/1997	Northern
Prof. Ahmed Ali Jenaif	19/8/1997	24/1/2000	Northern
Hasan Saad Ahmed	24/1/2000	27/1/2001	Kordofan
Hasan Osman Rizig	27/1/2000	22/2/2001	Northern
Ibrahim Mahmoud Hamid	22/2/2001	-	Eastern
Abdalla Musmar	-	To date	Darfur

TABLE 118: SUMMARY OF TABLE 117

TOTAL / REGIONS	KTM	EAST	KRDFN	NRTH	DFR	CENT	STH
7	0	1	1	3	1	1	0
%	0%	14%	14%	44%	14%	14%	0%

TABLE 119: SUMMARY OF NORTHERN STATES – REGIONAL SHARE OF GOVERNORS

TOTAL / REGIONS	KTM	EAST	KRDFN	NRTH	DFR	CENT	STH
93	8	3	12	37	14	18	1
%	9%	3%	13%	40%	15%	19%	1%

SOUTHERN STATES

All Governors, Tables 129 to 113 are from the Southern Region.

TABLE 120: GOVERNORS OF THE UPPER NILE STATE

GOVERNOR	FROM	TO
Lt. General Galwak Deng Garang	9/7/1989	30/7/1992
Colonel Bol Reet Koul	23/8/1992	5/9/1993
Jwan Tong	19/10/1993	14/2/1994
Musa Al Mak Kor	14/2/1994	20/4/1996
Alyous Atoke Ijwaj	20/4/1996	9/8/1997

GOVERNOR	FROM	To
Dr. Thimoni Tawfeeq Totlam	16/2/1997	16/2/1997
Mango Ajak Kole	4/6/1998	24/1/2000
Peter Sharlman	24/2/2000	24/2/2000
Dak Doke Bishop	22/2/2001	To date

TABLE 121: GOVERNORS OF THE UNITY STATE

GOVERNOR	FROM	To
Thomas Komi Kan	14/2/1994	17/1/1995
Michael Mibael Shole	27/5/1995	27/5/1995
Taban Deng Gaay	16/2/1997	24/1/2000
Hanna Samgouk	24/3/2000	24/2/2001
John Door Majouk	22/2/2001	-
Joseph Monytwell	-	To date

TABLE 122: GOVERNORS OF JONGLEI STATE

GOVERNOR	FROM	To
Alsheikh Beesh Akor	14/2/1994	9/8/1997
Riak Gaay Kok	16/12/1997	22/2/2001
Michael Mario	22/2/2001	-
Ismael Koyni	-	To date

TABLE 123: GOVERNORS OF BAHR AL JABAL STATE

GOVERNOR	FROM	To
Lt. General Aleson M Magaya	9/7/1989	6/8/1991
Lt. General Sterlino Areeka Mayit	6/8/1991	16/9/1993
Angelo Beeda	16/9/1993	14/2/1994
Ms Agnes Lokodo	14/2/1994	9/8/1997
Henry Jad Zakria	16/2/1997	22/2/2000
Lt. General James Loro	13/9/2000	To date

TABLE 124: GOVERNORS OF EASTERN EQUATORIAL STATE

GOVERNOR	FROM	To
Siris Baya Lwailala	14/2/1994	9/8/1997
Lt. Colonel Abdalla Kafeelo	16/2/1997	22/2/2001
Siris Baya Lwailala	22/2/2001	-
Abdalla Albirt	-	To date

TABLE 125: GOVERNORS OF WESTERN EQUATORIAL STATE

GOVERNOR	FROM	To
General Izaya bole	14/2/1994	9/8/1997
General Izaya Bole	9/8/1997	7/8/2000
James Niyama Niyandi	22/2/2001	-
Lt. General John Mathew	-	To date

TABLE 126: GOVERNORS OF WESTERN BAHR ALGHAZAL STATE

GOVERNOR	FROM	To
Lt. General Andrew Makor	9/7/1989	6/8/1991
General George Kangoor Arob	6/8/1991	14/2/1994
Ali Tameem Fartag	14/2/1994	9/8/1997
Charles Julu Yubo	16/2/1997	22/2/2001
Dr. Michael Millli Hesain	22/2/2001	To date

TABLE 127: GOVERNORS OF WARAB STATE

GOVERNOR	FROM	To
Arob Acher Akol	14/2/1994	9/8/1997
Arobe Acher Akol	16/12/1997	24/1/2001
Moses Mashar	24/1/2001	-
Bona Bole Bote	-	To date

TABLE 128: Governors of Northern Bahr Alghazal State

Governor	From	To
Joseph Ajwang	14/12/1994	9/8/1997
Kwaj Makui Miyar	16/12/1997	22/2/2001
Kong Dirodit	22/2/2001	-
Garang Agwuer	-	To date

TABLE 129: The Lakes State

Governor	From	To
Ramzi Monytwell Garang	14/2/1994	9/8/1997
General Naktore Magar Acheek	16/12/1997	24/1/2001
Lt. General Gabriel Shol Yak	24/1/2000	22/2/2001
John Angol	22/2/2001	-
Isaac Owan	-	To date

TABLE 130: Summary of Southern States – Tables 120 to 129.

Total / Regions	Ktm	East	Krdfn	Nrth	Dfr	Cent	Sth
51	0	0	0	0	0	0	51
%	0%	0%	0%	0%	0%	0%	100%

TABLE 131: Heads of Transitional Council for Southern Kordofan State

Name/Region	Duration	Khartoum	Eastern	Kordofan	Northern	Darfur	Central	Southern
Lt. General Bakri Hansan Salih		-	-	-	1	-	-	-

TABLE 132: Summary of Table 131

Total / Regions	Ktm	East	Krdfn	Nrth	Dfr	Cent	Sth
1	0	0	0	1	0	0	0
%	0%	0%	0%	100%	0%	0%	0%

Table 133:
Incumbent National State Ministers (Wuzaraa Dowla)

Name	Ministry	Khartoum	Eastern	Kordofan	Northern	Darfur	Central	Southern
Zibair. A. Hasan	Finance				*			
Azhari Altigni	Education			*				
Ali T. Fartag	Industry							*
Adam Ballouh	International Cooperation			*				
Ahmed M Fadl	Personnel Chamber						*	
Taj Alsir Majzoub	Personnel Chamber			*				
Mustafa Osman	Foreign Affairs					*		
Amin Hasan Omer	Information					*		
Mohamed Alsheikh Medani	Sport					*		
Omer Sulaiman	Personnel Chamber			*				
Mutrif Siddeeq	Personnel Chamber	*						
Omer Abdel Maroof	Defence						*	
Thomas Afwal	Health							*
Abdel Rahman Peter	Health							*
Sabana Jambo	International Cooperation							*
Abdel Rahman Nur Aldin	Working Forces					*		
Salman Alsafi	Federal Affairs			*				
Alayib Mustafa	Information					*		
Chol Deng	Peace							*
Marghani Mansoor	Education						*	
Abdel Gadir Ahmed Wahbi	Agriculture	*						
Musa Mohamed	Agriculture						*	
Ahmed Ibrahim Tahir	Presidency of Republic			*				
Nasr Aldin Ahmed Omer	International Cooperation						*	
Yusif Abdel Fattah	International Planning	*						
Ihsan Abdalla	Refugees					*		
Abdalla A. Safi Alnur	Federal Affairs						*	
John Door Majok	Federal Affairs							*
Dr. Ibrahim Abu Oaf	Federal Affairs					*		
Sayid Alhesaini	Communication	*						
Mariam Sir Alkatim	Tourism	*						

Name	Ministry	Khartoum	Eastern	Kordofan	Northern	Darfur	Central	Southern
Hasan Dhahawi	Social Planning				*			
Majzoub Alkhalifa	Work & Maintenance				*			
Ibrahim Shams Aldin	Defence				*			
Alfatih Irwa	Defence				*			
Ghazi Salah Aldin	Foreign Affairs	*						
Abdel Wahab A. Hamza	Finance				*			
Mohamed Kheir Zibair	Finance				*			
Gibrael Roraij	Foreign Affairs							*
Bardia Sulaiman	Council of Ministers	*						
Abdel Jabbar Hesain	Agriculture			*				
Dr isam Siddaiq	Presidency of Republic				*			
Alfatih M. Saeed	Agriculture						*	
Mariam O. Sir Alkhatim	Social Welfare				*			
Mirghani Mansour	Social Welfare					*		
Chol Deng Alak	Foreign Affairs							*
Idris M Abdel Gadir	Peace				*			
Usama Abdalla	Irrigation				*			
Kamal Abdel Lateef	Council of Ministers				*			
Ali Karti	Justice				*			
Azhari Altigani	Sport			*				
Ali Ahmed Osman	Industry				*			
Hasan Ahmed Taha	Finance				*			
Aayda Almadi	Finance	*						
Ahmed Al Majzoub	Finance				*			
Adam Ballouh	Animal Resources			*				
Mohamed Yousif A/Alla	Humanitarian Affairs					*		
Najeeb Alkheir	Foreign Affairs	*						
Ahmed Haroun	Internal Affairs			*				
Ahmed A. Alaas	Internal Affairs					*		
Ahmed Ali Fashosha	Defence						*	
F. Marshal Mansour Mohamadain	Defence	*						
Taj Alsir Mahjoub	Working Forces			*				
Mohamed Hasan Albahi	Aviation	*						

Name	Ministry	Khartoum	Eastern	Kordofan	Northern	Darfur	Central	Southern
Altayib Mustafa	Communications					*		
Siddeeq Almujtaba	Culture					*		
Mohamed Abu Zaid	Education						*	
Savannah Jambo	Finance							*
Sultan Dew Mathok	Federal Affairs							*
Joseph Diwair	Peace							*
Mango Ajak	Transport							*
Mikwaj Tonj	Federal Affairs							*
Mabor Marair	Health							*
Abbas Samsounj	Personnel Chamber							*
Mohamed Markazo	Roads and Bridges			*				
Hasan Sheikh Al Safi	Transport		*					
Ishraqa Mohmoud	International Cooperation	*						
Kamil Abdel Majid	Federal Affairs						*	
Ahmed Almahi	Federal Affairs				*			
Abbas Samsounj	Finance							*
Total		12	1	12	27	6	6	16

TABLE 134: SUMMARY OF TABLE 133

Total / Regions	Ktm	East	Krdfn	Nrth	Dfr	Cent	Sth
80	12	1	12	27	6	6	14?
%	15%	2%	15%	34%	8%	8%	18%

TABLE 135: HEADS OF THE NATIONAL ASSEMBLY/PARLIAMENT

Name	Duration	Khartoum	Eastern	Kordofan	Northern	Darfur	Central	Southern
Mohamed Alamin Alkhalifa	24/2/92 –1/4/96						*	
Dr. Hasan Alturabi	1/4/96 -- 12/12/99						*	
Ahmed Ibrahim Altahir	5/2/2001-To date			*				
Total				1			1	1

TABLE 136: SUMMARY OF TABLE 135

TOTAL / REGIONS	KTM	EAST	KRDFN	NRTH	DFR	CENT	STH
3	0	0	1	0	1	1	0
%	0%	0%	33%	0%	33%	33%	0%

TABLE 137: HEADS OF CONSTITUTIONAL COURT

NAME/ REGION	KHARTOUM	EASTERN	KORDOFAN	NORTHERN	DARFUR	CENTRAL	SOUTHERN
Jalal Ali Lutfi				*			
Hasam Mohamed Albeeli				*			
Mahdi Alfahal Altahir				*			
Mohamed Mahmoud Abu gisaisa				*			
Abdulla Ahmed Abdalla				*			
Ali Yahia Abdalla					*		
Ongay Kasia							*
Yousif Alwali				*			
TOTAL	0	0	0	6	1	0	1

TABLE 138: SUMMARY OF TABLE 137

TOTAL / REGIONS	KTM	EAST	KRDFN	NRTH	DFR	CENT	STH
8	0	0	0	6	1	0	1
%	0%	0%	0%	74%	13%	0%	13%

TABLE 139: HEADS OF JUDICIAL AUTHORITY (CHIEF JUSTICE PERSONNEL)

NAME	DURATION	KHARTOUM	EASTERN	KORDOFAN	NORTHERN	DARFUR	CENTRAL	SOUTHERN
Jalal Ali Lufi	29/7/1989-16/8/1994				*			
Ibaid Haj Ali	16/8/1994-15/2/1998						*	
Hafiz Alsheikh Alzaki	15/2/1998-			*				
Jalal Aldin M Osman	- To date				*			
TOTAL		0	0	1	2	0	1	0

Table 140: Summary of Table 139

Total / Regions	Ktm	East	Krdfn	Nrth	Dfr	Cent	Sth
4	0	0	1	2	0	1	0
%	0%	0%	25%	50%	0%	25%	0%

Table 141: Heads of National Security Authority 1/7/1989 To Date

Name/ Region	Khartoum	Eastern	Kordofan	Northern	Darfur	Central	Southern
Lt. General Nafayi Ali Nafayi				*			
Lt. General Mohamed A. Aldabi				*			
Lt. General Hasan Dahawi				*			
Lt. General Alhadi Abdalla				*			
Dr. Qutbi Almahdi				*			
Lt. General Awad Ibn Oaf				*			
Lt. General Abdel Kareem Abdalla				*			
Lt. General Ahmed Mohamed Alaas				*			
Lt. General Aljaili Almisbah				*			
General Yahia Hesain				*			
Lt. General Salah Abdalla				*			
Lt. General Mohamed Atta				*			
Total				12			

Table 142: Summary of Table 141

Total / Regions	Ktm	East	Krdfn	Nrth	Dfr	Cent	Sth
12	0	0	0	12	0	0	0
%	0%	0%	0%	100%	0%	0%	0%

DIRECTORS OF DIVISIONS OF INTERNAL SECURITY

For reasons connected with national security, we withhold names and Divisions of office occupants computed below.

TABLE 143: SUMMARY OF REGIONAL ORIGIN OF DIRECTORS OF DIVISIONS OF INTERNAL SECURITY

TOTAL / REGIONS	KTM	EAST	KRDFN	NRTH	DFR	CENT	STH
25	0	0	1	22	2	0	0
%	0%	0%	4%	88%	8%	0%	0%

TABLE 144: DIRECTORS AND DEPUTY DIRECTORS OF EXTERNAL SECURITY AUTHORITY, 1/7/1989 TO DATE.

NAME/ REGION	KHARTOUM	EASTERN	KORDOFAN	NORTHERN	DARFUR	CENTRAL	SOUTHERN
Lt. General Nafayi Ali Nafayi				*			
Lt. General Mohamed Mustafa Aldabi				*			
Lt. General Qutbi Almahdi				*			
Lt. General Alfatih Aljaili Almisbah				*			
Lt. General Abdel Kareem Abdalla				*			
Lt. General Ahmed Mohamed Alaas				*			
Lt. General Mutrif Siddeeq				*			
Lt. General Ahmed Hesain Diab				*			
Lt. General Yahia Hesain				*			
TOTAL	0	0	0	9	0	0	0

TABLE 145: SUMMARY OF TABLE 144

TOTAL / REGIONS	KTM	EAST	KRDFN	NRTH	DFR	CENT	STH
9	0	0	0	9	0	0	0
%	0%	0%	0%	100%	0%	0%	0%

DIRECTORS OF DIVISIONS OF EXTERNAL NATIONAL SECURITY

In the interest of national security, no names or exact offices will be given below. Information below is restricted to mere statistical summary.

TABLE 146: REGIONAL ORIGIN OF DIRECTORS OF DIVISIONS OF EXTERNAL NATIONAL SECURITY

TOTAL / REGIONS	KTM	EAST	KRDFN	NRTH	DFR	CENT	STH
18	3	0	1	13	1	0	0
%	16%	0%	5%	72%	1%	0%	0%

TABLE 147: DIRECTORS OF NATIONAL INTELLIGENCE AUTHORITY

NAME/ REGION	KHARTOUM	EASTERN	KORDOFAN	NORTHERN	DARFUR	CENTRAL	SOUTHERN
Lt. General Hasan Dahwi				*			
Lt. General Mohamed Mustafa Aldabi				*			
Lt. General Yasin Arabi				*			
Lt. General Awad Bin Oaf				*			
Lt. General Mohamed Hasan Alfadil				*			
TOTAL	0	0	0	5	0	0	0

TABLE 148: SUMMARY OF TABLE 147

TOTAL / REGIONS	KTM	EAST	KRDFN	NRTH	DFR	CENT	STH
5	0	0	0	5	0	0	0
%	0%	0%	0%	100%	0%	0%	0%

TABLE 149 : DIRECTORS AND DEPUTY DIRECTORS OF THE NATIONAL POLICE FORCE

Name/ Region	Khartoum	Eastern	Kordofan	Northern	Darfur	Central	Southern
F. Marshal Osman Alshafeey				*			
F. Marshal Awad Khojali	*						
F. Marshal Hasan M. Sideeq				*			
F. Marshal Abdel Munim Sulaiman	*						
F. Marshal Mohamed Haju Alkanzi		*					
F. Marshal Omer Alhaj Alhadari				*			
F. Marshal Salahi Mirhgani	*						
F. Marshal Fakhr Aldin Abdel Sadig				*			
F. Marshal Osman Yaqoub Ali		*					
TOTAL	3	2	0	4	0	0	0

TABLE 150: SUMMARY OF TABLE 149

Total / Regions	Ktm	East	Krdfn	Nrth	Dfr	Cent	Sth
9	3	2	0	4	0	0	0
%	33%	22%	0%	44%	0%	0%	0%

TABLE 151: DIRECTORS OF MAJOR SPECIFIED DIRECTORATES

Name	Directorate	Khartoum	Eastern	Kordofan	Northern	Darfur	Central	Southern
Lt. General Salah Alsheikh	Customs				*			
Lt. General Abdel Aziz Awad	Supplies	*						
Lt. General Adil Seed Ahmed	Orientation & Guidance						*	
Lt. General Mahia Aldin A Ridwan	Administration	*						
Lt. General Kamal Hasan Ahmed	Finance	*						
Lt. General Mahjoub H. Saad	Training				*			
Lt. General Omer Jaafar Osman	Khartoum Administration	*						

Name	Directorate	Khartoum	Eastern	Kordofan	Northern	Darfur	Central	Southern
Lt. General Mohamed Najeeb	Security						*	
Lt. General Taj Asir Aljazuli	Intelligence	*						
Lt. General Ammar Osman	Central Reserve Force						*	
Lt. General Abdel Baqi Bushra	Immigration and Passports						*	
Lt. General Mohamed Alhafiz Attiya	Popular Police			*				
Lt. General Mohamed Bahr	Petrol and Depots			*				
Lt. General Muhia Aldin Ridwan	Maintenance	*						
Lt. General Mohamed Hamid Awad	Wild Life					*		
Lt. General Salah Aldin Mohamed	Civil Defence					*		
Lt. General Abdel Raheem Yaqoub	Civic Records		*					
General Kamal Jaafar Osman	State Security					*		
Total		6	1	2	5	0	4	0

TABLE 152: SUMMARY OF TABLE 151

Total / Regions	Ktm	East	Krdfn	Nrth	Dfr	Cent	Sth
18	6	1	2	5	0	4	0
%	33%	6%	11%	28%	0%	22%	0%

TABLE 153: ADMISSION TO THE NATIONAL MILITARY COLLEGE, 1991-2000

Year	Batch	Total Intake	Khartoum	Eastern	Kordofan	Northern	Darfur	Central	Southern
1991	41	98	27	10	7	11	9	27	7
1992	42	93	30	11	5	10	7	21	9
1993	43	292	76	24	17	43	21	100	11
1994	44	375	103	22	19	35	14	172	10
1995	45	333	71	37	24	29	29	130	13
1996	46	435	97	43	29	45	33	174	14
1997	47	392	101	43	22	51	24	138	13

Year	Batch	Total Intake	Khartoum	Eastern	Kordofan	Northern	Darfur	Central	Southern
1998	48	358	97	39	27	29	20	136	10
1999	49	326	86	22	23	31	25	125	14
2000	50	293	87	27	15	26	17	110	11
Total		2995	775	278	188	310	200	1133	122

TABLE 154: SUMMARY OF TABLE 153

Total / Regions	Ktm	East	Krdfn	Nrth	Dfr	Cent	Sth
2995	775	278	188	310	200	1133	122
%	26%	9%	6%	10%	7%	38%	4%

TABLE 155: ADMISSION TO THE NATIONAL POLICE COLLEGE, INTAKES 1990-1999

Year	Batch	Total Intake	Khartoum	Eastern	Kordofan	Northern	Darfur	Central	Southern
1990	60	225	26	13	21	84	23	45	12
1991	61	222	47	11	15	82	14	45	8
1992	62	299	45	13	35	100	15	75	16
1993	63	250	62	12	17	83	12	59	5
1994	64	233	35	7	25	86	23	54	3
1995	65	170	45	2	17	55	9	35	7
1996	66	244	43	9	14	92	13	61	12
1997	67	257	55	12	15	103	17	50	6
1998	68	258	65	18	13	75	15	63	9
1999	69	150	45	5	7	30	6	54	3
Total		2308	468	102	179	790	147	541	81

TABLE 156: SUMMARY OF TABLE 155

TOTAL / REGIONS	KTM	EAST	KRDFN	NRTH	DFR	CENT	STH
2308	468	102	179	790	147	541	81
%	20	4%	7%	34%	6%	23%	3%

TABLE 157: APPOINTEES TO THE CUSTOM AND EXCISE DUTIES DEPARTMENT, 1990 ~ 2003

TOTAL / REGIONS	KTM	EAST	KRDFN	NRTH	DFR	CENT	STH
1400	458	60	83	488	61	211	39
%	32%	5%	6%	34%	5%	15%	2%

TABLE 158: SPECIAL TECHNICAL APPOINTEES (ENGINEERS, MEDICS, ECONOMISTS ...)

TOTAL / REGIONS	KTM	EAST	KRDFN	NRTH	DFR	CENT	STH
99	14	0	4	35	6	38	2
%	14%	0%	4%	35%	6%	38%	2%

TABLE 159: CURRENT AMBASSADORS OF SUDAN

NAME	COUNTRY	KHARTOUM	EASTERN	KORDOFAN	NORTHERN	DARFUR	CENTRAL	SOUTHERN
Khidir Haroun	USA				*			
A/Ghani Awad Alkarim	Canada				*			
Dr. Ibrahi Alsir Alkabbashi	Russia				*			
Bashir Mohamed Alhasan	Romania				*			
Ibrahim Mirghani	Austria				*			
Ahmed Jaafar Abdel Kareen	Germany				*			
Hasan Abdeen	UK				*			
Ali Yousif Ahmed	Belgium	*						
Abdel Mahmoud Abdel Haleem	India	*						
Hamid Ali Altinay	Iran	*						
Mirghani Mohamed Salih	China				*			

Name	Country	Khartoum	Eastern	Kordofan	Northern	Darfur	Central	Southern
Osman Mohamed Dirar	Libya				*			
Abdel Rahman Mukhtar	South Africa				*			
Awad Mohamed Alhasan	Pakistan						*	
Hasan Bashir	Chad	*						
Ismael Ahmed Ismael	Tunisia	*						
Hasan Ahmed Fageeri	Zimbabwe				*			
Muhia Aldin Salih	Emirates				*			
Osman Fafayi Osman	Saudi Arabia				*			
Osman Alsayid	Ethiopia				*			
Hafiz Ibrahim	Syria				*			
Ahmed Mamoud Yasin	Jordan						*	
Ahmed Abdel Haleem	Egypt				*			
Agnes Lokodo	Zaire							*
Ali Nimeiri	Kenya				*			
Siraj Aldin Ahmed Yousif	Yuganda					*		
Hasan Alfaki	Djibouti				*			
Siddeeq Yousif Abu Aagla	Indonesia				*			
Mohamed Adam	Malaysia				*			
Sid Ahmed Bakheet	Lebanon				*			
Awad Musi	Japan				*			
Mohamed Ahmed Abdel Ghaffar	Algeria				*			
Ahmed Meddi Omer	Morocco		*					
Mohamed Hasan Bakheet	Qatar							*
Alfareeq Alsanousi	Yemen				*			
Abdel Munim Mohamed Ahmed	Kuwait				*			
Ibrahim Mirghani	Geneva				*			
Adrew Kakore	Italy							*
Abdel Basit Badawi	France				*			
Zianab Ahmed Mahmoud	Sweden	*						
Abdel Haleem Abu Fatih	Holland			*				

Name	Country	Khartoum	Eastern	Kordofan	Northern	Darfur	Central	Southern
Baha Aldin Hanafi	Turkey				*			
Mohamed Salah Aldin	Bulgaria				*			
Salah Mohamed Ali	Zambia				*			
Mohamed Hasan Alamin	Senegal				*			
Dr. Sulaiman Mohamed Mustafa	Central Africa				*			
Mahjoub Albasha	Eritrea				*			
Ahmed Hamid Alfaq	Somalia				*			
A/Alla Hasan Salim	Spain				*			
Alfatih Irwa	UN							
Total		9	0	1	33	1	3	3

TABLE 160: SUMMARY OF TABLE 159

Total / Regions	Ktm	East	Krdfn	Nrth	Dfr	Cent	Sth
50	9	0	1	33	1	3	3
%	18%	0%	2%	66%	2%	6%	6%

TABLE 161: CONSULS OF SUDAN ABROAD

Consul	Country/City	Khartoum	Eastern	Kordofan	Northern	Darfur	Central	Southern
Almain Waqiaffalla	Ndjamena						*	
Salah Sirria	Abbeche (Chad)			*				
Isam Awad Alkareem	Kenya				*			
Abdel Lateef Mohamed Alhaj	Djibouti						*	
Abu Obaida Almahdi	Eritrea				*			
Omar Almangil	Ethiopia	*						
Altayib Aljazzar	Cairo						*	
Adil Ghaili	Alexandria				*			
Izzaldin Abdel Aziz	Benghazi				*			

Consul	Country/City	Khartoum	Eastern	Kordofan	Northern	Darfur	Central	Southern
Salah Mohamed Sagha	South Africa		*					
Osman Mohamed Abdalla	Uganda		*					
Ahmed Mohamed Giraishabi	Jiddah (Saudi)						*	
Jalal Alsheikh Altayib	Riyadh				*			
John Antonio	Central Africa							*
Alhadi Aljak	Zaire				*			
Adil Hasan	Jordan				*			
Mohamed Hasan Alkhawadh	Yemen				*			
Awad Abu Zaid	Emirates						*	
Altaj Ibn Ouf	Iran				*			
Mohamed Saeed Alhafian	Malaysia				*			
Ali Bunduq	China				*			
Yasir Altayib	Hong Kong	*						
Idris Mohamed Ahmed	France						*	
Usama Mukhtar	UK				*			
Omer Osman Elibaid	Russia						*	
Bashir Alturabi	Germany						*	
Adel Muttalab Abdel Rahman	Morocco				*			
Salah Seed Ahmed	Tripoli				*			
Adil Alaqeed	Somalia				*			
Tariq Shukri	India	*						
Mutasam Abdel Qadir	Kenya				*			
Izzal Din Musa	Nigeria						*	
Alaqib Safaldin	Italy		*					
Mawia Butrus	Turkey	*						
Total		4	1	3	16	0	9	1

Table 162: Summary of Table 161

Total / Regions	Ktm	East	Krdfn	Nrth	Dfr	Cent	Sth
34	4	1	3	16	0	9	1
%	11%	3%	9%	47%	0%	26%	2%

TABLE 163: AMBASSADORIAL CHIEFS SECURITY

Name	Country/ City	Khartoum	Eastern	Kordofan	Northern	Darfur	Central	Southern
Colonel Jaafar Sindeeg Jibreel	London		*					
Colonel A/Hafeezh Ibrahim A/Alla	Ciro						*	
Lt. Colonel Yasir Abdel Rahman	Baghdad	*						
Lt. Colonel Shareef A/Raheem Saeed	Sanaa				*			
Colonel Rasheed Musa Alzain	Riyadh	*						
Lt. Colonel Nasr Aldin M. Alzain	Tripoli	*						
Lt. Colonel Mawiya Jaafar Mohamed	Abu Dhabi	*						
Major Adil Hisain Ibrahim	Riyadh				*			
Major Nadawi Alsideeq Babikr	Benghazi	*						
Major Amir Abel Lateef Mahmoud	Jiddah (Saudi)						*	
Captain Mubarak Abakkar Jibreel	Jiddah (Saudi)						*	
Musaaed Siddeeq Omer Ahmed	Riyadh	*						
Lt. Colonel Hatim Osman A. Shareef	Jiddah				*			
Lt. Colonel Usama Moahmed Mustafa	Cairo				*			
TOTAL		6	1	0	4	0	3	0

TABLE 164: SUMMARY OF TABLE 163

Total / Regions	Ktm	East	Krdfn	Nrth	Dfr	Cent	Sth
14	6	1	0	4	0	3	0
%	43%	7%	0%	28%	0%	21%	0%

TABLE 165: SECRETARY GENERALS (PRINCIPAL OFFICERS) OF FEDERAL MINISTRIES

Name	Duration	Khartoum	Eastern	Kordofan	Northern	Darfur	Central	Southern
Dr. Yasin Alhaj Abdeen	17/3/1994-28/10/1995				*			
Lt. General Sulaiman Jaafar	28/10/1995-7/3/1999				*			
F. Marshal Salah M. Salih	7/3/1999-22/2/2001				*			
Total		0	0	0	3	0	0	0

TABLE 166: GENERAL SECRETARIAT OF THE COUNCIL OF MINISTERS

Name	From	To	Region
Hasan Sidheeq	4/5/1985	25/9/91	Northern
Sidheeq Alfaqi	10/7/1991	To date	Central

TABLE 167: SUMMARY OF TABLE 166

Ktm	East	Krdfn	Nrth	Dfr	Cent	Sth	Total
0	0	0	1	0	1	0	2

TABLE 168: GENERAL SECRETARIES OF THE MINISTRY OF HEALTH

Name	From	To	Region
Dr. Mohamed Ibrahim Alimam	29/1/1989	1/8/1989	Northern
Dr. Abdel Rahman Kabbashi	1/8/1989	11/12/1989	Northern
Dr. Kheiri Abdel Rahman	11/12/1989	16/9/1992	Northern
Dr. Mohamed Ahmed Abu Salab	13/2/1993	9/7/1995	Northern
Dr. Kheiri Abdel Rahman	9/7/1995	14/12/1996	Northern
Prof. Qurashi Mohamed Ali	14/12/1996	6/5/1998	Central
Dr. Bashir Ibrahim Mukhtar	6/5/1998	28/2/2001	Kordofan
Dr. Osman Sid Ahmed Osman	28/12/2001	To date	Northern

Table 169: Summary of Table 168

Ktm	East	Krdfn	Nrth	Dfr	Cent	Sth	Total
0	0	2*	5	0	1	0	8

* Incorrect entry in Table 168 or 169.

Table 170: General Secretaries of the Ministry of Work and Administrative Reform

Name	From	To	Region
Abdel Rahman Yousif Haydoob	?/1989		Northern
Abdel Rahman Yousif Haydoob	23/3/1997	To date	Northern

Table 171: Summary of Table 170

Ktm	East	Krdfn	Nrth	Dfr	Cent	Sth	Total
0	0	0	2	0	0	0	2

Table 172: General Secretaries of the Ministry of Aviation and Survey

Name	From	To	Region
Abdalla Mohamed Omer	26/2/1995	28/2/199	Northern
Abdel Wahab Jibreel	4/9/1999	1/3/2000	Northern
Ahmed Ismael Alazhari	1/3/2001		Northern

Table 173: Summary of Table 172

Ktm	East	Krdfn	Nrth	Dfr	Cent	Sth	Total
0	0	0	3	0	0	0	3

Table 174: General Secretaries of the Ministry of Trade

Name	From	To	Region
Mohamed Nuri Hamed	2/10/1989		Northern
Mohamed Nuri Hamed	8/8/1993	13/1/1994	Northern
Mohamed Sulaiman Fadlalla	22/1/1994		Northern
Mustafa A. Taha Sourij	10/7/1999	9/5/2000	Northern
Abdalla Idrin Habbani	9/5/2001		Central

Table 175: Summary of Table 174

Ktm	East	Krdfn	Nrth	Dfr	Cent	Sth	Total
0	0	0	4	0	0	0	4

Table 176: General Secretaries of the Ministry of Agriculture and Forestry

Name	From	To	Region
Musa Mohamed Musa	1/8/1989	1995	Kordofan
Dr. Abdel Jaleel Abdel Jabbar	26/1/1996	1998	Northern
Dr. Abdel Razzag Albashir	4/4/1998	9/5/2001	Central
Dr. Mohamed Mahmoud Alhannan	9/5/2001	To date	Northern

Table 177: Summary of Table 176

Ktm	East	Krdfn	Nrth	Dfr	Cent	Sth	Total
0	0	1	2	0	1	0	4

Table 178: General Secretaries of the Ministry of Irrigation and Natural Resources

Name	From	To	Region
Ahmed Mohamed Adam	16/6/1990	1/3/2001	Central
Mohamed Bahr Aldin Abdalla	1/3/2001	To date	Central

Table 179: Summary of Table 160
(Major error in this Table)

Ktm	East	Krdfn	Nrth	Dfr	Cent	Sth	Total
0	0	1	1	1	1	0	4

Table 180: General Secretaries of the Ministry of Foreign Affairs

Name	From	To	Region
Jaafar Abu Haj	4/6/1990		Northern
Ali Mohamed Osman Yasin	13/10/1991	14/9/1992	Kordofan

Name	From	To	Region
Omer Yousif Bireedu	14/9/1992	13/6/1995	Central
Awad Alkareem Fadlalla	12/6/1995	16/9/1996	Northern
Ali Abdel Rahman Alnimeiri	16/9/1996	8/3/1998	Northern
Dr. Hesain Abdeen	14/6/1998		Northern
Dr. Muttrif Siddeeg	1/3/2001		Northern

TABLE 181: SUMMARY OF TABLE 180

Ktm	East	Krdfn	Nrth	Dfr	Cent	Sth	Total
0	0	1	5	0	1	0	7

TABLE 182: GENERAL SECRETARIES OF THE MINISTRY OF HOUSING AND PUBLIC AMENITIES

Name	From	To	Region
Izzaldin Wahbi Alamin	89/10/23		Northern

TABLE 183: SUMMARY OF TABLE 182

Ktm	East	Krdfn	Nrth	Dfr	Cent	Sth	Total
0	0	0	1	0	0	0	1

TABLE 184: GENERAL SECRETARIES OF THE MINISTRY OF ROADS AND BRIDGES

Name	From	To	Region
Ibrahim Sharaf Aldin	21/4/2001	To date	Darfur

TABLE 185: SUMMARY OF TABLE 184

Ktm	East	Krdfn	Nrth	Dfr	Cent	Sth	Total
0	0	0	0	1	0	0	1

TABLE 186: GENERAL SECRETARIES OF THE MINISTRY OF NATIONAL COUNCIL RELATIONS

Name	From	To	Region
Baha Adin Sayid Ali	29/12/1996	To date	Northern

TABLE 187: SUMMARY OF TABLE 186

KTM	EAST	KRDFN	NRTH	DFR	CENT	STH	TOTAL
0	0	0	1	0	0	0	1

TABLE 188: GENERAL SECRETARIES OF THE MINISTRY OF INVESTMENT AND INTERNATIONAL COOPERATION

NAME	FROM	TO	REGION
Ahmed Mohamed Santour	1/5/2001	To date	Northern

TABLE 189: SUMMARY OF TABLE 188

KTM	EAST	KRDFN	NRTH	DFR	CENT	STH	TOTAL
0	0	0	1	0	0	0	1

TABLE 190: GENERAL SECRETARIES OF THE MINISTRY OF TOURISM AND ECOLOGY

NAME	FROM	TO	REGION
Retired Lt. General Sir Alkhatm Mohamed Fadl	16/3/1995	28/2/1999	Northern
Retired Lt. General Sir Alkhatm Mohamed Fadl	15/11/1999	5/11/2000	Northern
Retired Lt. General Muhia Aldin Mohamed Ali	17/2/2000	To date	Northern

TABLE 191: SUMMARY OF TABLE 190

KTM	EAST	KRDFN	NRTH	DFR	CENT	STH	TOTAL
0	0	0	3	0	0	0	3

TABLE 192: GENERAL SECRETARIES OF THE MINISTRY OF ORIENTATION AND GUIDANCE

NAME	FROM	TO	REGION
Dr. Shams Aldin Zein Ababideen	1/8/1989	30/11/1989	Central
Mohamed Albashir Abdel Hadi	1/3/2001	21/4/2001	Northern
Kamal Aldin Seed Ahmed	21/4/2001	To date	Northern

TABLE 193: SUMMARY OF TABLE 192

KTM	EAST	KRDFN	NRTH	DFR	CENT	STH	TOTAL
0	0	0	2	0	1	0	2

TABLE 194: GENERAL SECRETARIES OF THE MINISTRY OF ANIMAL RESOURCES

NAME	FROM	TO	REGION
Prof. Mohamed Saeed Harbi	18/9/1989	1993	Northern
Abdel Gadir Ahmed Wahbi	20/9/1993	9/2/1995	Northern
Alzain Abdel Rahman Yousif	16/7/1996	11/9/1999	Khartoum
Ahmed Almustafa Hasan	11/9/1999	29/3/2000	Darfur
Dr. Mohamed Salih Aljabalabi	29/3/2000	2001	Northern

TABLE 195: SUMMARY OF TABLE 194

KTM	EAST	KRDFN	NRTH	DFR	CENT	STH	TOTAL
1	0	0	3	1	0	0	5

TABLE 196: GENERAL SECRETARIES OF THE MINISTRY OF RELIEF AND REFUGEE AFFAIRS

NAME	FROM	TO	REGION
Dr. Ibrahim Abu Ouf	1/8/1989		Northern

TABLE 197: SUMMARY OF TABLE 196

KTM	EAST	KRDFN	NRTH	DFR	CENT	STH	TOTAL
0	0	0	1	0	0	0	1

TABLE 198: GENERAL SECRETARIES OF THE MINISTRY OF FEDERAL GOVERNMENT

NAME	FROM	TO	REGION
Adam Mohamed Badur	1/8/1989	7/9/1994	Central
Babikr Awad Ahmed	28/8/2000		Northern

TABLE 199: SUMMARY OF TABLE 198

KTM	EAST	KRDFN	NRTH	DFR	CENT	STH	TOTAL
0	0	0	1	0	1	0	2

TABLE 200: GENERAL SECRETARIES OF THE MINISTRY OF EDUCATION

NAME	FROM	TO	REGION
Ahmed Mohamed Kabboush	13/9/1989	22/3/1994	Northern
Abdel Basit Abdel Majid	26/2/1995	24/1/2000	Northern
Azhari Altigani	1/2/2000	To date	Kordofan

TABLE 201: SUMMARY OF TABLE 200

KTM	EAST	KRDFN	NRTH	DFR	CENT	STH	TOTAL
0	0	1	2	0	0	0	3

TABLE 202: GENERAL SECRETARIES OF THE MINISTRY OF SCIENCE AND TECHNOLOGY

NAME	FROM	TO	REGION
Dr. Mahmoud Hasan Ahmed	12/6/2001	To date	Northern

TABLE 203: SUMMARY OF TABLE 202

KTM	EAST	KRDFN	NRTH	DFR	CENT	STH	TOTAL
0	0	0	1	0	0	0	1

TABLE 204: GENERAL SECRETARIES OF THE MINISTRY OF TRANSPORT

NAME	FROM	TO	REGION
Faissal Mohemad Lutfi	10/8/1989	3/4/1997	Northern
Mudhawi Altiraifi	22/6/1997		Central

TABLE 205: SUMMARY OF TABLE 204

KTM	EAST	KRDFN	NRTH	DFR	CENT	STH	TOTAL
0	0	0	1	0	1	0	2

TABLE 206: GENERAL SECRETARIES OF THE MINISTRY OF SOCIAL
DEVELOPMENT AND WELFARE

NAME	FROM	To	REGION
Salah Muhia Aldin	14/9/1988	11/12/1989	Northern
Dr. Hasan Ahmed Taha	6/3/1995	22/3/2000	Northern
Dr. Mohamed Alhasan Makkawi	1/3/2001	To date	Nothern

TABLE 207: SUMMARY OF TABLE 206

KTM	EAST	KRDFN	NRTH	DFR	CENT	STH	TOTAL
0	0	0	3	0	0	0	3

TABLE 208: GENERAL SECRETARIES
OF THE MINISTRY OF SOCIAL PLANNING

NAME	FROM	To	REGION
Dr. Mohamed Osman Ibrahim	13/12/1995	13/1/1997	Northern
Ahmed Mohamed Shantour	13/1/1997	1/5/2001	Northern

TABLE 209: SUMMARY OF TABLE 208

KTM	EAST	KRDFN	NRTH	DFR	CENT	STH	TOTAL
0	0	0	2	0	0	0	2

TABLE 210: GENERAL SECRETARIES
OF THE MINISTRY OF RELIGIOUS AFFAIRS

NAME	FROM	To	REGION
Dr. Ahmed Khalid Babikir	1/10/1989		Northern

TABLE 211: SUMMARY OF TABLE 210

KTM	EAST	KRDFN	NRTH	DFR	CENT	STH	TOTAL
0	0	0	1	0	0	0	1

TABLE 212: GENERAL SECRETARIES OF THE MINISTRY OF SURVEY
AND CONSTRUCTION DEVELOPMENT

NAME	FROM	TO	REGION
Abdel Bagi Atta Alfadheel	7/4/1999	30/8/2000	Northern
Dr. Alfadil Ali Adam	30/8/2000		Darfur

TABLE 213: SUMMARY OF TABLE 212

KTM	EAST	KRDFN	NRTH	DFR	CENT	STH	TOTAL
0	0	0	1	1	0	0	2

TABLE 214: GENERAL SECRETARIES
OF THE MINISTRIES OF ENERGY AND MINING

NAME	FROM	TO	REGION
Abdel Rahman Sulaiman	13/9/1989	29/9/1994	Northern
Hasan Mohamed Ali Altoam	29/9/1994	To date	Northern

TABLE 215: SUMMARY OF TABLE 214

KTM	EAST	KRDFN	NRTH	DFR	CENT	STH	TOTAL
0	0	0	2	0	0	0	2

TABLE 216: SUMMARY OF GENERAL SECRETARIES OF FEDERAL
MINISTRIES; TABLES 196 TO 215

TOTAL / REGIONS	KTM	EAST	KRDFN	NRTH	DFR	CENT	STH
87	2	0	6	65	4	10	0
%	2%	0%	7%	74%	4%	11%	0%

TABLE 217: HEADS OF APPOINTMENT COMMITTEES OF NATIONAL PUBLIC SERVICE

NAME	DURATION	KHARTOUM	EASTERN	KORDOFAN	NORTHERN	DARFUR	CENTRAL	SOUTHERN
Alsheikh Abdel Rahim	1989-1996				*			
Nur Alhadi	1996-1998				*			
Awatif Ahmed Babibkir	1998-2001	*						
Sidheeq Altayib Bukhari	2001-2002						*	
Awatif Ahmed Babikir	2002-To date	*						
TOTAL		2	0	0	2	0	1	0

TABLE 218: SUMMARY OF TABLE 217

TOTAL / REGIONS	KTM	EAST	KRDFN	NRTH	DFR	CENT	STH
87	2	0	6	65	4	10	0
%	2%	0%	7%	74%	4%	11%	0%

TABLE 219: CURRENT PRESIDENTS OF UNIVERSITIES AND THEIR REGIONS, 1989-2002

No	PRESIDENT	UNIVERSITY	REGION
1	Prof. Muddathir Altingari	Khartoum	Northern
2	Prof. Mamoun Hemaida	Khartoum	Northern
3	Prof. Hashim Alhadi	Khartoum	Northern
4	Prof. Alzibair Bashir	Khartoum	Northern
5	Prof. Abdel Malik Abdel Rahman	Khartoum	Khartoum
6	Prof. Ibrahim Alamin Hagar	Alnilain	Darfur
7	Prof. Awad Haj Ali	Alnilain	Eastern
8	Prof. Ali Ahmed Babikir	Islamic Uni.	Northern
9	Prof. Siddeeg Nasir	Islamic Uni.	Northern
10	Prof. Mohamed Osman Nasir	Islamic Uni.	Northern
11	Prof. Mahmoud Musa	Juba	Darfur
12	Prof. Mohamed Ali Alsheikh	Juba	Kordofan

No	President	University	Region
13	Prof. Zakaria Bashir	Juba	Northern
14	Prof. Fathi Ahmed Khalifa	Juba	Northern
15	Prof. Babikir Ahmed Babikir	Juba	Northern
16	Prof. Ali Abdel Rahman	Sudan	Khartoum
17	Prof. Izzaldin Mohamed Osman	Sudan	Northern
18	Prof. Ahmed Altayib	Sudan	Northern
19	Prof. Ahmed Ali Alimam	Alqur'an	Northern
20	Prof. Ahmed Khalid Babikir	Alqur'an	Northern
21	Prof. Sulaiman Osman	Alqur'an	Northern
22	Prof. Tigani Hasan Alamin	Gezira	Kordofan
23	Prof. Mubarak Mohamed Ali	Gezira	Central
24	Prof. Ismael Hasan Hesain	Gezira	Northern
25	Prof. Faisal Alhaj	Sinnar	Northern
26	Prof. Ahmed Hasan Bairam	Sinnar	Northern
27	Prof. Hasan	Blue Nile	Northern
28	Prof. Qurashi Mohamed Ali	Alazhari	Central
29	Prof. Shamsaldin Zein Alabdeen	Alazhari	Central
30	Prof. Hasan Abu Shanab	Almahdi	Northern
31	Prof. Abdel Azeem Abbas	Almaddi	Northern
32	Prof. Abdel Raheem Osman	Almahdi	Central
33	Prof. Hasan Nowee	Bakh Alrida	Norhern
34	Prof. Ghaboush Tirtore Aldawi	Kordofan	Kordofan
35	Prof. Altaj Fadllala	Kordofan	Kordofan
36	Prof. Ibrahim Musa Tibin	Alnuhoud	Kordofan
37	Prof. Ibrahim Mukhtar	Aldalang	Kordofan
38	Prof. Khamees Kajo	Aldalang	Kordofan
39	Prof. Omer Alkurdi	Algadarif	Eastern
40	Prof. Mustafa	Kasala	North
41	Prof. Mahmoud Abbakar	Nyala	Darfur
42	Prof. Adam Hasan	Nyala	Darfur
43	Prof. Abdel Qadir	Red Sea	Northern
44	Prof. Ali Barri	Shandi	Northern
45	Prof. Abdel Ghaffar	Shandi	Northern
46	Prof. Ibrahim Alamin Hajar	Alfashir	Darfur
47	Prof. Mahmoud Musa	Alfashir	Darfur

No	President	University	Region
48	Prof. Fathi Ahmed Khalifa	Alfashir	Northern
49	Prof. Abdel Bagi Ahmed Kabeer	Alfashir	Darfur
50	Prof. Abdalla Abdel Hay	Alfashir	Darfur
51	Prof. Hasan Ali Alsaoori	Dungula	Northern
52	Prof. Mahmoud Hasan Ahmed	Dungula	Northern
53	Prof. Sinadi	Nile Valley	Northern
54	Prof. Faisal Alhaj	Nile Valley	Northern
55		Upper Nile	
56		Bahr Alghazal	

TABLE 220: SUMMARY OF TABLE 219;
REGIONS OF UNIVERSITY PRESIDENTS

Total / Regions	Ktm	East	Krdfn	Nrth	Dfr	Cent	Sth
54	1	2	7	30	9	5	0
%	2%	4%	13%	55%	17%	9%	0%

TABLE 221: MANAGERS OF BANK OF SUDAN, 1988 TO DATE

Name	Duration	Khartoum	Eastern	Kordofan	Northern	Darfur	Central	Southern
Mahdi Alfaki	1988-1990				*			
Alsheikh Sid Ahmed	9/9/1990-8/7/1993				*			
Sabir Mohamed Alhasan	8/7/1993-20/4/1996				*			
Abdalla Hasan Ahmed	21/4/1996-10/3/1996				*			
Sabir Mohmed Alhasan	10/3/1998-To date				*			
Total		0	0	0	5	0	0	0

TABLE 222: SUMMARY OF TABLE 221

Total / Regions	Ktm	East	Krdfn	Nrth	Dfr	Cent	Sth
5	0	0	0	5	0	0	0
%	0%	0%	0%	100%	0%	0%	0%

TABLE 223: MANAGERS OF SELECTED PUBLIC BANKS AND FINANCIAL INSTITUTIONS

No	MANAGER	BANK/ FINANCIAL INSTITUTION	REGION OF MANAGER
1	Saeed Osman Mahjoub	Nilain Bank	Eastern
2	Badr Aldin Mahmoud	Nilain Bank	Northern
3	Ibrahim Adam Habeen	Nilain Bank	Darfur
4	Aqee Allah Alnow	Nilain Bank	Northern
5	Omer Taha Abu Samra	Khartoum Bank	Northern
6	Dr. Sabir Mohamed Alhasan	Khartoum Bank	Northern
7	Ismael Mohamed Qurashi	Khartoum Bank	Northern
8	Mahmoud Yahia Alfadli	Khartoum Bank	Northern
9	Mohamed Salah Aldin	Khartoum	Northern
10	Hesain Ibrahim Almufti	Cooperative Development Bank	Northern
11	Alhaj Ahmed Osman	Cooperative Development Bank	Northern
12	Alkindi Yousif	Farmers' Bank	Northern
13	Ahmed Ibrahim Alturabi	Farmers' Bank	Central
14	Badr Aldin Mahmoud	Farmers' Bank	Northern
15	Mohamed Ali Amin	Estate Bank	Central
16	Abdalla Bashir	Estate Bank	Northern
17	Alfateh Ali Abdalla	Saving Bank	Northern
18	Abdalla Dafalla	Saving Bank	Central
19	Yousif Osman	Saving Bank	Northern
20	Altayib Ibrahim	National Workers Bank	Northern
21	Badr Aldin Taha	Agricultural Bank	Khartoum
22	Dr. haju Qism Alseed	Agricultural Bank	Central
23	Alkindi Yousif	Agricultural Bank	Northern
24	Abdalla Alhindi Alwaseela	Agricultural Bank	Northern
25	Dr. Bashir Adam Rahma	Animal Resources	Kordofan
26	Hashim Ali Mohamed Kheir	Animal Resources	Northern
27	Hatim Abdalla Alzibair	Animal resources	Northern
28	Alzibair Mohamed Alhasan	Omdurman National Bank	Northern
29	Ahmed Mohamed Ali	Omdurman National Bank	Central
30	Ahmed Musa	Omdurman National Bank	Northern
31	Alseed Osman Mahjoub	Sudan Development Bank	Eastern
32	Abdalla Alramadi	Sudan Development Bank	Khartoum
33	Mohamed Kheir Alzibair	Sudan Development Bank	Northern

No	Manager	Bank/ Financial Institution	Region of Manager
34	Abdel Wahab Ahmed Hamza	Sudan Development Bank	Northern
35	Dr. Adil Abdel Aziz	National Fund for Social Insurance	Khartoum
36	Mahil Abu Janna	National Fund for Social Insurance	Kordofan
37	Osman Sulaiman Mohamed Nur	National Fund for Social Insurance	Northern
38	Kamal Ali Medani	National Pension Fund	Northern
39	Ahmed Osman Alhaj	Strategic Reserve Bank	Northern

TABLE 224: SUMMARY OF TABLE 223; REGIONAL DISTRIBUTION OF MANAGERS

Total / Regions	Ktm	East	Krdfn	Nrth	Dfr	Cent	Sth
39	3	2	2	26	1	2	0
%	7%	5%	5%	67%	2%	12%	0%

TABLE 225: MOST RECENT DIRECTORS OF THE GEZIRA SCHEME, (BIGGEST IRRIGATED SCHEME IN SUDAN)

Name	Khartoum	Eastern	Kordofan	Northern	Darfur	Central	Southern
Izzaldin Omer Almakki				*			
Dr. Ahmed Albadawi				*			
Prof. Fathi Ahmed Alkhalifa				*			
Prof. Alamin Daffalla				*			
Ali Omer Mohamed Alamin				*			
Total				5			

TABLE 226: SUMMARY OF TABLE 225; REGIONAL DISTRIBUTION OF MANAGERS

Total / Regions	Ktm	East	Krdfn	Nrth	Dfr	Cent	Sth
5	0	0	0	5	0	0	0
%	0%	0%	0%	100%	0%	0%	0%

TABLE 227: DIRECTORS OF NATIONAL ZAKAT (ISLAMIC TAX) CHAMBER AND THEIR REGIONS

NAME	KHARTOUM	EASTERN	KORDOFAN	NORTHERN	DARFUR	CENTRAL	SOUTHERN
Mohamed Ibrahim Mohamed				*			
Dr. Abdel Munim Alqosi				*			
Dr. Ahmed Majzooub				*			
Dr. Abdel Gadir Alfadni				*			
TOTAL	0	0	0	4	0	0	0

TABLE 228: SUMMARY OF TABLE 227

TOTAL / REGIONS	KTM	EAST	KRDFN	NRTH	DFR	CENT	STH
4	0	0	0	4	0	0	0
%	0%	0%	0%	100%	0%	0%	0%

TABLE 229: MAJOR PUBLIC TRADING COMPANIES AND THEIR MANAGERS

No	COMPANY	GENERAL MANAGER	REGION
1	Lulu (Jewell) Palace	Alrsheed Faqwwri	Northern
2	Shakireen	Omer Bashir Mohamed	Kordofan
3	Dhifaf	Ysir Hasan Omsan	Northern
4	Qidira Albitoul	Mutasam Rahma	Central
5	United Sudan for Services	Faisal Ishaq Omer	Northern
6	Alhadaf	Kamal Hasan Ali	Northern
7	Green Flag (Araya Alkhadra)	Alsayid Bajouri	Northern
8	Kordofan	Mahil Abu Janna	Kordofan
9	Cooptrade	Osman Ibrahim Ahmed	Northern
10	Alsalma	Abdel Ghaffar Ahmed	Northern
11	Alwakeel	Adil Seed Ahmed	Northern
12	Altairan (Aviation)	Sideeg Abdel Lateef	Northern
13	Sahiroun	Abdel Lateef Ishmaig	Northern
14	Altarif	Sami Saeed	Northern
15	Diamond	Dia Aldin Abdel Rahman	Northern
16	Zhilal	Asim Aljak	Central

No	Company	General Manager	Region
17	Gum Arabic	Mustafa Ahmed Taha	Northern
18	Bank Notes	Isam Alzein Almahi	Northern
19	Shikan Insurance	Osman Alhadi	Northern
20	Aldar Alistithmaria (for Investment)	Abdalla Abbas Habeeb	Northern
21	Dan Fodio	Ibrahim Musa Khalifa	Northern
22	Islamic Insurance	Rabee Hasan Ahmed	Central
23	Sugar Trade	Hamza Ginnawi	Northern
24	Abr Alqarrat Intercontinental	Omer Ali Abdalla	Northern
25	Rowsam International	Alsir Ahmed Yousif	Kordofan
26	Khartoum of Gum Arabic Products	Khalid Farah	Central
27	Bashair Littaqa (Energy)	Ahmed A. Jibreel	Northern
28	Ariab Litaadeen (Mining)	Abdel Aziur Ahmed	Northern
29	Sudan Petrol Company	Hamad Alneel Abdel Qadir	Khartoum
30	Petrotrans	Sulaiman Dawood	Northern
31	Pipe Lines	Yousif Salih Ahmed	Northern
32	Algezira	Mohamed Ahmed Fageeri	Northern
33	Azzah for Transport	Osman Gadim	Kordofan
34	Red Sea for Sea Transport	Awad Haj Ali	Northern
35	Alfarabi	Mohamed A. Alhadhari	Central
36	Sudan Banknotes Printers	Hasan Omer Abdel Rahman	Northern
37	Alkanar	Ibrahim Karti	Northern
38	Saroud	Abdel Aati Siddeeg	Northern
39	Medical Supplies	Mandour Almahdi	Khartoum
40	Higleeg	Yousif Mohamed Yousif	Central
41	Alyarmouk	Abu Bakr Mohamed Hasan	Northern
42	Petroneed for Trade	Salah Altayib	Northern
43	Almuhagir Altalimi	Alfirazdaq Yaqoub	Khartoum
44	Awab for Services	Husam Alsayid	Northern
45	Awab for Trade	Mohamed Omer	Northern
46	Sudan Cottons	Abdeen Mohamed Ali	Northern
47	Sudan Oil Seeds	Ahmed Saad	Khartoum
48	Sudan Company of Milk	Mohamed Osman Almirghani	Northern
49	Alshaheed for Roads and Bridges	Azhari Fadl	Northern
50	Jiad lilsinaa (Car Assembly)	Alamin Mohamed Alamin	Northern
51	Sudatel (Telecommunication)	Abdel Aziz Osman	Northern
52	Khartoum Centre	Abdel Gadir Mimmat	Northern

TABLE 230: SUMMARY OF TABLE 229

TOTAL / REGIONS	KTM	EAST	KRDFN	NRTH	DFR	CENT	STH
52	4	0	4	38	0	6	0
%	7%	0%	7%	73%	0%	11%	0%

TABLE 231: PRIMARY SCHOOLS ENROLMENT 1999-2000 BY STATE (SOUTH BY REGION)

STATE	POPULATION AT SCHOOL AGE	OVERALL %	ENROLLED	% ENROLLED	REGION
Northern	113981	1.7%	107738	94.5%	Northern
River Nile	187095	2.8	151762	81.1	Northern
Khartoum	785827	11	678850	86.8	Khartoum
Gezira	686881	10.3	527630	86.8	Central
Sinnar	267314	4	137822	51.6	Central
Blue Nile	143336	2.2	51130	35.7	Central
White Nile	335800	5.1	183874	54.8	Central
Algdharif	309363	4.6	144385	46.7	Eastern
Kasala	307959	4.6	101109	32.8	Eastern
Red Sea	154128	2.3	65908	42.8	Eastern
North Kordofan	317158	5.8	171678	54.1	Kordofan
West Kordofan	277615	4.2	84162	30.3	Kordofan
South Kordofan	290648	4.4	100663	34.6	Kordofan
North Darfur	338639	5.1	152193	44.9	Darfur
West Darfur	378044	5.7	75238	19.9	Darfur
South Darfur	633609	9.5	171541	27.1	Darfur
Upper Nile	349898	5.3	117963	33.7	Southern
Bahr Elghazal	485959	7.3	65482	13.5	Southern
Equatorial	292493	4.4	48364	16.5	Southern
TOTAL	6655747		3137492	4.71 AV	

TABLE 232: SUMMARY OF TABLE 231, PERCENTAGE OF ENROLMENT BY REGION

%/REGION	KTM	EAST	KRDFN	NRTH	DFR	CENT	STH
%	76.8%	40.5%	39.7%	87.8%	30.6%	54.7%	21.2%

We note that lack of education in the last two Regions is clearly reflected in their level of destitution, unemployment and relative lack of development.

TABLE 233: SECONDARY SCHOOLS ENROLMENT FOR THE YEAR 1999/2000 BY STATE

STATE	POPULATION AGES 14-16	ENROLLED	% OF ENROLMENT
North	36888	13460	36.5%
Rive Nile	61818	22073	35.7
Khartoum	280582	98386	35.1
Gezira	227294	29716	13.1
Sinnar	85812	20980	24.4
Blue Nile	47012	4436	9.4
White Nile	106902	19428	18.2
Algadharif	104408	8530	8.2
Kasala	109796	11781	10.7
Red Sea	51047	11682	22.9
North Kordofan	110052	17618	16.0
West Kordofan	88588	11492	13.0
South Kordofan	94284	6252	6.6
North Darfur	110172	18038	16.4
West Darfur	130626	6655	5.1
South Darfur	216756	29922	12.4
Upper Nile	102305	3081	3.0
Bahr Alghazal	165895	4310	2.6
Equatorial	88244	3549	4.0
TOTAL	2218482	338389	15.35

TABLE 234: SUMMARY OF TABLE 233; PERCENTAGE OF ENROLMENT BY REGION

%/REGION	KTM	EAST	KRDFN	NRTH	DFR	CENT	STH
%	35.1%	13.9%	11.9%	36.2%	11.3%	16.2%	3.2%

TABLE 235: GROWTH OF SUDANESE UNIVERSITIES, 1990/1991 - 1998/1999

University/ Year	90/91	91/92	92/93	93/94	94/95	95/96	96/97	97/98	98/99
Khartoum	9474	13154	12188	17002	17022	22118	27789	27794	26740
Omdurman Islamic	4559	6581	1902	20765	30751	28805	23595	25182	35615
Holy Qur'an	2407	3187	6060	8449	10639	11832	10890	12399	12823
Science & Techn.	2739	5053	7672	9015	10145	19150	20708	23475	23731
Juba	1557	1763	1998	2019	2287	2234	2613	3468	4177
Gezira	2499	4721	7432	8653	12041	14188	13917	14243	14031
Nile Valley	304	1238	2253	3067	2751	3069	4295	4782	5991
Nilain	26128	20454	17500	22375	16137	14924	15070	15260	17327
Kordofan	186	727	1509	1895	1374	1537	2104	2314	2571
Alfashir					1643	2030	2630	3280	3980
Aldalang					924	1136	1166	1549	2292
Bahr Al Ghazal			116	223	342	393	563	916	1058
Upper Nile				159	271	319	639	427	818
Nyala					628	964	1163	1154	1900
Zalengay					238	420	534	336	615
Alazhari				368	730	1237	1874	2418	3015
Shandi					456	1071	1419	1189	2777
Dongula					658	795	1073	1482	1682

Table above shows spectacular growth of universities based in the Northern, the Central and Khartoum Regions in comparison to those in other Regions.

TABLE 236: HOSPITAL BEDS PER 100,000 POPULATION BY STATE FOR THE YEAR 2000

REGION	BEDS PER PER 100,000	HOSPITALS PER 100,000	NO OF BEDS	NO OF HOSPITALS	TOTAL POPULATION
Khartoum	111	0.8	5281	39	4,740,000
Gezira	79	1.3	2664	43	3,374,000
White Nile	83	1.1	1217	17	1,476,000
Blue Nile	42	1.1	265	7	636,000
Sinnar	90	1.1	1059	13	1,173,000
River Nile	156	2.5	1405	23	900,000
Northern	146	5.2	1435	30	582,000
Kasala	74	0.8	1131	12	1,525,000
Gadharif	67	1.0	954	15	1,409,000
Red Sea	103	2.3	748	17	721,000
North Kordofan	88	0.9	1299	14	1,483,000
SouthKordofan	46	0.6	512	7	1,111,000
West Kordofan	54	0.8	602	9	1,124,000
North Darfur	38	0.6	554	9	1,455,000
South Darfur	22	0.3	603	8	2,760,000
West Darfur	14	0.2	219	4	1,577,000
Equatorial	94	1.3	1190	16	1,261,000
Bahr Al Ghazal	42	0.4	954	9	2,321,000
Upper Nile	68	1.2	993	17	1,453,000
SUDAN AS WHOLE	74.2	1.0	23076	309	31,081,000

TABLE 237: HOSPITALS AND HOSPITAL BEDS PER 100,000 IN ALL REGIONS

TOTAL / REGIONS	KTM	EAST	KRDFN	NRTH	DFR	CENT	STH
Hospitals	0.8	1.4	0.8	3.9	0.4	1.2	1
Beds	111	81.3	62.7	151	24.7	73.5	68

TABLE 238: MEDICAL DOCTORS PER 100,000 POPULATION, YEAR 2000

STATE	DOCTORS RATIO	DENTISTS RATIO	SPECIAL-LISTS RATIO	DOCTORS TOTAL	DENTISTS TOTAL	SPECIA-LISTS TOTAL	POPULATION TOTAL
High Trainee Doctors				2238			
Khartoum	35.0	3.6	11	1663	171	524	4,740,000
Gezira	6.2	0.3	2.4	211	13	83	3,374,000
White Nile	4.6	0.1	1.7	69	1	25	1,470,000
Blue Nile	5.3	0.4	0.6	34	3	4	636,000
Sinnar	6.0	0.3	1.7	71	4	21	1,173,000
River Nile	8.5	0.8	2.3	77	8	21	900,000
Northern	13.5	0.7	2.5	79	4	15	582,000
Kasala	4.2	0.3	0.7	64	4	20	1,525,000
Gadharif	4.6	0.2	1.0	65	4	13	1,409,000
Red Sea	10.4	0.2	4.1	77	2	30	721,000
North Kordofan	5.5	0.3	1.8	82	3	27	1,483,000
South Kordofan	1.7	0	0.3	19	0	4	1,111,000
West Kordofan	2.1	0	0.2	24	0	3	1,124,000
North Darfur	1.5	0.1	0.5	23	1	8	1,455,000
South Darfur	2.0	0.1	0.4	50	1	12	2,760,000
West Darfur	1.0	0.1	0.2	17	1	3	1,577,000
Equatorial	3.7	-	-	47	-	-	1,261,000
Bahr Elghazal	1.4	-	-	34	-	-	2,321,000
Upper Nile	3.3	-	-	48	-	-	1,453,000
SUDAN OVERALL	16.0	0.7	206	4992	222	814	

TABLE 239: SUMMARY OF DOCTORS PER 100,000 POPULATION BY REGION (TABLE 238)

TOTAL / REGIONS	KTM	EAST	KRDFN	NRTH	DFR	CENT	STH
Specialists	11	1.9	0.8	2.4	0.4	1.6	0.0
G.Ps	35	6.5	3.1	11	1.5	6.5	2.8

Tables 238 and 239 show drastic shortage of general and specialists doctors in all Regions in comparison with Khartoum and the Northern regions.

TABLE 240: CONSTRUCTED AND UNDER-CONSTRUCTION HIGHWAY ROADS IN SUDAN

No	Road	Region	KM Length	Completed	Remaining Km	% Done
1	Sinnar-Singa- Damazeen	Central	237	237	0	100%
2	Obeid-Kazgail	Kordofan	47	47	0	100%
3	Kost-Obeid	Central	307	307	0	100%
4	Muglad-Higleeg	Kordofan	235	235	0	100%
5	Rabak-Jabalain	Central	69	69	0	100%
6	Medani-Managil	Central	57	57	0	100%
7	Hasahias-Tabat	Central	38.5	38.5	0	100%
8	Jabalain-Rank	Southern	97	7	90	7%
9	Obeid-Bara	Kordofan	57	10	47	17%
10	Obeid-Khiway	Kordofan	103	103	0	100%
11	Khiway-Nuhood	Kordofan	103	3	100	3%
12	Nuhood-Umkeddada	Darfur	238	0	238	0%
13	Umkeddada-Alfashir	Darfur	168	7	161	4%
14	Slfashir-Nyala	Darfur	215	60	155	30%
15	Zalingay-Algineina	Darfur	168	One Bridge	168	0%
16	Managil-Gurashi	Central	37	0.7	36.3	2%
17	Doka-Gallabat	Eastern	54	54	0	100%
18	Umrwaba-Rashad-Abu Jibaiha	Kordofan	191	0	191	0%
19	New Halfa-Khasm Algirba	Eastern	47	47	0	100%
20	Aljaili-Shandi	Northern	130	130	0	100%
21	Shandi-Atbara	Northern	140	140	0	100%
22	Atbara-Hia	Northern	274	0	274	0%
23	Omdurman-Dongula	Northern	484	218	266	45%
24	Albaja-Ousali	Northern	14	14	0	100%
25	West Nile	Khartoum Northern	120	70	50	58%

Notes on Table above:

Western Road extends 1209km. 163km was completed during Nimeiri (1969-1985). The remaining 995km still await funding.

The planned Southern Kordofan Road,191km, is relegated to speeches of politicians.

The picture in the Northern Region is different. Challenge Road Atbara Aljaili, 270km of the Northern Region has been fully completed. The Northern Nerve Road, Omdurman- Dongula, 484 has gone a long way. 232mk of it has been completed.

Alfashir, Kafra Road connecting Darfur with Libya has been planned for a long time. More recently, this road has been rerouted to connect Kafra in Libya with Dongula in the Northern Region. No comment!

WATER AND ELECTRICITY

We concede that our statistics for this section is far from complete. What is known is that electricity work has concentrated in Khartoum, the Central and Northern Regions. The provision of electricity for other Regions varies from little to none.

Water problems remain acute in deprived Regions of Darfur, Kordofan, the East and the South.

CONCLUSION OF PART II

Our evidence as presented above, is based on statistics that are hard to dispute. Whenever we speak out, we get accused of Regionalism, tribalism and racism. Our work here shows that it is our opponents who practise Regionalism, tribalism and nepotism. This is crystal clear in appointment to high office, allocation of resources and exploitation of national wealth.

We do not believe that qualification for high office is a preserve of certain Regions. We also do not accept the assumption that commitment to national interests, experience, honesty and integrity for high office predominates in certain areas in the country to the exclusion of others.

Our next work will focus on the qualities of those who have been placed in charge of others. We will expose their corruption, breach of human rights, thwarting the national Constitution and other excesses. We would like here to apologise for innocent citizens who have been scathed by some of the information contained in this manuscript.

Lastly, we would like to warn our current leaders, that they cannot hope to remain in office forever, while at the same time preside over injustice. Knowledge of national issues, relations with State and others, citizen rights, etc., is no longer a preserve of the few. Our advice is simple and we say it to end this work: "Be just: That is Next to Piety" (Koran, Almaaida, Verse 8).

Index

River Nile 69, 195, 196, 202, 203, 205, 207, 232-234, 280, 281, 304, 339, 342

Salah El Din, Ghazi 208, 211

Sandal, Sulaiman 24, 38-40, 44, 50, 51, 54, 56, 59, 61, 68, 145

Saudi Arabia 161, 163, 164, 197, 319

Secondary school 26, 129, 136, 140, 141, 143, 154

Seedling, Nabta 193, 200

Shakir 183-185, 294

Shammar, Ali 167

Shogar, Ali 168, 169, 222

Slamat, Salamat

Soccer 50, 54, 132, 133, 138

South Sudan's Liberation Movement (SSLM) 185

SPLA, SPLM 23, 30, 31, 35, 40, 50, 51, 70, 158, 169, 170, 171, 182-189, 197, 212, 215, 218, 223, 230, 232, 236, 247, 249, 252

Sub-Saharan Africa 17, 56, 135, 210

Sudan Liberation Movement (SLM), SLA 57, 185

Sudan's Armed Forces 221

Sudanese Communist Party (SCP) 183, 212, 224

Sudanese School Certificate, Leaving Cert. 152

Sudanese Socialist Union (SSU) 142, 143, 149, 150

Suleiman, Bishara 222, 275

Taha, Osman Mohamed, Vice President 1, 12, 211, 246, 247, 264, 283, 293, 295, 297, 298, 309, 324, 330, 335, 338

Tahir, Tigani Adam 12, 209, 210, 248, 282-284, 286, 287, 289, 290, 292, 303, 308, 310, 311

Tama 13, 14

Tergem 222

Thong Thong 223

Thuraya, Satellite, Mobile phone 3, 4, 62, 213, 218, 219

Tibir 64

Tina 125-127, 130, 135-138, 140, 141, 153

Togot, Ahmed Lisan 15, 38-40, 42-46, 48, 50, 51, 54, 56-59, 61, 63, 68, 73, 168, 169

Tuar 141, 155

Tuar 141, 155

Tuareg, Turban 34, 57, 58, 71

Turabi 164, 171, 172, 211, 246, 247